HAVING WORLD ENOUGH
AND TIME

HAVING WORLD ENOUGH AND TIME

OCTOBER 2013

To

NEVINE HAIDER

Tom Sluberski

THOMAS RICHARD SLUBERSKI

To order additional copies of this book, contact:
Xlibris LLC
1-888-795-4274
www.Xlibris.com
Orders@Xlibris.com
52752

CONTENTS

PART I: WHERE I WAS
"Had We But World Enough and Time"

A bit trendy (for its time!) and academic, but does reflect the tumultuous state of America in the 1960s, along with my own developing outlook. I wish now that I had written one of these every five years.

One of a series of articles and studies on satire I wrote as a student at Concordia Seminary and Washington University in the 1960s.

Another study focusing on satire, written for a graduate seminar at Washington University.

PART II: HOW I GOT HERE
Having time to "sit down and think"

PART III: WHERE I AM NOW
"Now Let Us Sport Us As We May," "At Once Our Time Devour," "And Make Our Time Stand Still"

PART IV: WHAT'S NEXT?
"Time's winged chariot," "Eternity," "The grave"

> A study of eschatology, "testing the doctrines," the background, context, and reasons why the church confesses the doctrines she does.

> A series of background papers combining exegesis, systematics, church history, philosophy, and contextual studies. At the time of writing, I thought I wanted to be a systematician.

ON THE TITLE OF THE BOOK

From the poem "To His Coy Mistress" by Andrew Marvell (1621-1678), the first line of which is, "Had we but world enough, and time . . . ."

To His Coy Mistress

by Andrew Marvell

Had we but world enough, and time,
This coyness, lady, were no crime.
We would sit down and think which way
To walk, and pass our long love's day;
Thou by the Indian Ganges' side
Shouldst rubies find; I by the tide
Of Humber would complain. I would
Love you ten years before the Flood;
And you should, if you please, refuse
Till the conversion of the Jews.
My vegetable love should grow
Vaster than empires, and more slow.
An hundred years should go to praise
Thine eyes, and on thy forehead gaze;
Two hundred to adore each breast,
But thirty thousand to the rest;
An age at least to every part,
And the last age should show your heart.
For, lady, you deserve this state,
Nor would I love at lower rate.

But at my back I always hear
Time's winged chariot hurrying near;
And yonder all before us lie
Deserts of vast eternity.
Thy beauty shall no more be found,
Nor, in thy marble vault, shall sound
My echoing song; then worms shall try
That long preserv'd virginity,

And your quaint honour turn to dust,
And into ashes all my lust.
The grave's a fine and private place,
But none I think do there embrace.

Now therefore, while the youthful hue
Sits on thy skin like morning dew,
And while thy willing soul transpires
At every pore with instant fires,
Now let us sport us while we may;
And now, like am'rous birds of prey,
Rather at once our time devour,
Than languish in his slow-chapp'd power.
Let us roll all our strength, and all
Our sweetness, up into one ball;
And tear our pleasures with rough strife
Thorough the iron gates of life.
Thus, though we cannot make our sun
Stand still, yet we will make him run.

What draws me to the poem:

Its "speaker" is impatient. Patience is one of the many virtues I lack as
well. He's anxious to get to the point, to cease the wooing and get to the
lovemaking. He assures his beloved that, yes, *if* they had all the time in
the world, he would happily "sit down" and "think which way to walk,
and pass our long love's day." He even suggests some distant, exotic spots
for such activities: the Ganges, for her to find rubies, and the distant river
Humber, which he could sit beside and complain. He would love her from
"ten years before the Flood," and she "could refuse till the conversion of the
Jews" at the end of the world, if she so chose. He'd pass whole centuries in
praise of each part of her anatomy, especially her heart. He grants that she
deserves all this and more.

BUT THEY DON'T HAVE THE TIME! "Time's winged chariot" is
always at their backs, and the deserts of eternity stretch out in their future.
In the grave, she will no longer be beautiful. Nor will she be able to hear
his song. Worms will get at her "long preserv'd virginity." Her honor, and
his lust, will both turn into dust. No one embraces in a grave.

NOW IS THE TIME to "do it"—while she is still young and fresh and beautiful and, obviously, "willing" (evidenced by her blushing).

Now, he says, is the time to "sport us while we may." He suggests their lovemaking ought to be like the "am'rous birds of prey," which devour their time at once rather than "languish" any more: putting their "all" into it, to "roll all our strength, and all our sweetness, up into one ball" and "tear our pleasures with rough strife, through the iron gates of life."

Because they cannot *stop time* ("make our sun stand still"), they can make it "run."

Seize the day! *Carpe diem!* This is the spirit that motivated me to write the essays collected here, and now prompts me to put them into a volume.

Sections of this poem introduce each of the four parts of this volume.

PREFACE

Marvell's poem provided me a title and theme for this collection of "edgy" essays from around the world and across the disciplines. We don't know how long we will live, or how well or where. That said, we may reach a moment at which we can look *back* and ponder what the gift of many years, long life, and wide experience means. I have been granted not only a long life, but a childhood, an education, and a career that gave me time—as Marvell phrases it—to "sit down and ponder . . . which way to walk and pass" my days. I was granted so many opportunities to admire, contemplate and praise so much of what is out there. I did have time to "sport" and even at times "devour" what life has had to offer. Time, in many ways, did "fly," yet I had both world and time enough that I was able to do and see more than I ever expected.

Still, I too hear "time's winged chariot hurrying near." These essays, I hope, benefit from, and show not only a changing perspective, but a growth from youth to maturity—to the extent that I have matured. They are only a selection. Some I no longer agree with. Most I would now change and alter, but growing up, I never thought I would have had enough time to do all that I wanted to do. Like the poet, I felt I had to "seize the day" (*carpe diem*). I am glad I did. Had I known, however, I had so much more time. I think I would have paused along the way more often. Now I am more able to do that kind of reflection and introspection.

Shakespeare put it well in *Julius Caesar*: "There is a tide in the affairs of men, which, taken at the flood, leads on to fortune; omitted, all the voyage of their life is bound in shallows and miseries. On such a full sea are we now afloat." The Bronxville Rotary Club used that quotation to review a presentation I had made to them. They said:

> On very short notice, Dr. Tom Sluberski—a professor at Concordia and a true renaissance man—gave a most entertaining speech on his travels to St. Petersburg in the early 1990s. This was a remarkable time in Russian history: the Berlin Wall had fallen only a few years before Yeltsin was democratically elected as president, there was a failed coup over President Gorbachev, the Communist Party was banned, and the Soviet Union ceased to exist. Dr. Sluberski was asked to go to St. Petersburg for at

least one year to represent Lutheran interests and education. He initially refused, comfortable in his position at Concordia and not willing to shift his destiny so late in life. Concordia's president, Ralph Schultz, convinced him that this was an opportunity not to be missed. Bathed in that rapidly changing milieu of a country in great flux, Dr. Sluberski's simple assignment quickly expanded to encompass greater deeds. The "tide" that carried him to St. Petersburg led to further adventures and fortune, none of which would have come about if he had not accepted this initial assignment.

There are waves and tides that come our way. We never know which to ride, and which will prove mere ripples. Only looking back do we see which were the important ones, those that led to so much undreamed of when they came our way.

One of the most inspiring and accurate insights into aging is the one Alfred Lord Tennyson offers in his poem "Ulysses." Ulysses speaks as an old man, after a lifetime of glorious experiences, and he knows he "cannot rest from travel." He wants to "drink life to the lees," "always roaming with a hungry heart." He has seen "men, manners, climates, councils, governments, myself not least." He has become part of all that he has met and exclaims, "How dull it is to pause, to make an end." "Old age hath yet its honor and its toil . . . but something ere the end . . . some work may yet be done. To strive, to seek, to find, and not to yield." I find this becomes only more compelling as I grow older.

These essays are not necessarily representative, complete, or presented in strict chronological order; but they show to some degree where I was, how I got to where I am now, and my thinking along the way: how my mind has changed through the years and how my world expanded.

The earliest date from almost fifty years ago—my years in college, seminary, and graduate school; then presentations from my professional career and a leap forward to my arrival in Brazil and Russia. A short byway into a providential foray into the world of sports, and the volume concludes with "Times Winged Chariot," essays on death, dying, and the afterlife.

This collection is my own *A Mind in Frame*, that being the title of my last book, on the thought of another British poet whose work I've especially prized, Thomas Traherne (1636?-1674). This collection is read best not necessarily from front to back, but selectively, depending on the reader's interest. To help place each item included here in my own wandering biography, I've organized a timeline of my life; I include it at the back of this volume because it may be a useful "family tree" for those who want to understand the genesis of these writings.

September 2013 Oviedo, Florida

PART I

WHERE I WAS

"Had We But World Enough and Time"

From Andrew Marvell's "To His Coy Mistress"

CHAPTER ONE

HOW MY MIND HAS CHANGED

"How My Mind Has Changed" was written in the 1960s—heady times for the USA, the Lutheran church and Concordia Seminary in St. Louis. A bit trendy and academic, but it does reflect its era. It was chiefly the later overseas study, the parish, academia, and world events that changed my mind in different ways. I now wish I had written a "period" piece like this every five years or so. [Topics: Billy Graham, Eisenhower, liturgics, evolution, fundamentalism, pietism, Henry Reimann, Francis Pieper, Anglo-Catholic]

This article, more appropriately, should be entitled "How My Mind Is Always Changing" because my mind continues to change; a theologian, like a woman, has the prerogative of changing his mind. Not that change necessarily implies growth or advancement, but it does indicate flexibility and life—attributes, I might add, also of the Holy Spirit.

To illustrate the extent to which my mind has changed these past few years, it is first necessary to characterize my state of mind when I entered junior college in 1958. Like those of others then entering the ministry of the Lutheran Church—Missouri Synod, my theology was fundamentalist, my politics were right-wing Republican, my morality pietistic and my worship practice was free Protestant.

In high school I engaged in endless controversy with science teachers on the question of evolution, was lulled by the folksy Eisenhower administration, gave up dancing as a lustful pastime of the flesh, and ridiculed papist ritualism. But at this writing, even though I can understand why others continue to avow these positions, I can no longer stand before God or view the world in these ways. In these four areas, at least, I have made almost a complete about-face and the process of turning has been exhilarating.

Not one of these "new" positions, however, came without struggle and wavering, but in the process I think I understand more clearly how God works through people and events to change minds and hearts. This revelation has in turn made me a more mature Christian, with a personal faith better equipped to take the knocks of the twentieth century. These "object lessons" of the Holy Spirit have, in effect, forced me either to respond to or react from a Christian perspective, relying on the wisdom only He gives.

A) In 1958, I could confidently point to the Billy Graham New York TV Crusade as the most important theological event of that year, but I now see significant theological meaning also in the secular realm. Just as significant for my theological change of mind was one man whom I chose to call my mentor in absentia: Prof. Henry Reimann. Of course, my present stance cannot nor should not be attributed entirely to him, but his example did much to influence the general direction of the change: exegetical findings could be assimilated, Pieper could be built on, the liturgical renewal embraced, the sixteenth century Confessions doxologically affirmed as my twentieth-century confession because of Prof. Reimann's coordinating insight. More important, I learned the rudiments of independent and creative theological thinking. After his untimely death, my interest rapidly changed from systematics to exegesis; but soon, with the question "Is that all?" I turned to the area of "Christianity and culture" and began work on a Masters in English at Washington University simultaneously with my seminary degree. On vicarage I found this area, too, less relevant than it first appeared. The problems of the parish suggested the whole new world of Christian social ethics, family, politics, and technology. Paralleling these changes of interest, I found also a change in the questions I think important. There is a time for the isogogical question, a time for the three *genera*, a time for the survival of the historical vestments, but now is the time I am concerned about the social implications of the Christian *kerygma*.

B) Events of the Sixties: the civil rights struggle, the assassination of a president, the first man in space, and the "hotline" have irrevocably globalized my theology and forced me to reexamine my political convictions. I lost respect for the Republican Party and took a critical stance against the Democrats. The implications of the Christian message (as I interpreted them) led me to sympathize with those who were working toward a social democratic system through existing institutions. Social concern is now an integral part of both my theology and my view of the Christian ministry. My relationship with Jesus Christ has not changed, but the implications of the relationship have changed me. On vicarage, I found myself more often aligned with the leaders of social protest (even though at times they were humanists) than with the Lutheran clergy, who were enmeshed in a corrupted "doctrine of the two kingdoms." C) I suppose the censorious and inhibited attitudes of a certain type of Christian, as much as anything I read or experienced, contributed to the decline and fall of moralism in my life. I can no longer sing "The world is very evil" (hymn No. 605) without the qualification: God said, "It is good." The poem "God's Grandeur by Gerard Manley Hopkins, conveys a similar sentiment: The world is charged with the grandeur of God. There lives the dearest freshness deep down things . . . Because the Holy Ghost over the bent world broods . . . With warm breast and with ah! bright wings. Or to paraphrase a notorious pope (Leo X): "God has given us this world, let us enjoy it." D) After losing battle after battle on the subject at the senior college with a roommate from Bronxville, my Puritan worship attitudes began to change. A Fort Wayne pastor who in his person embodied the liturgical renewal and certain Anglo-Catholic authors (T. S. Eliot, Evelyn Waugh, and George Herbert) helped to make liturgical worship and the Catholic heritage emotionally satisfying as well as intellectually valid. Admittedly, it was all romantic and medieval, but a beginning had been made. However, when I saw the Lutheran liturgical tradition prostituted for aesthetic kicks, for love of the past, or for upper-class identification, I began to modify radically my position in that movement. I can no longer naively accept all that is perpetrated in the name of "renewal," and I believe I have given my "medievalism" a seemly burial. The liturgy must be twentieth century or, otherwise, we have a new Protestantism (worse than the old): a protest, as it were, against modernity, a protest against both the present and the future. To summarize: my theology is now confessional, my political ideal is more social democratic, the freedom of the Christian man has preempted priggishness, and the liturgical renewal informs my worship. It would seem, then, that my mind's changes were more attitudinal than doctrinal: the change was from knowing the truth to doing the truth, from individualism to ecumenical globalism, from inhibition to freedom. A year in another environment—vicarage— with different traditions and concerns should provide a perfect test situation to see whether I changed my mind merely in reaction to corruptions of otherwise sound points of view rather than because I was responding to the guidance of the Holy Spirit. Only the latter alternative will stand the test of our time and our eternity.[Some of the wider and later ramifications of the changes evidenced in this essay are elucidated in other chapters in this volume: the global, the ecumenical, the exegetical, the cultural, the systematic, the political, and the apologetic.]

CHAPTER TWO

AGAINST THE LAUGHTER HATERS
CONTRA MISOGELASTICS!

"Against the Laughter Haters: *Contra Misogelastics*," was a paper written for an apologetics seminar. I had been considering making apologetics the focus of my career, convincing the skeptic of the truth of Christianity.

{Topics: Stan Freberg, Max Eastman, Elton Trueblood, Jonathan Swift, Robert Short, G. K. Chesterton, C. S. Lewis, Alexander Pope, Robert McAfee Brown, Ronald Knox, David Head, Paul Harms}

A casual acquaintance with Christian tracts and literature, radio and television programs, art and movies would probably convince most outsiders that Christians are the most serious, the most somber, the most sober people in the world.

Too often, the only spoken humor permitted the public image of the church is the isolated (and therefore sterile) joke which might open a sermon. The joke columns or page fillers in Christian literature are often carefully separated as unclean things from the real "meaty" articles.

Max Eastman, an influential humor theorist, in his book *The Sense of Humor*, avowed that "it is only in our own too-Christian times that laughter was banished out of [religion] and tears alone established as an appropriate approach to the deity. Humor is of all things most unlike religion. And so it is not surprising that the mystics should seem wanting in the sacred gift of humor, and that humorists should be not often of a prayerful turn. A prayer is indeed the intense opposite of a comic laugh."

To the non-Christian, then, Christianity is not humorous (and far too many Christians would solemnly agree). There are those Christians who firmly believe that humor is frivolous, and satire, vicious. Christianity, therefore, according to this reasoning, is no laughing matter, and satire is no Christian matter.

There are, however, a growing number of Christians in our century who agree with Kierkegaard that "Christianity is the most humorous point of view in the history of the world," and far from being a failing, humor can be a powerful weapon in the contemporary world.

Our society has powerful defenses against the Gospel, and these defenses are not only spiritual but also cultural and intellectual. This kind of barrier will not be broken down by raising the volume of our message or extending the length of the siege. Instead, we need a Trojan horse to get inside the walled-off minds of those of our contemporaries who are "allergic" to God, who dismiss Christianity as irrelevant, who cannot separate religion from culture. There are satirists who are attempting to meet the challenge with a combination of the Trojan horse and Pegasus—not only entering in through the unguarded gate but also flying over the walls. These satirists are not only indicting the world for its lack of faith, but also the church for her lack of humor.

This article will attempt to point out some issues of the Christian use of satire by evaluating one genre of Christian satire (the radio and television spot) in the twentieth century, by placing satirical apologetic within the history of the church, and finally by listing possible contributions of satire to the church.

Some recent Christian radio and television spots are representative and illustrative of the possibilities of satire for Christian apologetics. In their use of mass media, electronics, and advertising (the "hallmarks" of the twentieth first century) these attempts are particularly appropriate for reaching the "world come of age."

The United Presbyterian Church late last summer released a ten-second television "spot" picturing a congregation at prayer. A pastor prays for those who are not present "this morning because of problems, illness, and other hardships." As he prays, animated figures appear on the screen, illustrating what the "absent brethren" are really doing: playing golf, lying on a chaise lounge, sipping a cool drink, and boating. The honorable intentions of the church are ironically juxtaposed with the actions of the members—resulting in incongruity and irony. The brunt of this satire, however, is aimed more at the non-participating church members, than at the real "outsider."

The Roman Catholic Radio and Television Apostolate of the St. Louis Archdiocese has developed six radio spots. The scene of one is the lobby of

a movie theater, where a cashier asks how old a boy is. The father drowns
out his son's "twelve" with "He's only eleven." The boy asks his dad why
he lied, to which the father replies, "What's a few months?" and besides,
"I'll buy you popcorn with the money we saved." The boy says in real
admiration, "Gee, Dad, I wish I could cheat as well as you."

The best of the six is about integration. This spot takes the form of
a phone call, which is an invitation to attend a neighborhood meeting
concerned about Negroes moving into the area. "We've got to protect our
property!" The man replies that he doesn't think he wants to get in on the
plan. The other asks in astonishment, "You're kidding?" To which the first
replies "No, I'm not, but I wish you were."

Perhaps the most successful attempt at satirical radio broadcasting is
Stan Freberg's commercials for the United Presbyterian Church. Much
study, effort, thought, and money went into three advertisements for
religion. They are geared to reach the "growing mass of people who—as
believers or unbelievers, churched or un-churched—are impervious to
traditional methods of religious communication. The spots are beamed at
the affluent young adult who thinks religion is chiefly a matter of being
good and life chiefly a matter of getting ahead. They carry no 'message'
as such. Instead, they gently needle the seemingly self-sufficient young
American and suggest that "life is distorted without God."

Although these commercials must be heard to be fully appreciated
(radio is a "back of the mind" medium which allows no time for close
analysis, as does newsprint), it is nevertheless helpful to see how theory is
carried out in practice.

A pastor and a "prospect" are discussing church attendance. (Note how
the pastor uses the best non-directive counseling approach!):

Man:	Well, I can't this Sunday . . . I'm playing golf, and uh . . .
Pastor:	The following Sunday?
Man:	I promised to take the kids to the beach.
Pastor:	Umm-hum.
Man:	A man's got to spend some time with his kids, you know.
Pastor:	Yeah, sure.
Man:	Besides, ahh . . . we find we get along just fine without church. You know. It's up to the individual. Uh, gee, look at the time. I've got to run. But anyhow, we'll trot along to church one of these days.
Pastor:	Um-humm, well, how about two weeks from Sunday?

Man: Oh, I never plan that far ahead. Two weeks. The whole
            world could blow up by then. Heh,—heh.
Pastor: That's right.

[MUSIC :] Where'd you get the idea
            You could make it by yourself?
            Doesn't it get a lit-tle lonely sometimes,
            Out on the limb . . . without Him . . . .
            It's a great life, but it could be greater,
            Why try and go it alone,
            The blessings you lose may be your own.

Freberg, the son of a Baptist minister, refused his usual $50,000 creative fee and even donated $1,500 toward the total cost of $13,000 for these "spots." He says the trick is "to disarm them, through entertainment of some sort, then once you have captured their attention, tell them what you have to offer in the simplest, most entertaining way possible. I have used, when you come right down to it, an almost espionage approach to sneaking up on them." This is how Troy was taken!

An opinion poll was made by C. E. Hooper Inc. on the effectiveness of these spots. They found that 99% of the listeners polled remembered what they heard; 85% found them interesting; 73% helpful; 88% in good taste; 49% not amusing; 79% wondered about living with God; 29% thought about church; 39% talked with others about the spots; 39% felt personally affected; 85% said they were church members. Approximately 14% of the city of St. Louis heard the spots.

In California it was found that occupation, education, religious affiliation, frequency of church attendance, or self-evaluated religiosity didn't affect the recall appreciably, nor did it make any difference whether the listener liked or disliked the spot.

Religious satire is not, however, peculiar to the twentieth century. God's spokesmen have been using it for centuries. Edwin Good's *Irony in the Old Testament, The Interpreter's Dictionary of the Bible* articles on "Humor" and "Irony and Satire in the Bible," and Elton Trueblood's *The Humor of Christ* are a good introduction to the nature and extent of this phenomenon in Holy Scripture.

The Satirical Letters of St. Jerome and the sermons of Bernard, Bromyard, and Wyclif demonstrate that satire and humor were not lost to the church even in the dark (but not dreary) ages. In fact, Theodore Maynard in his

Pillars of the Church observes that many of the saints "had a keen sense of humor; so much so that one is almost tempted to say that it is hardly possible to become a saint without it." The consensus of the fathers would be with St. Teresa of Avila who wrote: "From silly devotions and sour-faced saints, good Lord, deliver us!"

Satire is not merely an ornamental recurrence, however. Satire makes at least five positive contributions to the apologetic task of the church. Particularly useful are the *attention, impression, admonition, correction*, and *persuasion* functions of satire.

1) Satire not only catches our *attention*, but it arrests it. Satire is an effective "bait" to be used by twentieth century fishers of men. Like the parables of Jesus, satire that is well done traps our interest. No one falls asleep on a good joke. This is, perhaps, one reason for the surprisingly large recall of the Freberg advertisements. Robert Short, in this connection, has shown the possibilities and the function of humorous "bait" in his book *The Gospel According to Peanuts*.

2) Moreover, the use of satire creates a salutary *impression* of Christianity. Satire subtly indicates a sunny, good-natured, happy outlook on life. The satirical writings of such men as Jonathan Swift, C. S. Lewis, G. K. Chesterton, and R. A. Knox have pulled the image of Christianity out of the doldrums. The satire of these men communicates the love and pity inherent in all Christian criticism. Free and open, never priggish or fanatical, these men have gained a hearing for the faith in places usually inaccessible to Christianity. The British public enjoys the sparkling wit of their writings almost in spite of their pronounced Christian bias. The use of satire also indicates sophistication, intelligence, and talent. It takes a quick mind and an intelligent writer to stay one jump ahead of a reader. This is precisely why the college graduate is more drawn to the sharp satire of the *New Yorker* and *Playboy* than to the insipid moralizing so rampant in Christian publications.

What is more, satire communicates the security inherent in the satirist's position. It is only the secure man who can joke about a serious situation creatively. It may well be that in our times the last stronghold of meaningful satire will be the church, as mobility and relativity infect more areas that were traditionally stable in our culture.

3). Christian satire can also serve as an *admonition*, a rebuke—a judgment upon men, institutions, and ideas. It is the peculiar gift of satire to juxtapose the temporal and the eternal, thereby exhibiting the inherent incongruity of life. This forces, as Stanley Hopper put it, the "conscious inward infinitely upon its sense of moral impotence and ethical responsibility . . . Thus in its profoundest sense, irony may assist in bringing the rebellious soul, the soul curved in upon itself, to the point of moral choice . . ."

Satire thus forces us to ask the religious question by stripping away our defenses and our pride. The soul is made aware of its imperfections and its sin. Satire then becomes like the "law"—a schoolmaster to lead us to Christ. Alexander Pope combined his understanding of the admonition and the correction functions of satire in these words.

> As with a moral view designed
> To cure the vices of mankind:
> His vein, ironically grave,
> Expos'd the Fool, and lashed the Knave.

Swift was another effective employer of this function of satire.

4). Satire is *corrective* when it focuses upon ideas and actions that are perversions of the faith. In this way the Christian sees more clearly the disjunction between his profession and his practice.

Certain twentieth-century Christian satires have as their explicit or implicit intent the reformation and the information of the church. In this category belong Charles Merrill Smith's *How to be a Bishop Without Being Religious*, which exposes the organizational climbing and the debased motivations all too evident in the church; Robert McAfee Brown's *The Collected Writings of St. Hereticus*, which parodies and caricatures the seminarian and the Sunday school teacher, the pastor and the congregation exceptionally well. Other good examples: "Pen-Ultimates"; "Eutychus and his Kin"; S. J. Forrest's *What's the Use*; and David Head's audacious three books on prayer: *He Sent Leanness* (prayers for the natural man), *Stammerer's Tongue* (prayers for the infant Christian), and *Shout for Joy* (prayers of the angels).

The essays of Fr. Ronald A. Knox are probably among the best religious satires of our century. They exemplify the corrective possibilities of satire not only for the church, but also for the world. Aspects of the ecumenical movement are caricatured in "Reunion all Round" and "Absolute and Abitofhell." Form Criticism is ridiculed in his "Studies in the Literature of Sherlock Holmes," "The Identity of the Pseudo-Bunyon," "The Authorship of 'In Memoriam,'" and "Materials for a Boswellian Problem." "A New Cure for Religion" and "The New Sin" castigate society's attitude toward religion and sin.

5). And as well there is the *persuasive* function of satire. Paul Harms has succinctly stated his understanding of this phenomenon in a *Triangle* article:

"What some of the most profound thought and most persuasive argument, finely drawn, fail to achieve, a bit of humor does. Humor cracks through our defenses. When our defenses are down, we accept and often embrace that which we would otherwise have resisted on psychological, theological, and philosophical grounds."

Alexander Pope put it (rather arrogantly) in poetry:

> Yes, I'm proud, I must be proud to see
> Men not afraid of God, afraid of me;
> Safe from the Bar, the Pulpit, and the Throne,
> Yet touched and shamed by Ridicule alone.

The difficulty of standing up against the onslaught of laughter puts a grave responsibility into the hands of the satirist. Norman Vincent Peale almost gave up the ministry because of the ridicule directed at his position, such as one Christian pastor's evaluation: "I find Paul appealing and Peale appalling."

Thus, we see that satire can be used as a tool of Christian apologetics, for the function of satire closely parallels the function of apologetics. We can, furthermore, go a step further and maintain that satire and humor are of the essence of Christianity. G. K. Chesterton believed that the "test of a good religion" was "whether or not you could joke about it." C. S. Lewis observed that "it is the heart not yet sure of its God that is afraid to laugh in His presence." Leslie Weatherhead adamantly capped the argument when he affirmed that the "opposite of joy is not sorrow, but unbelief." The

Christian stance is viewed as foolish by the world, but from his stance in faith, the Christian is able to glimpse how ironic and humorous the actions and attitudes of blundering mortals must look from God's point of view.

Yes, we must be *"against misogelastics,"* against the laughter haters, just as much as the second-century apologists were against Celsus, for those who do not laugh deny the fullness of Christianity as well as undercut the mission of the church in the contemporary world.

CHAPTER THREE

FRIAR JOHN: THE ANTIPODAL APOSTLE IN CHAUCER'S "THE SUMMONER'S TALE"

This is a graduate seminar paper written at Washington University, a *very* secular institution. At the time, there was an interesting cooperation between Washington University and Concordia Seminary, allowing students to study at both schools at greatly reduced cost, which enabled me to get two degrees (M.A. and M.Div.) simultaneously. This study gave me an opportunity to approach issues from a secular as well as a religious standpoint using the accepted methodology in each field of study. This is another in a series of studies of satire. Only two are included in this volume.

(A brief synopsis of the tale: Chaucer attacks a previous story in his *Canterbury Tales*, told by a friar who had decried summoners as corrupt. Summoners were those who brought people to attend ecclesiastical courts. The summoner satirizes the lengthy sermons and high living of friars. A friar makes his living by preaching and begging. He is supposed to record the names of people who give him money, but he erases the names as soon as he leaves the house. When he goes to a sick man's house, he asks for an extravagant meal of a roasted pig's head and asks for money to build his own cloister. The sick man gets angry and says he has given too much to friars through the years. The friar then uses three parables about the sin of anger. The sick man then says he has one gift that should be shared equally among the friars. He is sitting on it. The friar puts his hand under the sick man's butt, and the sick man farts. The friar is furious and goes to a local lord, who is not very sympathetic and instead wonders how the flatus might be shared equally among the thirteen friars of the order. A squire suggests having the friars stand around a cartwheel while someone farts. The lord rewards the squire with a new coat to show how impressed he is with what was done to the friar.)

When the critical material available on "The Summoner's Tale" is compared in quantity and quality with that on other individual *Canterbury Tales*, it would appear that "The Summoner's Tale" either is overlooked or is insignificant. To some extent, this phenomenon may be attributed to "bad press." "Disorganized," "lacks solidarity," "does not add up to much," "remains an extended anecdote," "deliberately ill-constructed," "an example of elementary humor," "the humor of stable-boys and swineherds" are a few negative estimates of the tale.[1]

Perhaps another factor that has inhibited appreciation is the fragmented approach to the "Summoner's Tale." Until recently isolated puns,[2] literary sources,[3] and similar piecemeal studies[4] have engaged scholarly attention, and no one has bothered or has been able to detect structural unity or an organizing principle in the tale. However, since Germaine Dempster in 1932 suggested that dramatic irony is a key to a number of the *Canterbury Tales*,[5] there have been at least three good articles which attempt to relate structure to meaning.[6]

When Mrs. Dempster combined a knowledge of the sources[7] and an understanding of irony, she perceived dramatic irony as the main point of the tale.[8] She demonstrated that Chaucer strengthens the basic irony in his source and heightens contrast and humor by intensifying the friar's lust for gold, the friar's sermon on anger, and the friar's parables on "ire."

Though characterization is important to the ironical nature of the tale, Mrs. Dempster perhaps overstates her case when she suggests that Chaucer suppresses ironies already latent in the plot and adds others only when they serve the external purpose of characterization.[9] The dramatic irony of the tale appears to rest on far more than characterization. Chaucer, more than likely, capitalizes on the satirical potential of his material. Dempster's research, however, suggested a direction, and her emphasis on dramatic irony, on hypocrisy, and on anger proved to be germinal to much later criticism.

Without inordinate stress on characterization, Earle Birney develops Dempster's concept of dramatic irony. The story, as he sees it, rests upon "expectation monstrously and comically frustrated." Chaucer weaves ironical foreshadowings, ambiguities, and reversals into the basic tale; for this reason, most of the "apparent digressions in the interests of framework satire will be seen . . . to be contributions to this central irony."[10] With "foreshadowings" as the key to structure, other aspects of the tale besides characterization are opened to analysis, but when characterization is taken as the main point of the tale much detail will be considered extraneous. Birney's sane and evocative reading of the tale evidences the value of his method.

In his article "The Structure of Irony in the Summoner's Tale" (closely echoing Birney's "Structural Irony within the Summoner's Tale"), John Adams concentrates on hypocrisy as the abuse underlying the structure. Although gluttony, avarice, and anger are also mentioned in the tale, hypocrisy is the generic sin of which other sins are merely species. "The Summoner's Tale" can be interpreted as a veritable compendium of the standard abuses of the friars. Birney's reading is rescued from fragmentation by his qualification that moral failings are included not to be exposed but rather as integral parts of the structure. The essential feature of Chaucer's criticism of the friar is that it is dramatic. "Each criticism is dramatically realized through the character and action of this particular friar."[11] Because Adams contrasts words with actions, the standard with the abuse, he interprets the tale much as Birney but from a different perspective.

The weakest part of his article is his comments on the sermon against anger. Adams rightly observes that what Thomas needs is not so much a sermon on anger but a sermon on sloth. The sermon the friar preaches is really "morally irrelevant" to Thomas's spiritual needs. Further, the morals the friar wrenches from his parables on anger are irrelevant to the main purposes of the stories. The sermon, therefore, is a satiric commentary on the irrelevant preaching of the friars.[12] Adams, however, does not connect the sermon with the rest of the tale, nor does he sufficiently develop the satire inherent in the sermon.

Thomas Merrill concentrates on this omission in his article, "Wrath and Rhetoric in the Summoner's Tale." His approach appears to be less unified and instructive, but in explicating the sermon Merrill includes not only the insights of others (from dramatic irony to the workings of hypocrisy, from the use of puns to source criticism) but also his own consideration of the tale in its larger context to illuminate the satirical elements of the sermon.

Within this larger view, the satire of the sermon and of the tale itself are extended and deepened. On one level is the ironic presentation of a hypocritical friar's preaching a sermon on anger to someone who does not need it (Thomas) and immediately thereafter himself falling victim to the sin. On another level, when the tale is put into its larger framework, particularly in connection with the argument between the summoner and Friar Huberd, the "Summoner's Tale" in effect becomes a retaliatory device. The summoner's primary motive for including the digression on anger (comprising about one-fifth of the tale) is to discredit hot-tempered Huberd.[13] There is yet another level of irony. When the tale is considered from Chaucer's point of view, the satire is compounded with dividends not only against Friar John and Friar Huberd, but also against the teller of the tale (the summoner).[14]

The value of seeing the tale in a wider context is evident in Merrill's treatment of the anti-ire parables. Each of the parables illustrates the consequences of anger, and by extension each applies to Friar John, to Friar Huberd and *also* to the summoner. With this method of interpretation Merrill not only defends the importance of the sermon; more important, he provides a larger context and a clearer focus to the tale and its individual parts. Thus a seeming "digression" on anger becomes the "absolute moral standard against which the posing of two 'moralists' is illuminated into comedy."[15]

THE THESIS OF THIS ESSAY:

> The trend in criticism of "the Summoner's Tale" seems to be turning attention from isolated details to the wider context of the tale ("the Friar's Tale," "the Parson's Tale," and "the Prologue"). Following this trend, this paper will attempt to demonstrate that the satire of "the Summoner's Tale" can best be understood by comparing the deeds, words, and thoughts of the portrait of Friar John to the Christian ideal.[16] This is one method of appreciating the totality of the tale and its individual parts as well as its relationship to the other *Canterbury Tales*. By allusion, by foreshadowings, and by undertone (both conscious and unconscious) a point of reference is delineated, a moral landscape is sketched, and an absolute moral standard is erected from which and to which the action and characters are to be compared and contrasted.
>
> In effect, "the Summoner's Tale" portrays Friar John as an antipodal apostle. His actions, his words, his motives, and his

ideals are totally opposed to those of a Christian apostle. Yet the profession and the professions of Friar John lead the reader to expect a modicum of apostolic character.

By profession he is a Christian friar, a latter-day disciple of Jesus Christ, and a man from whom one should expect Christian behavior; by his many professions, the reader is led to expect a model Christian friar.

> I walke, and fisshe Cristen mennes soules,
> To yelden Jhesu Crist his propre rente
> To sprede his word is set al myn entente (1820=23).[17]

Moreover, he asks Thomas to see whether the Gospel is more like "oure professioun,/ Or hirs that swymmen in possessioun" (1925=26). He asserts that

> We fare as seith th' apostle; clooth and foode
> Suffisen us . . .

> The clennesse and the fastynge of us freres
> Maketh that Crist accepteth oure preyeres. (1881=84).

Friar John goes on to say that it is this similarity to the apostles that enables

> Oure orisons been moore effectueel,
> And moore we seen of Cristes secree thynges,
> Than burel folk (1870=73, cf. 1913).

The essential hypocrisy of this friar's profession and professions is the central irony in "the Summoner's Tale." The words *"peccavi nimis cogitatione, verbo, et opere"*[18] from the confession of sins in the Mass provide a convenient organizing principle for Chaucer's characterization of Friar John.

First, the actions or the "opera" betray the antipodal character of his apostleship. The activity of Friar John and his comrades after he had preached in church suggests a comparison to Christ's sending the disciples two by two into every city to preach the good news (Luke 10:1 ff.). However, there was a third person in the friar's company—"a sturdy harlot" (1754) to carry the loot (an addition to the company surely not envisioned by Jesus Christ). What is more, the presence of the sturdy harlot betrays Friar John's confidence of getting a sackful that day. The tenth chapter of Luke further states that Christ enjoined the disciples to "carry neither purse, nor scrip, nor shoes" (Luke 10:4), yet Friar John traveled "with scrippe and tipped staf" (1734, cf. 1776). Furthermore,

> His felaw hadde a staf tipped with horn,
> A peyre of tables al of yvory,
> And a poyntel polysshed fetisly (1740=43).

What is more, the friar went

> hous by hous, til he
> Cam til an hous ther he was wont to be
> Refresshed moore than in an hundred placis (1765=68).

This too is inconsistent with Christ's standard which was that the disciples were "To remain in the same house, eating and drinking such things as they give: for the laborer is worthy of his hire. Go not from house to house" (Luke 10:7).

The purpose, of course, of the friar's going from house to house was his begging.

> In every house he gan to poure and prye,
> And beggeth mele and chese, or elles corn (1738=39).[19]

The true disciples, however, "forsook all, and followed Him" (Luke 5:10, cf. Matthew 4:19). Also, St. Paul emphasized that he "preached . . . the gospel of God *freely*" (II Corinthians 11:7). He received no wages for his work, but Paul supported himself by making tents. There can be no doubt that the Christian ideal put no stress on money or begging. Even Friar John paid lip service to the ideal when he appropriated one of the Beatitudes=—"Blessed are the poor in spirit, for theirs is the kingdom of heaven" (Matthew 5:3)==as a prophecy of friars (1923). Yet, Friar John appears to be more concerned with wealth than with the soul of Thomas.

He consistently confuses a lesser goal with a higher, and his lust for the tangible instead of the intangible is ironically judged when he receives the intangible "fart" instead of the tangible "yifte" which he so desired. Friar John truly is a "parfit leche" (1956) in more ways than one, but Thomas might rightly have said, "Physician heal thyself" (Luke 4:23).

When the impropriety of Friar John's method of begging is compared to the apostolic ideal, the cleavage is widened. The friar stresses that those who give to his cause will have their name written down (1743, 1752) whereas Christ told His disciples not to do "your alms before men, to be seen of them: otherwise ye have no reward of your Father which is in Heaven." (Matthew 6:1). As will be seen, those who gave alms to these friars in reality received no reward at all for their gifts. Elsewhere, Christ warns that "When thou doest alms, let not thy left hand know what thy right hand doeth" (Matthew 6:3). In effect, the friar implicitly denies the letter and the spirit of these injunctions, encouraging the almsgivers "to be seen of men" and to know what their "right hand doeth." Of course the essential irony of the begging practice of the friars inheres in their deceptive practice of writing down the names "ascaunces that he wolde for hem preye" (1745). In this manner he serves them with "nyfles and with fables" (1760), and then erases the names "whan that he was out at dore" (1757). This practice may be evaluated by the words of St. Paul, "Such are false apostles, *deceitful* workers, transforming themselves into the apostles of Christ. And no marvel, for Satan himself is transformed into an angel of light" (II Corinthians 11:13, 14). The deceptions of Friar John evidence the insincerity of his apostleship.

Thomas is said to be a "sike man," which indirectly adds yet another failing to the lengthening list against Friar John. The disciples were bidden to "heal the sick" (Luke 10:9), not to beg or steal from them.

Although the tale makes no explicit judgment about Friar John's maintenance of the vow of chastity, there is a hint, which when taken in conjunction with a warning from the Bible, evidences questionable practice. It is said pejoratively of certain men in the "last days" that "they creep into houses, and lead captive silly women laden with sins, led away with diverse lusts" (II Timothy 3:6). The Friar asked for the "dame" almost immediately, and flattered her and "hire embraceth in his armes narwe,/ And kiste hire sweete, and chirketh as a sparwe/With his lyppes" (1803=05). He knew wherein his strength lay.

He proceeds to order his dinner from the wife (1839=42), even though the apostolic command was that they were to eat "such things as they give"

(Luke 10:7). His interest in food militates against his constant avowals of "fasting." He swears that he was a "man of litel sustenaunce" (1844), but he emphasizes gifts of food in his begging (1739).

Another characteristic that contributes to the completely hypocritical nature of Friar John and his world is his need to take the case of the "yifte" to court. Thomas is the friar's brother both by decree (1946) and by the brotherhood implied in a common Christianity. However, after Friar John was insulted, he went to the lord for redress (2189). He vows vengeance (2211) and amendment (2193). These desires, coupled with the fact that Thomas is a brother, nicely contradicts Paul's concern that "brother goeth to law with brother."

> Now therefore there is utterly a fault among you, because ye go
> to law with one another. Why do ye not rather take wrong? Why
> do ye not rather suffer yourselves to be defrauded? (I Corinthians
> 6:6, 7)

This picture of an antipodal apostle is created under the guise of factual reporting which requires some knowledge of the moral landscape to which Chaucer has constant reference.

Secondly, by every word that comes out of the mouth of the friar, Chaucer undergirds his portrait of an antipodal apostle.

Friar John would have had Thomas believe that friars are characterized by "humblenesse" (1870, cf. 1884, 1913), that "the world (will go) al to destruccioun, if yow lakke oure predicacious" (2109=10), and that "whoso wolde us from this world bireve,/He wolde bireve out of this world the sonne" (2111, 13). Pride often goes before a fall, and Jankyn's biting reference to "your noble confessour" (2165) hinted at the judgment which was to come. "Whosoever shall exalt himself shall be abased" (Matthew 23:12).

When Thomas calls Friar John "O deere maister" (1781), he goes unrebuked by the friar, although Friar John grudgingly acknowledges the impropriety (though not the injustice) of the greeting when called "maister" by the lord.

> No maister, sire, quod he, but servitour,
> Thogh I have had in scole that honour.
> God liketh nat that 'Raby' men us calle (2185=87).

What the friar alludes to is an extensive section in Matthew, in which Christ lists the marks of the Pharisees, and commands his disciples not to be like them.

> But be ye not called Rabbi: for one is your
> Master, even Christ, and all ye are *brethren*.
> Neither be ye called masters: for one is your
> Master, even Christ (Matthew 28:8=11).

The irony of Thomas calling Friar John "maister" is heightened when it is remembered that Thomas was a lay *brother*. What is more, the appended warning proves to be true. Friar John does "exalt himself" and was "abased" both by Thomas and by Jankyn. The proud are humbled.

Flattery is another counter-apostolic characteristic of Friar John. The second sermon illustration of the friar (2056=2079) has as its application that the best way to deal with a man of exalted degree is to flatter him. Even though Friar John tells Thomas, "Of me thou shalt not been yflattered" (1970), flattery remains his method. He addressed him previously, "O Thomas, freend, seyde this frere, curteisly and softe" (1769=71). He divulges part of the reason for his flattery when he says that

> ful ofte
> Have I upon this bench faren ful weel;
> Heere have I eten many a myrie meel (1770=74).

This sycophantic characteristic of Friar John is evident also in his relationship to the lord.

> doun to the court he gooth
> Where as there woned a man of greet honour,
> To whom that he was alwey confessour
> This worthy man was Lord of that village (2162=65).

Friar John, however, has no kind word (nor any word) for his servants or with Jankyn, for they have nothing to give. His actions can be unfavorably juxtaposed to the methods of St. Paul, who said, "For neither at any time used we flattering words nor a cloak of covetousness" (I Thessalonians 2:5). Significantly, the Parson "rekene flaterie in the vices of Ire" (X, I, 617).

Equally revelatory is Friar John's fascination with numbers. The tale opens with his mathematical solution to a spiritual problem. How can one escape so many days in purgatory? Friar John suggests to the congregation that twenty-nine days might be eliminated by condensing the "trental" into one day (1724=1732). Moreover, the priests are explicitly criticized for singing only one Mass a day (1728). There is, however, *one* soul that Friar John ought to have been more concerned about in his travels that day, because the friar's concern with numbers and quantity ironically turns back upon himself. He, in effect, suggested the very method of his own punishment to Thomas. In an involved reasoning process by which Friar John tries to prove to Thomas that he ought to have given all his money to one convent, he asks Thomas,

> What is a ferthying worth, parted in twelve?
> Lo, ech thyng that is oned in himselve
> Is moore strong than what it is toscatered (1967=9).

The sound of "ferthyng" resembles the sound of "fart," and the "twelve" and "toscatered" are ironically twisted by Janykn to compound the irony of his answer (2270=74).

The lord himself is aware of the mathematical interests of the friar and seizes upon this interest to avoid the real issue of Thomas's insult (2214=15).

> I trowe the devel putte it in his mynde.
> In ars-metrike shal ther no man fyndes (2220=22).

Of course "ars" is a pun on the word "ers" of the devil in the prologue to the tale (1705) as well as the source of Friar John's insult. In connection with Janykn's solution the lord observes that "Jankyn spak, in this matere, as wel as Euclide dide or Ptholomee." Friar John discovers to his chagrin that people can never be manipulated mechanically and by enumeration. Before the convent was begun, the friars ought to have "counted the cost" (Luke 14:28) in terms of human beings instead of material "tyle" (2105).

Another way words betray Friar John's counter-imitation of Christ is the matter of swearing. Christ enjoins His disciples,

> Swear not at all, neither by heaven . . . nor by the earth. But let
> your communications be, Yea, Yea; Nay, Nay: for whatsoever is
> more than this cometh from evil (Matthew 5:34, 35).

Ironically, however, Friar John *swore* "on his professioun" (2135) that Thomas's gift would be distributed to "every frere" (2134-37). Those words betray the falsity both of his "professioun" and of his professions. Those words come from an "evil" friar and came to an "evil" end. That the story revolves around just such a distribution (ironically misused) is indeed poetic justice.

No commentator appears to have adequately traced the source of Thomas's "yifte." However, when the "yifte" is connected with "swearing" two Biblical parallels are evident. Both parallels appear in the book of Genesis.

> Abraham said unto his eldest servant of his house, 'Put, I pray thee, thy hand under my thigh' (Genesis 24:2).

> Israel called his son Joseph and said unto him, 'Put, I pray thee, thy hand under my thigh, and deal kindly and truly with me; bury me not in Egypt (Genesis 47:29).

Both the Genesis accounts and "the Summoner's Tale" have as their subjects "swearing" and a hand on the thigh. However, Chaucer overturns the positive intention of Genesis, which resulted in a "blessing" for the servant and for Joseph. Instead, Friar John receives a curse. (The hand under the thigh can be compared to putting one's hand on a Bible in a courtroom.)

Angry words break into the tale in response to a charge of deception. Friar Huberd, who can no longer restrain himself, cries out, "Nay, ther thou lixt, thou somonour" (1761). This is the first suggestion of the important anger theme of the tale. Friar John is well aware of the nature of anger, and he presents a thorough case against it. The devil, he says, sets hearts afire with anger (1982). Moreover, anger is one of the seven deadly sins (2005), and brings "destruccion," "homycide," "pryde," and "sorwe" (2005=16). Furthermore, God has forbidden it (1834). When, therefore, Thomas's wife asks the friar to "chide" her husband on his anger (1824), the friar graciously complies by preaching a sermon on the evils of anger which comprises one-fifth of the length of the entire tale.

The sermon brings no response from Thomas, but the friar's begging does. When Friar John gets down "on his knee" to beg (2120), Thomas "wax wel ny wood for ire" (2121). As an angry response to Friar John's tactics, Thomas is driven to play the crude practical joke on the friar, even though he had just heard a long sermon against anger. The irony is protracted by the friar's angry response to the practical joke. He "stirte as dooth a wood leoun" (2152), left "with a ful angry cheere" (2158), and "grynte with his teeth, so was he wrooth" (2161). The comedy is compounded when he appeared before the lord in a rage.

There is more to the satire than Thomas's angry response after a long sermon against anger, or even the anger of the preacher who does not practice what he preaches. There is also an implicit link with Christian morality. It is written in the book of James, "Let every man . . . be slow to wrath. For the wrath of man worketh not the righteousness of God" (James 1:19). As things develop, Friar John should have controlled his wrath and not have gone to the lord with his grievance. Moreover, it is written in the book of Proverbs, "Make no friendship with an angry man; and with a furious man thou shalt not go" (Proverbs 22:24). If Friar John had heeded this advice in the case of Thomas, perhaps he would not have received the gift he did. What is more, Jesus said, "Whosoever is angry with his brother without a cause shall be in danger of the judgment" (Matthew 5:22). Ironically, Friar John *is* subjected to judgment—Jankyn's—and loses. Anger, like the other antipodal apostle characteristics of Friar John, is integral to the dramatic irony of "the Summoner's Tale," comparing and contrasting, as it does, the content of the sermon with the actions of hearer and preacher as well as judging everything in a scriptural context.

Friar John uses words in an anti-apostolic way not only by boasting, by flattery, by arithmetic, and by swearing, but also (and most detrimentally) by his preaching. The tale opens with a reference to Friar John's preaching, and preaching is integral to the structure of the tale. To Thomas, Friar John says that the sermon is "after my symple wit," and "in prechyng is my diligence,/ and studie in Petres wordes and in Poules" (1818-19). Friar John has an extremely high regard for preaching (2109) especially his own, but this high regard is not matched by his audience (2281-86), one of whom would have repaid him with "th firste smel of fartes thre" (2284).

The extended sermon of Friar John is in reality a parody of what a Christian sermon ought to be (2116 ff.). It is unorganized. Its theme comprises the diverse subjects of abstinence, alms-giving, patience, and anger. Moreover, it is insensible to the spiritual needs of the hearer (Thomas). Thomas appears to be suffering more from sloth than from anger, but in this way the sermon participates in the action of the tale and contributes to the denouement. Furthermore, the sermon is extremely secular in content. All three major *exempla* of Friar John have little connection to Christianity, and the rhetorical style by which the friar delivers his message serves to heighten the contrast with the biblical passage. The biblical stress is on simplicity:

> . . . take no thought how or what ye shall speak: for it shall be given you in that hour what ye shall speak. (Matthew 10:21).

> But though I be rude in speech, yet not in knowledge; but we have been thoroughly made manifest among you in all things (II Corinthians 11:6).

This latter statement of St. Paul might be rephrased to refer to the preaching practices of Friar John. "Though I be high-flown in speech, yet not in knowledge, but by this means I have been thoroughly made manifest (as an antipodal apostle) among you in all things."

Closely connected to his misuse of words in the sermon is his talent in "glosynge." Not all his words are "after the text of hooly writ" (1790-93). Those words are true on a more pervasive scale than Friar John intended. He goes on to say,

> For it is hard to yow, as I suppose,
> And therefore wol I teche yow al the glose.
> Glosynge is a glorious thing, certeyn (1790-93).

The stress on difficulty is ironically reversed in the coda to the tale which can be understood as a gloss on the text of the tale. The riddle Thomas presents to the Friar proved to be unanswerable by Friar John, by the lord, or by the lady, but Jankyn solved the dilemma "nat all after the text." In reality that is not the problem Friar John came to have solved, but his sermons are not exactly what the people needed nor are they faithful to the text. Just as Friar John ignores the text in his preaching, so Jankyn ignores Friar John in his solution, yet he does solve the difficulty Friar John poses:

> To parte that wol nat departed be,
> To every man yliche, with meschaunce! (2213-15).

Glossing is another example of the hypocrisy of the friars, for by it they could prove whatever they wished (1919), but in reality the actual text of Scripture judges rather than supports their activities.

It is easier to demonstrate that the deeds and words of Friar John are counter to those of a real apostle of Jesus Christ. However, it may be that Chaucer attempts to illustrate the thoughts and ideals, the true nature of Friar John, by his deeds and words. "The Parson's Tale" investigates the roots of sin whether in thought, word, or deed. By reference to "the Parson's Tale," it is possible to demonstrate that Friar John is guilty of most of the seven deadly sins, and by extension, it is possible to suggest some of the thoughts and ideals he had. The thought is usually prior to either the word or the deed, and thus it is not necessary to attempt to "mind-read" to discover the antipodal apostle characteristics in the *cogitatione* of Friar John.

Friar John is manifestly guilty of the root sin of pride, whose branches are said to be "Inobedience, Avautinge, Ipocrisie, Despyt, Arrogance, Impudence, Swellings of herte, Insolence, Elacion, Impatience, Pertinacie, Veyne Glorie" (X (I) 390-93). The parson goes on to say that envy springs by nature from malice and,

> malice hath two speces: that is to seyn, hardnesse of herte in wikkednesse, or elles the flessh of man is so blynd that he considereth nat that he is in synne, or rekketh nat that he is in synne, which is the hardnesse of the devel. That oother spece of malice is whan a man werreyeth trouthe, what he woot that it is trouthe; and eek whan he werreyeth the grace that God hath yeve to his neighbor; and al this is by Envye (X (I) 485-88).

Friar John is hard of heart and does not consider that he is wicked. He wearies truth both in his begging and in his avowals in connection with the death of Thomas's child.

What is more, it is amply demonstrated that Friar John is wrathful. The parson, however, deepens the interrelationships of anger with other failings of Friar John. A certain kind of anger has a wicked determination to take vengeance (X (I) 544). Furthermore, pride increases anger by chiding and wicked words (X (I) 550). "Homicyde" (X (I) 560), "hate" (X (I) 565), "swering" (X (I) 585), "lesynges" (X (I) 608), "flateringe" (X (I) 612), "cursynge" (X (I) 617), "chidynge and reproche" (X (I) 622) are all connected with anger.

The parson's commentary on "Accidie" describes Friar John particularly when he talks about the "newe shepherdes" who have "no fors of hir owene governaunce" (X (I) 720 ff.). The coldness which freezes the heart of man could well describe the attitude of Thomas, the lord, the lady, and Jankyn towards Friar John.

Avarice is connected to idolatry by the parson, and this may be the god which Friar John follows since he is definitely not a follower of the Christian God. Friar John did desire "erthely thynges."

In Friar John's interest in "rich metes" and "outrageous apparailinge of mete" (X (I) 832) when he ordered his dinner from the wife evidences traces of "Glotonye."

The "seconde finger" of Lecherie applies to the friar. The parson describes it in the words of Solomon, "who-so toucheth and handleth a womman, he fareth lyk him that handleth the scorpioun that stingeth." (X (I) 852). "The fourthe finger is the kissinge." (X (I) 855). The friar, by implication, commits the sin of lechery when he kisses the wife.

A paper could be written merely comparing the deeds, words, and thoughts of Friar John with the homily of the Parson. These few suggestions and parallels with the seven deadly sins indicate the nature of the thoughts of Friar John and his ideals.

Friar John is not merely a caricature of what a disciple should be, but he is worse than an antipodal apostle. If he is compared to a portrait of men in the last days written in the second letter to Timothy, Friar John takes on aspects of the very Antichrist himself.

> (1) This know also, that in the last days perilous times shall come, (2) for men shall be lovers of their own selves, covetous, boasters, proud, blasphemers . . . unthankful, unholy, (3) . . . incontinent, fierce, despisers of those that are good, (4) . . . heady, high-minded; lovers of pleasures more than lovers of God; (5) Having a form of godliness, but denying the power thereof: from such turn away. (7) For of this sort are they which creep into houses, and lead captive silly women laden with sins, led away with divers lusts, (9) But they shall proceed no further: for their folly shall be manifest unto all men, (13) But evil men and seducers shall wax worse and worse, deceiving and being deceived.

This description added to Christ's warning to "Beware of false prophets, which come to you in sheep's clothing, but inwardly are ravening wolves. Ye shall know them by their fruits." (Matthew 7:15, 16), adds the last damning piece of evidence to the case against Friar John.

The antipodal apostle characteristics of Friar John evidenced in his thoughts, words, and deeds are integral to the structure of "the Summoner's Tale." Each of his failings is ironically and dramatically portrayed. Thus, Chaucer does not employ the contrasts between a true and false apostle merely for momentary comedy. Nor does he intend to list a compendium of the standard abuses of the friars merely to criticize them. Instead, each of the vices of the friar contributes in five ways to a larger whole: to the plot, to the characterizations, and to the satire.

In connection with the plot the antipodal apostle theme is used throughout the tale to under gird the final comedy.

> Twelve spokes hath a cartwheel comunly.
> And bryng me thanne twelve freres, woot ye why?
> Thrittene is a covent, as I gesse (2257-2259).

The solution to Thomas's riddle, understood in the light of Friar John's contrary apostolic actions, is a fitting climax and integral part of this key theme of "the Summoner's Tale." When Jankyn said that Friar John deserved the "firste fruyt" because "he is a man of greet honour" (2276, 77), and when he commented that the "noble usage of freres yet is this/ The worthy men of hem shul first be served" he pointed out another connecting link in the counter-apostle theme of the tale. In the New Testament, Christ is spoken of as the "first fruits" (I Corinthians 15:20, 23). In Proverbs, it is "the Lord" who is to be honored "with the first fruits" (3:9). There is one passage, however, which—when juxtaposed with the kind of first fruits Jankyn is proposing—adds yet another dimension to the irony.

> Ourselves also, which have the first fruits of the Spirit, even we ourselves groan within ourselves, waiting for . . . the redemption of our body (Romans 8:23).

Jankyn suggests a different kind of "spirit" (if spirit can be understood in its wider sense as "wind" and as the "intangible"). Friar John probably did "groan" within himself when that kind of "first fruit" was suggested. Contributing to the denouement of the tale is Friar John's assertion "that the wekman worthy is his hyre" (1973). This statement, too, is turned against him. He receives just what he is "worth."

And certeinly he hath it weel disserved.
He hath to-day taught us so muche good
That I may vouche sauf, I sey for me
He hadde the firste smel of fartes thre (2280-84).

It would seem that the lord and lady concurred.

On a second level, the antipodal apostle then provides a point of view, a way of looking at the action and the characters, and a referent for judgment. Friar John's constant claims to worth and holiness, when juxtaposed with the absolute moral standard of the New Testament, provide the basis for an *alazon* whose clay feet are easily displayed by a *eiron* (both Thomas and Jankyn). In effect this is one basis for the satire of the tale, the contrast between the "is" and the "ought."

A third way the antipodal apostle theme contributes to the structure of "the Summoner's Tale" is in its interconnecting links to a "world" outside the tale. "The Summoner's Tale" was told in retaliation to "the Friar's Tale," and Friar John was "created" (narrative fiction) by the summoner as an analogue of Friar Huberd. The scene at the beginning of "the Friar's Tale" is matched by a similar scene at the beginning of "the Summoner's Tale."

This worthy lymytour, this noble Frere,
He made alway a maner lourying chiere
Upon the Somonour (1265-68).

This Somonour in his styropes hye stood;
Upon this Frere his herte was so wood
That lyk an aspen leef he quook for ire (1665-67).

The argument between the summoner and the friar is, in effect, a miniature of the ongoing argument between the mendicants and the seculars of Chaucer's day. ("The Parson's Tale" and "the Prologue" provide supplementary material on the attitudes and actions of the unapostolic religious of the day.) Obviously, the summoner is not unscathed in this argument, because Chaucer did not favor either side. For this reason the satirist is satirized by his very criticism of Friar John and Friar Huberd. The summoner has some of the same faults he criticized in the friar. He too is an angry man and participated in the senseless quarrel with Friar Huberd. Therefore, when the tale and chief characters (Friar John, Thomas, and by extension, Friar Huberd and the summoner) are placed into the implicit and explicit moral landscape of scriptural injunction and Chaucer's understanding of Christianity, each in turn is satirized.

The tale is meant not only as a criticism and a satire of the mendicants and secularists, but the tale can be seen in a fourth way in the light of its universal implications. Men are like Friar John. "Original sin" or "propensity for evil" infects all the relations of men, making them exploiters, deceivers, and hypocrites. Humanity usually does seek the material instead of the spiritual, and the gift for their efforts (anxiety, meaninglessness, and death) often turns out to be a raw practical joke, something just as insubstantial as Thomas's gift.

Finally, and closely connected to the last point, is the attitude the counter-apostle theme promotes in the reader. By the end of the tale the reader learns not to take the friar's claims of sanctity and Christianity too seriously. By contrast, by allusion, and by comparisons the actions, the words, and the thoughts of Friar John are obviously not those of an ideal apostle and servant of Jesus Christ. For this reason the practical joke of the friar appears to be "just." God's eternal justice is imaged as worldly, comic justice. Friar John, as a fraud, receives precisely what he deserves. If the friar appears to be a worthy apostle (like the Parson) and evidences any of the Christian virtues, the reader might have some sympathy for the friar. Then the tale could be read as the story of a maligned friar, but because of the constant comical juxtaposition of the biblical "ought" with what Friar John actually "is" the story is supremely satirical. The reader is able to laugh at a "man of God" with a clear conscience, and with the feeling that there is justice at work in the world after all.

Notes

1   Earle Birney, "Structural Irony Within the *Summoner's Tale*" *Anglia*, LXXVIII (1960), 205.

2   Paull F. Baum, "Chaucer's Puns," *PMLA*, LXXI (1956), 225-246. Baum does, however, disprove Robinson's statement that "Puns are unusual in Chaucer, and it is not always easy to determine whether or not they are intentional." Furthermore, he illustrates that the humor of the tale is far more subtle than anal word play by delineating the rhetorical devices Chaucer employs in the isolated puns.

3   F. Tupper, "Jerome and the *Summoner's Tale*," *MLN*, XXX, N. 1 (1915), 8, 9.

4   Daniel S. Silvia, "Chaucer's Friars: Swans or Swains?" *English Language Notes*, I (June 1964), 248=250, and others.

5   Germaine Dempster. *Dramatic Irony in Chaucer*. (Stanford, 1932).

6   John F. Adams, "The Structure of Irony in the *Summoner's Tale*," *Essays in Criticism*. XII, n. 2 (April 1962), 126-132. Thomas Merrill, "Wrath and Rhetoric in the *Summoner's Tale* Tale," *Texas Studies in Literature and Language*, IV, n. 3 (Autumn 1962), 341-350. And Birney.

7   "Li dis de la vescie a prestre" by Jakes de Baisiu, *Seneca, Jerome against Jovinian, and Scripture*.

8   Dempster defines dramatic irony as the "Irony resulting from strong contrast, unperceived by a character in a story, between the surface meaning of his words or deeds and something else happening in the story." p. 7.

9   Ibid., pp. 45, 46.

10 Birney, pp. 206, 207.

11 Adams, pp. 126, 127.

12 Ibid., p. 127.

13 Merrill, p. 342.

14 See above for a development of this view.

15 Merrill, p. 346.

16 This is evidenced mainly by a comparison with Holy Scripture, but it is underscored by the *Parson's Tale*.

[17] All references to Chaucer's works are from the second edition of *The Works of Geoffrey Chaucer*, edited by F. N. Robinson (Cambridge, Mass., 1957). Subsequent references to this work will be enclosed in the parentheses and included in the body of the paper.

[18] "I have sinned exceedingly in thought, word, and deed."

[19] Cf. 1734, 1743-44, 1746-52, 1755-58.

PART II

HOW I GOT HERE

Having time to "sit down and think"

From Andrew Marvell's "To His Coy Mistress"

CHAPTER FOUR

THE RELIGIOUS LEADER
AS INTELLECTUAL
IN JUDAISM,
ROMAN CATHOLICISM, AND
LUTHERANISM /PROTESTANTISM

"The Religious Leader as Intellectual in Judaism, Roman Catholicism, and Lutheranism" was a paper delivered first to an academic conference (Association of Lutheran College Faculties) growing out of the end of the seven-year cycle of dialogues among these major faith groups. It is obviously directed not just at Lutherans. Anti-intellectualism is always a danger in the church. Education is sometimes seen as incipient secularism.

{Topics: seminary, college president, academic gown, dialogue, rabbis, theological education, traits of the clergy, Tertullian, Richard John Neuhaus}

Is there a future for a well-educated clergy in the Protestant and Lutheran churches in America? Will Lutheranism continue to produce leading theologians in this country? Do Lutheran pastors need or use the kind of undergraduate and seminary education now required for ordination?

The seven-year cycle of official Jewish/Roman Catholic/Lutheran dialogues recently drew to a close. The papers given during these dialogues were generally presented by academics (college or seminary professors) not parish priests, pastors, or rabbis. This absence of parish clergy among the presenters highlighted a more general problem.

The three traditions (Judaism, Roman Catholicism, and Lutheranism) have often had differing perceptions of the need for intellect and learning at the parish level, and all three have experienced major changes in emphasis in the last few generations. The differences in perception are now so widespread in the three faith traditions that real problems are becoming apparent in religious colleges and seminaries as well as in the churches and synagogues of America

To analyze the issues, it will be helpful to analyze briefly:

I.   The changing perceptions of the clergy in America;
II. The changing traditions of Judaism, Roman Catholicism, and Protestantism//Lutheranism relating to intellect and learning in the rabbi, priest, and pastor;
III. Some possible courses of action for those who wish to maintain at least a semblance of a "learned" or intellectual clergy in American Lutheranism/Protestantism.

I.   ONCE UPON A TIME IN AMERICA (changing perceptions of the clergy in the United States)

Perhaps the major changes in the intellectual status of the clergy in America can best be illustrated by pointing out that before the Civil War, some 90 percent of all college presidents in the United States were ordained ministers. Ministers before the nineteenth century in America were often perceived to be the intellectual leaders of their communities. Cotton Mather in his "Directions for a Candidate of the Ministry" stated that one should first cultivate piety, then cultivate "that Learning and those Ingenious and Mollifying arts, which may distinguish you from the more Uncultivated Part of Mankind."

By the nineteenth century, however, the prestige of the clergyman had fallen on hard times, in part because of a strong anti-intellectual tradition within American Christianity. Here and there were those who said things like "None of the twelve disciples went to college" or "A pastor should care more about people than books." Many of the denominations saw little need for an intensive, let alone classical, education on the American frontier. Bishop Pierce, a Southern Methodist, said in 1872, "The best preacher I ever heard had never been to college at all—hardly to school. It is my opinion that every dollar invested in a theological school will be a damage to Methodism." As late as 1926, fully 40 percent of the ministers of the seventeen largest white denominations in America did not have a college degree. Only 33 percent were graduates of both college and seminary (Niebuhr 274ff).

The academic community, which previously looked to clergy for leadership, completely reversed itself. A former president of Cornell, Andrew White, agreed with a late-nineteenth—century member of the British government who said, "A candidate for high university position is handicapped by holy orders." Eliot, a former president of Harvard, stated that "Multitudes of educated men . . . had come to be suspicious of the intellectual abilities of the clergy, and this was a potent cause for the decline of the ministry during the last forty years." In another context, Eliot also wrote that ministers "as a class and as a necessary consequence of the ordinary manner of their education . . . are peculiarly liable to be deficient in intellectual candor . . . . No other profession is under such terrible stress of temptation to intellectual dishonesty." It is now rare to find an ordained clergyman as the president of any large or influential college or university (Niebuhr 278ff). Even in the Lutheran Church—Missouri Synod, the change is evident. The three most recent presidents of Concordia College, Bronxville, for example, have not been ordained.

II. IT'S A CHANGING WORLD! (How the Roles of Rabbi, Priest, and Pastor Evolved)

A. The title *rabbi* means "teacher." The name was given early in the Christian era to men learned in Jewish law who were also teachers. Learning was central; study was the central ritual. (Neusner pp. 5ff). Traditionally, rabbis did not function like a priest or a pastor. Today, however, the duties of rabbis are often very similar to those of Christian clergy: performing ceremonies relating to birth, confirmation, marriage, and death, as well as teaching, preaching, counseling, and administration (Rosten 300-301). Synagogues were once primarily places of study; they are becoming more like Jewish community centers (Hertzberg 97ff). Still, of the leaders of the three faith traditions, rabbis are expected to fill learned and intellectual roles more often than are most priests and pastors (Polnar xiv, 1, 4, 127, 139,211).

If you've analyzed the countless rabbi, priest, and pastor jokes, you've probably noticed that generally the rabbi gets the witty or intelligent lines. For example: a new worldwide flood is foretold, and nothing can be done to prevent it. In two weeks, water will cover the entire earth. The protestant (perhaps Lutheran) clergyman tells his flock, "See what your sin and disobedience have brought us! Repent so that you will be saved." The Catholic priest asks his parish to "Pray the rosary and say numerous 'Our Fathers' so that perhaps this tragedy can be averted." The rabbi simply tells his flock, "We have two weeks to learn how to live under water."

B. Titles to some extent do dictate expectations: "priest" (the preferred Roman Catholic title for the clergy) denotes a more sacramental role, whereas "pastor" (the preferred Lutheran title) indicates shepherding. Yet Paul in the New Testament usually lists prophecy and teaching first as tasks for the clergy. The earliest Christian manual on church morals and practice, the *Didache*, also accords first place to prophets and teachers. Evidently, it was Clement of Rome who first made the connection between the Old Testament Aaronic priesthood and the New Testament ministry. In the Eastern tradition, Chrysostom in his "On the Priesthood" describes a pastor as an instructor of people from the pulpit, a learned theologian able to refute heretics and pagans (Niebuhr 1-83). Priests were often among the few in the Middle Ages who were literate and thus were often drafted as civil servants. The Council of Trent established special institutions called seminaries for educating the clergy. Prior to Trent, clergy training sometimes consisted of study at the universities accompanied by an informal apprenticeship (Niebuhr 61, 167).

C. The Lutheran Reformation began in the university, and although Luther was sometimes critical of the universities of his day (calling them "asses' stalls and devil's training centers"), few changes were actually made in universities located in Lutheran territories, according to Solberg. Luther did call for the establishment of higher schools of learning to supply pastors, teachers, and civic leadership. He thought that teaching was the "best, and greatest, and most useful office there is" next to preaching. Strong efforts were made to produce well-trained and effective parish clergy; most notably at the University at Marburg, founded in 1525, to prepare pastors in theology and the humanities. Preaching was not taught but rather the ability to read and interpret texts. Significantly, the Lutheran Confessions stress "right" preaching and the "right" administration of the sacraments. Sometimes Lutherans are criticized for putting too much stress on head knowledge and pure doctrine, but at least, these words demand intelligence and learned skills. Although it was Zwingli who introduced the academic gown of the secular scholar into the church and pulpit, less than a year later, Luther wore it (the *Shaube*) in October of 1524 (Niebuhr 24, 147).

The ideal of an educated clergy continued in the early years of Lutheranism in America, although even Muhlenberg was concerned that too much emphasis on the scholarly preparation of ministers would delay unduly the training of missionary pastors for America (Niebuhr 24, 147).

As soon as the immediate and extensive demand for Lutheran clergy in America subsided, Lutherans were again able to indulge their desire for a learned clergy (among the best educated in any American denomination). The *Handbook of the Lutheran Church—Missouri Synod*, for example, lists education as the first prerequisite for ordination: "He shall have completed the prescribed courses of study and have received a diploma from one of synod's seminaries." For a colloquy, official transcripts of the applicant's secondary, collegiate, and seminary training, including a full description of non-credit academic work, are requested. The "Rite of Ordination" in the *Occasional Services, A Companion to the Lutheran Book of Worship* asks the candidate for ordination "to accept, teach, and confess," "to be diligent in your study of the Word," and "nourish them with the Word."

There was a time in America when (as in Judaism and Roman Catholicism) the Lutheran pastor was the only or the most educated person in the community. Those times have changed for all three faiths. In fact, studies indicate that Lutherans, like other American denominations, value skills in preaching, counseling, youth work, and group dynamics much more highly than intellect or theological knowledge. Consider also that the most visible clergy in America today, those of the electronic church, are seldom well educated and not perceived to be particularly learned. Yet in the popular mind they are usually considered to be among the most successful in the general Christian community, especially when success is measured in terms of money, name recognition, congregational size, or the number of prayer breakfasts conducted at the White House.

Most Lutheran education of the clergy (undergraduate and seminary) is perceived to be primarily academic (concerned with the training of the intellect), at least until recently. The exception, of course, was the internship or vicarage year. Seminarians returning from this year sometimes would turn their backs on much of their prior education and sign up for primarily "practical" courses in counseling, administration, education, and evangelism. In the Missouri Synod, this phenomenon was labeled the "fourth year" syndrome. Their year "in the field" taught students that parishes seem to be less interested in a pastor's academic training than in personality, sense of humor, compassion, and listening skills. Sermons are often evaluated not on exegetical prowess, but on whether they are interesting and well-delivered. "Good examples" and "interesting stories" are deemed more important than a preacher's ability to provide insights into a biblical text. In short, the priorities of the seminary (and often those of the seminarian) appear to be different than those of most congregations.

Recently, studies relating to Lutheran clergy by Schuller, Brekke, and Strommen have indicated that the laity do not expect or necessarily want intellectual clergymen. In fact, intelligence is one of the least desired traits in Lutheran clergy (Schuller, 123, 164-167).

On the other hand, compounding the problem, another recent study described characteristic traits of clergy in the 1970s and '80s. People who study for the ministry have primarily helping personalities. They are often extroverts, people oriented, and sociable. They need and cultivate interpersonal relationships. They like groups, like to be leaders, and tend to stress the outer world of people and events rather than the inner world of ideas. Their judgments are usually made on the basis of values rather than analysis and logic (Harbaugh 70). Apparently, the expectations and desires of American congregations are influencing the type of person who studies to become a minister, even though much college and seminary preparation for ministry remains primarily academic. If these trends continue, the ministry and the church will be even more "perplexed" in Niebuhr's words.

III. A FUTURE FOR THINKERS

How to maintain at least a semblance of a learned and intellectual clergy in or out of the parish in American Lutheranism.

Most Lutheran clergy, looking back on their college and seminary education, appreciate its rigor and stress on much that was admittedly academic. But in the last decades there has been a decreasing interest in and emphasis on the classical training that used to be the mark of a Lutheran clergyman. Lutheran seminaries currently require far less language study, for example. What is more, grades, rank in class, and academic skills are not as important for seminary admission as they once were. Those entering seminary, moreover, are sometimes not the best students, and some students who excel in and particularly prize academics often consider entering the campus ministry or academia.

It is true that many pastors do not use the Greek, Hebrew, Latin, and German they spent so much time learning. It is also true that the American parish leaves precious little time for original research. The answer, however, is not to encourage those pastors who care about such things to go into teaching or the campus ministry. In fact, adding an additional four years to the usual time span spent in obtaining a doctorate seems a roundabout way of becoming a college professor.

As a way of maintaining a learned and intellectual tradition within American Lutheranism, the following steps should be considered:

A) David Schuller suggests that professional or theological study be considered a lifelong process not complete after a fixed number of years. He points to the Underwood study that calls for "education at the boundary points" between theology and ministry, theory and action, university and church, individual and group. The Underwood study branded some seminary education as too academic and irrelevant and much field education as too isolated and segmented (244).

B) Schuller also says that seminary education should have four goals: the acquisition of knowledge, the development of professional skills, personal (human) growth, and deepening of Christian commitment (244).

C) Most readers would agree that good grades alone, especially in academic subjects, do not qualify someone to lead a congregation. Yet there are valid reasons why Lutheranism has always insisted on a learned clergy and should continue to do so. Every Lutheran clergyman in or out of the parish is concerned about words and the Word. The clergy have to care about history and tradition and how to adapt, if need be, the past for our day. Preaching and teaching are based on learning and intelligence. Contemporary concern about seminary reformation seems to center on the area of spiritual formation. Spiritual formation is hard to define and harder to impart, but it need not conflict with academic preparation. Indeed, the two are quite compatible.

D) Some want our seminaries to be more closely related to large universities. This linkage might be a mistake. Yes, the theological school can be seen as an intellectual center of the church and, rightly or wrongly, theology has been called the "Queen of the Sciences," the science of God. But the danger is the importing to American shores of a problem common in Europe where the theological faculties have little relationship to the church and are usually not accountable to the church.

E) Others suggest that seminaries ought to have different curricula for those who want to teach and do serious research and those who wish to be pastors. That attitude led the Lutheran Church—Missouri Synod to develop two seminaries, one considered more "practical" than the other and having fewer academic requirements. This arrangement did not work well at all. The two seminaries have, in recent years, grown quite similar in requirements and student body. Which of us knows at the time we choose a seminary, moreover, where our calling in life will take us?

F) Circuit (the old *Winkel*) conferences are one place where "lifelong" learning might be fostered. Unfortunately, not much solid material is studied in these conferences. Leaders do not spend much time in advance preparation, and consequently, few clergy expect much from the meetings.

Yet there are notable exceptions around the country, of course. The Ad Fontes group of pastors sponsors significant periodic theological conferences in Ephrata, Pennsylvania. A circuit in Dayton, Ohio led by Pastor Mel Younger has organized a weekly study group which studies a book of the Bible in Greek or Hebrew. Two books are selected for the monthly circuit meetings, one to be used in the morning session, the other in the afternoon. Neuhaus, in *Freedom for Ministry* (which should be required reading for Lutheran clergy), has stated that every pastor should have time for at least two hours of prayer and study a day.

G) Church colleges and religion departments usually have first crack at future clergy. Often, the love of learning and research instilled at this undergraduate level is carried on to seminary and then into church service. More attention should be paid to who is recruited for the ministry and what kind of undergraduate education they have.

H) There continues to be a large number of Lutheran clergy and laity who study, do solid research, and read challenging works. One survey showed that the readers of *Lutheran Forum* bought an average of twenty-six books a year. This love of learning is reflected in the readership of other Lutheran publications as well. These publications foster continued study and are evidence of a very extensive, committed, and enthusiastic cadre of well-educated Lutheran clergy and laity. May their tribe increase.

Many of us have Luther's "Prayer of a Pastor" over our desks:

I would gladly give my mouth and tongue and heart to Thy service. I would teach the people. I would also learn continually and would meditate upon Thy Word more diligently. Use me as Thine own instrument. Never forsake me. Were I to be left alone, I would easily make a failure of all things.

Most pastors are grateful for the rigorous education that was demanded of them. Studies show that students remember and continue to appreciate the most those instructors who challenged them to do their best. The goal of clergy undergraduate and seminary preparation in the Lutheran church has traditionally been to produce "a man for all seasons." Tertullian is famous for his comment that "Athens has nothing to do with Jerusalem." Time and again, history has proved him wrong. This generation is being challenged to do so once again.

Greeley, Andrew M. *The American Catholic*. New York: Basic Books, 1977.

Harbaugh, Gary L. *Pastor as Person*. Minneapolis: Augsburg, 1984.

Hertzberg, Arthur. *Being Jewish in America*. New York: Shocken Books, 1979.

Neuhaus, Richard John. *Freedom for Ministry*. New York: Harper and Row, 1979.

Neusner, Jacob, ed. *Understanding Rabbinic Judaism.* New York: Ktav Publishing House, 1974.

Niebuhr, H. Richard & Williams, Daniel D., eds. *The Ministry in Perspective.* New York: Harper and Row, 1956.

Polnar, Murray. *The American Experience.* New York: Holt, Rinehart, and Winston, 1977.

Schuller, David. "The Formation of Clergy for Ministry Today." *Lutheran World.* 17 (1970). 231-245.

Solberg, Richard W. *Lutheran Higher Education in North America.* Minneapolis: Augsburg, 1985.

CHAPTER FIVE

CHRISTIANITY AND LITERATURE:

THE JOHN THE BAPTIST FUNCTION OF LITERATURE

Originally presented as "Lutherans and Literature: The John the Baptist Function of Literature," as a guest lecture delivered at Concordia, St. Paul, Minnesota. It is really an "apologia" for teaching SECULAR literature at a Christian institution of learning.

{Topics: Werner Elert, Melanchthon, Don Deffner, H. Richard Niebuhr, Tertullian, Peter Abelard, Erasmus, pornography, Matthew Arnold, mimesis, Sir Philip Sidney, Coleridge, Wordsworth, semantic, Vladimir Nabokov, Lord Byron, W. H. Auden, Terence, Rousseau, Alexander the Great, Rainer Maria Rilke, Albert Camus, William Golding, Ingmar Bergmann, J. D. Salinger, Flannery O'Connor, Bo Giertz}

Lutherans and Evangelical Protestants should have no problem with the discipline of literature and language, Luther wrote,

> I am persuaded that without knowledge of literature pure theology cannot at all endure, just as heretofore, when letters have declined and lain prostrate, theology too has wretchedly fallen and lain prostrate; nay, I see that there has never been a great revelation of the Word of God unless He has first prepared the way by the rise and prosperity of languages and letters as though they were John the Baptists. Certainly, it is my desire

that there shall be as many poets and rhetoricians as possible, because I see that by these studies, as by no other means, people are wonderfully fitted for grasping the sacred truth and for the handling of it skillfully and happily.

Therefore I beg of you that at my request (if that has any weight) you will urge your young people to be diligent in the study of poetry and rhetoric.

—March 29, 1523, Letter to Eoban Hess (1)

As a mature man, Luther indicated that he was sorry that he had not devoted more attention to history and poetry because he recognized that "much time is required for personal experience and that literature could have enabled him to know more about life and avoid many errors." He would, therefore, include even Terence and Plautus in the school readings in spite of objectionable features because they portray real people in real situations so well. (2)

Similarly, Philip Melanchthon stated "that religion be rightly taught . . . implies as a necessary condition sound instruction in letters."(3) Traditionally Lutherans have included thorough training in language and letters in the education of clergy and theologians and encouraged such study where possible in schools and universities. Werner Elert in his *Structure of Lutheranism*, which summarizes what Lutheranism has been and should be, states that "the poet seems to have the easiest task when it is a matter of giving artistic expression to belief in God as part of the consciousness of being in the world. Apparently he need only speak of God to show his piety. If he does this, he can certainly take part directly in the proclamation of the Gospel."(4)

Given these enthusiastic endorsements of literature and language by so many prominent Lutherans, my task should be easy: to indicate something of what it means to be a Christian, a Lutheran, a student, and a professor of literature; what it means to take seriously the Lutheran confessions; what it means to be familiar with and use the theories and methods of the discipline of literary study; what it means for the church and the Christian to use literature.

As an instructor in a small college, I teach a wide range of courses and have had to cease being a specialist. I have taught British literature, world masterpieces, drama, Old Testament, introduction to religion, the history of Christian denominations, and even an art, music, and literature appreciation course, but perhaps the primary reason I was asked to be a part of this particular lecture series is that ten years ago I developed a course entitled "Christianity and Contemporary Literature" at Concordia College in Bronxville, New York, which almost immediately became rather popular, at times offered twice yearly. Later, I joined the Conference on Christianity and Literature (a subgroup of the Modern Language Association) and even organized and hosted the Northeast Regional Conference on Christianity and Literature at Concordia, Bronxville. This is probably one of the first times a Lutheran college has hosted such a conference. As chairman of the Northeast Region I also planned our conference held at New York University. It is surprising how few Lutherans are involved in this kind of research.

When I entered Concordia College, St. Paul, as a student in 1958, I intended not only to enter the ministry but also to major in English. The "literary" life was so lively then with Professors Otto, Treichel, and Poggemeier; the dramatic productions (especially the Minnesota Centennial of Lutheranism which we took on tour); the student newspaper; and the literary organizations called Tri-A and SAB. At Concordia Senior College in Fort Wayne—with Professors Essig, Rubel, and Rossow—the solid foundation in literary and theological studies was continued. However, I do not remember anyone on the undergraduate level ever indicating any problems about being a professor or student of literature for a Lutheran. Most of the literature professors were also ordained and had served parishes.

It was only at Concordia Seminary in St. Louis with Dr. Donald Deffner, who taught a course relating Christianity to literature, and in graduate school that I discovered that the discipline of literature could pose problems for the Christian. (5)

Your invitation gives me the chance to explore why the discipline of literature can pose problems for Christians in general and Lutherans in particular, but I also want to stress the opportunities the discipline of literature provides for Christians and the church.

An outline:

I.   Some problems the discipline of literature poses to Christians (including Lutheran Christians)
II. Some misuses of literature by Christians and others

III. Some possible uses of literature by Christians and the church

IV. Some problems the discipline of literature poses to Christians (including Lutherans)

A. It might be helpful to begin by referring to H. Richard Niebuhr's seminal work, *Christ and Culture*, especially to his helpful categorization of various Christian approaches to culture. In his schema the types of Christianity which have the most problems with literature are those Christians he labels "against" culture. This view has some basis in Scripture, especially in the First Letter of John and the Book of Revelation.

"Do not love the world or the things in the world. If anyone loves the world, love for the Father is not in him. For all that is in the world, the lust of the flesh and the lust of the eyes and the pride of life, is not of the Father but is of the world" (1 John 2:15-16). This verse is paralleled by "Come ye out from among them and touch not the unclean thing" (2 Cor. 6: 17).

A direct line extends from this approach to some of the church fathers, especially Tertullian, who writes specifically about the teaching and learning of literature. Tertullian (AD 120):

"We must also ask about schoolmasters and the other teachers of letters though their affinity with all manner of idolatry is really beyond question. In the first place, they are bound to praise the Gods of the heathen, rehearse their names, genealogies, stories, and all their ornaments and attributes. Let us look into the necessity of a literary education. Let us recognize that it can be partly allowed and partly avoided. It is more allowable for Christians to learn letters than to teach them. The principles involved in teaching and learning are different. When a Christian teaches literature, he comes upon occasional praises of idols. In teaching them, he commends them; in handing them on he confirms them; and in mentioning them he bears testimony to them. But when a Christian learns these things, already understanding what idolatry is, he does not accept or admit them, all the more so if he has understood it for some time (from *On Idolatry*)." (6).

Peter Abelard (1079-1142) asked, "What has Horace to do with the Psalter, Virgil with the Gospel, Cicero with the Apostle?"(7) Even Erasmus of Rotterdam, supposedly a Renaissance man, asked in the same vein, "What has Aristotle to do with Christ?"(8) These views are echoed also within the domain of literature. Samuel Johnson (1709-1784) wrote, "Contemplative piety, or the intercourse between God and the human soul, cannot be poetical" (in his *Life of Waller*). (9) Niebuhr places the monastic and the Mennonite movement in this school of thought. At times, spokesmen of the Moral Majority make similar statements.

Niebuhr is particularly critical of Christians who oppose culture. Briefly he tries to show that when we become Christians, our language, our thought patterns, our culture do not change. We are saved as human beings within a specific cultural context. Niebuhr believes these well-meaning Christians really are denigrating human reason; they are forgetting that sin is not only in the culture but also in our own nature. The Christians who oppose culture tend to be legalistic and parochial, tending to overlook Christ's lordship over both nature and history and the Spirit's part in ongoing creation. (10)

Niebuhr lists other Christian stances on culture that are not as hostile, including those Christians who feel they are "above the culture" (sometimes the Roman Catholic and Anglican position). This attitude can lead to such unfortunate situations as the Index of Forbidden Books and film censorship boards. (11) There are also Christians who see Christianity as a part "of culture" (culture Protestantism), who minimize or deny any supernatural quality to the Christian faith, stressing only its positive secular and cultural uses and influence. This view has little basis in Scripture.(12) When I was in graduate school at Washington University, a few of my friends considered themselves agnostics or atheists, but they sent their children to Sunday school so they would be prepared later in life to appreciate and understand the biblical allusions of Chaucer, of Shakespeare, and of Milton.

Lutherans, according to Niebuhr, are those who see Christianity and culture in paradox, citizens of two worlds, caught in a tension and a duality. Thus Lutherans should have fewer problems with culture, with citizenship, and with the arts. He mentions Luther's return from the Wartburg to censure those who were destroying the stained glass windows, paraments, and statues in Wittenberg. Niebuhr also alludes to the many substantial Lutheran contributions to music, art, and literature through the ages, and he finds the scriptural basis for the Lutheran stance particularly in the writings of St. Paul. (13)

However, Niebuhr seems to prefer yet another type of Christian stance toward culture: those who see Christianity as the "transformer" of culture. It is a view he sees as represented by St. Augustine, John Calvin, and the Reformed tradition in general, based on such New Testament passages as John 3: 17, Colossians 1: 15ff, and Philippians 4:8.(14)

    B. In addition to the problems some Christians seem to have with culture and literature because of their reading or misreading of the New Testament, some authors and literary critics have added additional stumbling blocks. Obviously pornography, faulty value systems, anti-Christian, and anti-religious sentiments create difficulties for the Christian reader, just as Dickens's Fagin and Shakespeare's Shylock have been comparably difficult for Jewish readers.

    C. But on a more theoretical plane there are those like Matthew Arnold, who believe that eventually poetry will take over the role of religion in society, (15) or D. H. Lawrence, who as a novelist considered himself "superior to the saint, the scientist, the philosopher, and the poet, who are masters of different bits of man alive, but never get the whole hog" (*Why the Novel Matters*).(16)

    D. Sometimes well-meaning Christian authors have other concerns. Gerard Manley Hopkins feared that his poetic gift might "distract him from his religious vocation," and he burned most of his poetry when he was ordained a priest. (17)

Before indicating some of the ways I think Christians and others misuse literature, a brief history of the discipline of literary criticism will be helpful. The outline of M. H. Abrams and Giles Gunn, in the book *Literature and Religion*, is easy to understand and brief. Basically, they believe every literary critical theory must take into account at least four elements: the world which the work creates and reveals; the audience which the work reflects; the writer of the work; and the work itself. Rather strangely in the history of Western literature, one of these aspects has usually been seen as a key to understanding the other three in various periods of history.

The oldest criticism in the West is that of Plato and Aristotle. They stressed the *world* which the work creates and reveals. *Mimesis* (imitation) is the keyword they used. Plato thought that a work of literature imitates what is essential or basic about reality itself whereas Aristotle believed that literature completes and fulfills nature rather than merely imitating it. Aristotle said, "nature is never so unified or fully realized" as it is in literature. Plato was concerned that literature unfortunately appealed to the inferior faculties of man, his emotions and his passions, whereas Aristotle believed that literature arouses and excites our passions and emotions only to allay them (catharsis). Plato, in fact, feared poets and storytellers. He once wrote that if a poet should visit his ideal state, he would be welcomed as someone special but then sent away. (18)

Later, in the Renaissance, criticism began to stress the *audience* of the work as the key factor. *Instruction* is the watchword. Literature is evaluated pragmatically. Sir Philip Sidney, a good spokesman for this viewpoint, in his book *Defence of Poesie* tries to answer the Puritan charges that poetry was immoral and provocative. He cites in response the long-civilizing influence of poetry, how it "imitates the real less than it invents and represents the possible." According to Sidney, the purpose of poetry is "not to please the emotions but to instruct the mind, or if to please at all, then merely in order finally to persuade." Sidney believes that poetry can lead people to virtue, "to contemplate and then imitate a better world than our own where virtue always prospers and vice always perishes." According to this theory, then, literature is a means to an end, and it is evaluated as good or bad on the basis of whether or not it achieves its aims. (19) Horatio Alger and O'Henry would probably rank very highly as authors if evaluated by these criteria. Unfortunately, many well meaning Christians might think that this view is the only proper Christian one.

In the Romantic era, the stress was on the writer or *author* who creates the work. Wordsworth and Coleridge especially propound this view. Coleridge, for example, believed that the question "What is poetry?" is nearly the same question as "What is a poet?" He believed that the poet imitates the ongoing work of creation, saying that the poet brings the whole soul of man into activity "by that synthetic and magical power, to which we have exclusively appropriated the name of imagination."(20) This view seems overstated and, to some people, perhaps even blasphemous.

The theory of criticism we have come to call "modern" or semantic sees the key in *the work itself.* The stress is on objectivity, focusing on the nature and structure of the writer's language. The chief interest in modern criticism seems to be in "language's capacity to generate images and symbols by which literature is composed and particularly in the relations between words in all their contextual specificity and realities which they specify." Some modern critics believe that literature can express some thoughts that are inexpressible with other kinds of language (i.e. technical prose). Others think that the kind of meaning, not the way in which poetry communicates, is the difference. (21)

Most of today's critics are probably eclectic, using the best ideas in all these approaches. However, these approaches are not only the domain of the professor of literature. All readers of literature ought to evaluate what they look for in a work of literature and why, because if primary stress is placed on any one of the four elements of a work (the world which the work creates and reveals, the audience the work affects, the author of the work, or the work itself), the evaluation of the work will differ dramatically.

In addition to the problems of literary critical theory, there are other pitfalls in reading a literary work into which both Christians and others frequently fall.

II. Some misuses of literature by Christians and others.

    A. Literature is misused when meanings not intended by the author are read into the work. For example, often Christian readers surmise that "Godot"—in Samuel Beckett's *Waiting for Godot* —is "God." Yet Beckett has stated that he did not intend this interpretation. The reader can still "use" the work in this way as long as it is clear that it is a personal interpretation. Well-meaning Christians and "hip" ministers are especially prone to this misuse.

Sometimes our Christian enthusiasm carries us along into reading into a work Christian messages and meanings.

    B. Literature is misused when a work is judged inferior only because one disagrees with the values represented or is offended by some of the scenes or the language used. My first course in graduate school, "Practical Criticism," was intended to train students in the discipline of literary criticism. One of the works read was Vladimir Nabokov's *Lolita* (the story of the seduction of a thirteen-year-old girl by her stepfather). A number of people in the class thought it was not good literature and should not have been read. They were apparently unable to surmount a theme which they found disgusting, although the meaning of the work transcended the plot. Some people similarly dislike John Updike and Norman Mailer because they disapprove of their views on women.

C. Literature is misused when the reader always looks for a moral lesson. Some works do not have one and do not need to have one. Tolstoy, one of the greatest Christian writers of all times, unfortunately, later in life disparaged all literature (even some that he had written), which did not convert or teach a moral. (22) Yet we know that some good literature may in fact be amoral or immoral (the poetry of Percy Bysshe Shelley or Lord Byron, for example).

D. Literature is misused when the author's personal beliefs or attitudes are confused with those of a narrator or a character in his work. In interpreting poetry, it is always the hardest task for an English literature instructor to get students to say "the speaker" or "the speaking voice" instead of "the author says." In fiction, one of the writer's stock-in-trade techniques is the use of an "unreliable narrator." Bernard Malamud's short story "Black Is My Favorite Color" uses a narrator who says he is not prejudiced, and an integral component of the story is the reader's slowly growing realization that the author is "unreliable" (not believable), that in spite of what he is saying in the story, he is prejudiced.(23)

E. Literature is misused when the reader expects it always to be inspirational or always to have a happy ending or always to equate an inspirational with a happy ending. Life is not that way, and literature reflects life.

These and a host of other misuses of literature reflect the general problem of not dealing fairly with the work of literature in its own right. However, as long as the integrity of the work is respected, there are a number of ways literature can be used by Christians and the church while remaining fair to the work, fair to the audience, and fair to the Christian faith.

III. Some possible uses of literature by Christians and the church.

"What good is literature?" is obviously a very different question from "What is good literature?" The latter question would take another seminar.

A. CONVERSION: In my "Christianity and Contemporary Literature" course, I depend heavily on a theory proposed by Giles Gunn (whose outline on literary criticism was referred to above) (24) He calls it the "hypothetical" or "conjectural" approach to a work of literature. "If you will grant me my initial premise or set of conditions, then such and such would, or at least could, follow from them." Some have called this the "willing suspension of disbelief" or withholding of judgment. A reader who reads a book that deals with material, ideas, or experiences different from his own, going along with the author, walking "a mile in a characters shoes," that reader may change his mind and perhaps even his life and his attitudes. My favorite expression is "this book may change your life." We have all seen it happen, but we do not capitalize on it enough. C. S. Lewis once wrote, "If you want to remain an atheist, be very careful what you read." Literature can make people ready for conversion. (25)

B. Literature can also be used to TRANSMIT JUDEO-CHRISTIAN VALUES AND CULTURE. This tradition pervades Western literature, and the church should not shrink from stressing this fact. It is extremely difficult to teach the work of most Western writers because many students do not know the Bible and the frequent allusions to it made by these writers. I have, in fact, taught a mini-dogmatics or systematics class based solely on contemporary secular literature.

C. Literature can be used as MODELS of poetry and prose to teach style, technique, rhetoric. This makes for better sermons, better hymns, better Christian literature (and not just Sunday school materials and devotional literature). Just as many of the Latin and Greek classics were saved for posterity by Christian educators during the Middle Ages who used them as models, not necessarily for their content, so today reading improves writing style and content.

D. Literature can ENLIVEN sermons, not just for illustrations but also for the technique of making a point, for telling a story, and for expressing concerns. Literary examples often can prove to be a bridge to the academic and the intellectual community.

E. Literature can be used as a DIAGNOSTIC tool. Sometimes artists are more perceptive than the general public, and some literature seems to call attention to changes in society and the way we look at ourselves. As Shakespeare put it, "The purpose of playing . . . both at first and now, was and is, to hold as 'twere, the mirror up to nature; to show Virtue her own feature, scorn her own image, and the very age and body of the time his form and pressure" III. ii. Literature can also flesh out new trends and make them more visible. "The Age of Anxiety" got its name from a poem of W. H. Auden.

F. Literature can CORROBORATE certain aspects of the Christian message and values. "*Teste David cum sibella*" ("The muses sacred and profane agree" from the "*Dies Irae*," a Judgment Day hymn). Neophyte or unsure Christians particularly seek to know that the Christian faith is not so unique that it does not relate to the human tradition. The almost biblical understanding of sin and evil in William Golding's *Lord of the Flies* is doubly effective because it is "proven" without reference to the Bible or the Christian tradition.

G. Literature can give us insights into the FULLNESS of human nature, both the good and the evil, both ancient and modern. As Terence (185?-159 BC) put it, "*Homo sum; humani nil a me alienum auto.*" ("I am a man; nothing that is human is alien to me.") This is one of the many reasons Christians ought to be careful about supporting indiscriminate censorship. We cannot overlook or allow society to overlook the potential we all have within us for violence or for heroism, for perversity or for noble acts. I doubt whether anyone would go out and commit a murder because he reads *Crime and Punishment* or molest a child after reading *Lolita*, even though the characters in the books "get away with it . . ."

H. Literature can be read for KNOWLEDGE, not the knowledge perhaps of a scientist or a sociologist but the knowledge that can delve more deeply. This is knowledge that is not a formula or a definition of human nature, but a knowledge about ourselves as a member of the human race. Every year, students thrill to Siddhartha's quest for wisdom in Hesse's novel of the same name, realizing that they are not alone in the search.

I. Literature can be read for ENJOYMENT, a re-creation as well as recreation. For many of us there is no better enjoyment than a good book, but I am talking about something more profound. Walter Pater, in one of the most memorable passages in literary criticism, points out what the awakening of the literary sense can be—a veritable extension and lengthening of life.

> "One of the most beautiful passages of Rousseau is that in the sixth book of the *Confessions*, where he describes the awakening in him of the literary sense. An indefinable taint of death had clung always about him,

and now in early manhood he believed himself smitten
by mortal disease. He asked himself how he might make
as much as possible of the interval that remains; and he
was not biased by anything in his previous life when
he decided that it must be by intellectual excitement,
which he found just then in the clear, fresh writings of
Voltaire. Well! we are all *condamnes* as Victor Hugo says:
we are all under sentence of death but with a sort of
indefinite reprieve; we have an interval and then our
place knows us no more. Some spend this interval in
listlessness, some in high passions, the wisest—at least
among 'the children of this world in art and song.
For our one chance lies in expanding that interval, in
getting as many pulsations as possible into the given
time. Great passions may give us this quickened sense
of life, ecstasy and sorrow of love, the various forms
of enthusiastic activity, disinterested or otherwise,
which come naturally to many of us. Only be sure it is
passion—that it does yield you this fruit of a quickened,
multiplied consciousness. Of such wisdom, the poetic
passion, the desire of beauty, the love of art for its own
sake, has most. For art comes to you proposing frankly
to give nothing but the highest quality to your moments
as they pass, and simply for those moments' sake." (26)

Reading good literature thus extends our actual "lived
lives" by making the moments we spend in reading more
intense, more involved, more meaningful.

J.   Literature can be used for its PERSUASIVE and formative influence.
     Alexander the Great thought he learned more from Homer than
     from his tutor Aristotle. "He received more bravery of mind by
     the pattern of Achilles, than by hearing the definition of fortitude"
     (27) Congregations might well foster circles of reading. Pastors
     might well consider buying certain key works in multiple copies
     to distribute to those not yet ready to talk. I often give copies of
     Thornton Wilder's *Bridge of San Luis Rey* to those who are touched
     by the premature death of someone they love or J. D. Salinger's

Franny and Zooey to someone contemplating suicide or touched by the suicide of another.

K. Literature can be used to make us BETTER STUDENTS of Holy Scripture, better interpreters, better theologians. In fact, if the history of biblical criticism is analyzed, it will be clear that almost every new breakthrough in interpretation, every new critical methodology (including lower and higher criticism) was first developed in interpreting the classics. Our understanding of metaphor, simile, image, and genre are all honed by reading secular literature. It is only the Bible school mentality that does not see the carry-over of secular to sacred studies. Exegesis and explication are basically literary skills.

L. Perhaps at least one reference should be made to the way a writer can use his Christian faith in his writing and TO ENCOURAGE CHRISTIANS TO WRITE. The Christian faith is stocked with potential themes for literature. Christianity also provides the writer with a point of view, one shared by many others. Literature in the twentieth century may be weakened by the fact that the Western world no longer shares a point of view, that each writer must also create his own myth, a world in which his characters live, move, and have their being. The Christian faith provides ready plots, allusions, characters, situations to enrich literature. I am somewhat hesitant to refer to an attitude that is frequently expressed, namely that the artist is almost godlike in his creative powers, that he imitates the act of creation each time a work is created, but a Christian writer will see this also as a gift from God. Tolkien and even the *Star Wars, Empire Strikes Back, Return of the Jedi* phenomena are good examples of modern myths pervaded by the Judeo-Christian influence, yet not quite the same.

M. There are other uses for literature for the Christian and the church, some are a bit esoteric, others are somewhat irrelevant for this audience, but the above should give some direction for Lutherans considering using literature. I conclude with a use that is the subtitle of this article: the John the Baptist or forerunner use of literature. As Martin Luther phrased it, when literature is in decline, theology is in decline:

> "Without knowledge of literature, pure theology cannot at all endure. There has never been a great revelation of the Word of God UNLESS HE HAS FIRST PREPARED THE WAY BY THE RISE AND PROSPERITY OF LANGUAGE AND LETTERS, AS THOUGH THEY WERE JOHN THE BAPTISTS" (28).

Indeed, some believe the Reformation might not have happened without the Renaissance, especially because of the rebirth of interest in the classical texts (including Homer, Plato, Aristotle, Plautus, Terence, Virgil, and Cicero).

Just as John the Baptist preached repentance, so literature can indicate our true situation, the ways in which we have fallen short as human beings; It can alert us to the real issues, can raise questions that must be answered and can be answered by Christianity. As Rainer Maria Rilke (1875-1926) put it in his poem "Archaic Torso of Apollo": "There is no part of it that does not see you. You must change your life." (29) De Rougement put it a different way, "Art is a calculated trap for meditation."(30)

That is why in my Christianity and Contemporary Literature classes most of the assigned works are not Christian! In part I do this because the course is a safety valve on a Christian campus. Half of our students are not Lutheran; many have little interest in religion and are often turned off by the usual religion offerings (Bible, church history, doctrine). They seem to take this course because they think it is not as "religious" as the other religion offerings. "You read a lot of interesting modern novels, plays, short stories, and poems" is the kind of press the course gets. What the students do not at first realize is that though most of the books may not be Christian, they are all profoundly religious. I use these secular (and at times anti-Christian) books as John the Baptists, as forerunners, as way-preparers.

I usually begin the course with a best seller current to the time such as *The Exorcist, 2010: A Space Odyssey, Equus, Marat/Sade*. We then discuss the issues the book raises about what it means to be human in the twentieth century, what kinds of problems modern man has, and what are the options open to us to solve these problems.

We continue by reading some of the modern classic non-Christian answers to the problems of humanity such as *The Plague* (existentialism), which I think is one of the few books which is an intellectual threat to Christianity because it analyzes the Christian faith honestly and then presents many logical alternatives and answers. We sweat out this book year after year. We often read *Lord of the Flies* for the way it corroborates the Christian view of original sin and evil. *Siddhartha* presents not only a quasi Hindu/Buddhist point of view, but it also shows the universal youthful quest for wisdom. We read a lot of poetry by William Butler Yeats, William Ernest Henley, Archibald MacLeish, and Thomas Hardy, who are noted for their non-Christian or post Christian conceptions of man and his place in the universe.

Usually we read Archibald MacLeish's *J.B.* to see if the student can sort out the difference between humanistic and Christian answers, and the difference between the message of the Book of Job and this mode of rendering the story. (Most students cannot do so at first but soon catch on.) We also read the libretti of some modern rock operas like *Godspell, Jesus Christ Superstar,* and *Tommy,* comparing and contrasting their messages with the Scriptures. Generally, a few movies are discussed such as *Star Wars, The Seventh Seal, Winter's Light* along with other such hits.

Generally, the only Christian works we read in the course are J. D. Salinger's *Franny and Zooey,* C. S. Lewis's *The Lion, the Witch and the Wardrobe* and *The Last Battle* (from The Chronicles of Narnia series), the short stories of Flannery O'Connor together with her novel *The Violent Bear It Away,* and selections of the poetry of T. S. Eliot, Gerard Manley Hopkins, and W. H. Auden. This year, I am also including Walker Percy's novel *The Second Coming* and Bo Giertz's novel *The Hammer of God* (one of the few good Lutheran novels). These come at the end of the course—by then, the students trust me not to shove religion (or, more specifically, Christianity) down their throats. Discussion is sometimes heated, tempers flare, and more traditional students are at first puzzled.

I like to think what I am doing is preparing the students for the hearing of the Gospel. By the end of the course, they seem to begin to see a need for Christian answers; they begin to see that there are Christian answers to very real questions, Christian solutions to very real problems. We thus avoid those old campus jokes: Under the sign that states "Jesus is the answer" a student scrawls "What is the question?" Under the sign that states "Jesus saves" a student writes "Green stamps?" This approach would work doubly well on secular campuses.

Of course, like John the Baptist, a Christian professor of literature must finally say about all non-Christian literature: "I indeed baptize you with water unto repentance; but He that cometh after me is mightier than

I, whose shoes I am not worthy to wear; He shall baptize you with the Holy Ghost and with fire" (Matthew 3:11).

Even if this literature is the voice of one crying in the wilderness, it is still only preparing the way for the Lord; it is not the way itself.

ENDNOTES

1. Martin Luther, *Luther's Correspondence* II, trans. and eds: Preserved Smith and Charles M. Jacobs (Philadelphia: United Lutheran Publication House, 1918): 176-177.
2. Ibid. IV.
3. Roland Mushat Frye, *Perspectives on Man* (Philadelphia: Westminster Press, 1961), p. 171.
4. Werner Elert, *Structure of Lutheranism.* I (St. Louis: Concordia Publishing House, 1962), 462.
5. Among other Lutheran Church—Missouri Synod professors active in this this area are Francis Rossow, Duane Mehl, Warren Rubel, and Paul Boecler.
6. H. Richard Niebuhr, *Christ and Culture.* (New York: Harper & Brothers, 1951), pp. 45-82.; Frye, p. 59.
8. Ibid.
9. Evidently, Johnson believed that the poet dealt only with the works of God and not God directly.
10. Niebuhr, pp. 45-82. 11. Ibid . . , pp. 116-148. 12. Ibid., pp. 83-115.
13. Ibid., pp. 149-189. 14. Ibid., pp. 190-229.
14. Ibid.
15. Matthew Arnold, "The Study of Poetry," in *The Norton Anthology of English Literature.* 4th ed. II (New York: Norton. 1979):1444-1445.
16. Ibid. p.2225.
17. Eversole, Findley, ed. *Christian Faith and the Contemporary.* (New York: Abingdon Press, 1 2, p. 120.
18. Giles Gunn, ed., *Literature and Religion.* (New York: Harper & Row, 1971), pp. 5-7.
19. Ibid., p. 7.
20. Ibid., pp. 8-9. 21. Ibid. pp. 9-11
22. Niebuhr, pp. 56-65.
23. This short story can be found in *A Malamud Reader* (New York: Farrar, Straus, and Giroux, 1972), pp. 449-459.
24. Gunn, pp. 8ff.
25. Ibid., pp. 23-29.
26. Walter Pater, "The Renaissance" in *The Norton Anthology of English Literature.* 4th ed.}.

27. Ibid., pp.1582-1583. 27. Frye, p. 23.

28. See the first page of this essay.

29. The concept of art as "judge" merits more attention than it is given here. One thinks of the comment by the museum guard to some visitors, "The works are not on trial, you are."

30. Charles L. Rice, *Interpretation and Imagination* (Philadelphia: Fortress Press, 1970), p. 24.

CHAPTER SIX

THE DUDA LECTURE:
SACRED SURPRISES IN SECULAR CINEMA

"Sacred Surprises in Secular Cinema" was the title of my inaugural lecture for the Duda Endowed Professorship (Chair) at Concordia College, New York (2002), which I held for five years. It was combined with a film/slide presentation and a banquet with film as the theme.

{Topics: Jaroslav Pelikan, Martin Scorsese, D. W. Griffith, Catholic League of Decency, Michael Medved, Milos Forman, Hannibal Goodwin, Herbert Booth, Paul Thomas Anderson, Paul Schraeder, Peter Weir, Steven Spielberg}

First, I want to express my thanks to the Duda family for their foresight and generosity in establishing the *first* endowed chair at Concordia College. May their tribe increase! And also to the college for electing me the first holder of this chair and enabling me to present this lecture in partial fulfillment of the expectations of the endowment. This is quite an honor!

Tonight's illustrated lecture entitled "Sacred Surprises in Secular Cinema" is meant to be just a partial glimpse into the larger study that I am engaged in on the long term—something along the lines of the sacred in secular cinema.

I have been frequently surprised, and pleasantly so, in my viewings of films and study of them, so I thought that focusing on just a few sacred surprises in secular cinema this evening with some film clips might not only be a good introduction to what I am doing, but it might also be entertaining and educational.

The Duda Chair Lecture

Sacred Surprises in Secular Cinema

Presented by
The Rev. Dr. Thomas R. Sluberski,
holder of the Duda Chair in Religion

Thursday, 26 April 2001 at 8:00 PM

Sommer Center for Worship and
the Performing Arts

Special thanks to the Village Lutheran Church for sponsoring
the showing of the videos seen tonight through their licensing
arrangement with Christian Video International.

The Duda Chair in Religion

The purpose of appointing an individual to an endowed chair is to recognize excellence in teaching and scholarly achievement, provide special resources for the appointee's further scholarly endeavor and enable the appointee to contribute in a publicly recognized way to the intellectual life of Concordia College in particular and the academy of higher education in general.

The Duda Chair in Religion was established at Concordia College in honor of Andrew, Ferdinand and John Duda by their family who reside in Oviedo, Florida. The Duda Chair in Religion is given under the endowment of the Duda Foundation, which made possible the Rev. Dr. Thomas Sluberski's research for a two-year period. One member of the family, Betty Duda, is a former chair of the college's Board of Regents and recipient of an honorary doctorate from the college. Concordia College is honored to have Dr. Duda and her husband, John, as generous friends of the college.

An informal guide to tonight's 2001 Duda Chair illustrated lecture, Sacred Surprises in Secular Cinema

I. Why this topic, this year, for this occasion?
II. The intended audience(s)?
III. What NOT to expect this evening and why:
   Films on obviously religious subjects
   Foreign, art and science fiction films
   Films in which God appears or speaks
   Films about Jesus Christ
IV. Sacred surprises in some examples of secular cinema:
   Magnolia
   Rocky and *Raging Bull*
   The Year of Living Dangerously, Almost Famous, Grand Canyon and *Pulp Fiction*
   The Matrix, Amistad, and *Places in the Heart*
   American Beauty
V. "What do we then do?" to quote *The Year of Living Dangerously* (and Count Leo Tolstoy)
VI. Not the end, but to be continued…

At the conclusion of the lecture you are invited to submit your own nominees for surprisingly sacred scenes in films you have seen on the sheets of paper provided. Leave them on the table at the exit.

Let me offer an outline of my topics:

I.   Why This Topic This Year for This Occasion in This Place?
II. The Different "Audiences"
III. The Type of Film to Be Analyzed
IV. Definitions of the Sacred
V.   What Do We Then Do?
VI. To Be Continued

I.   WHY THIS TOPIC THIS YEAR FOR THIS OCCASION IN THIS PLACE?

First, I've become increasingly aware of the enormous influence movies have on all sectors of American life. Young people in school or university probably see far more films than they read books, and that ratio seems to extend across the population.

And I don't mean so much "going to the movies" or a movie theatre, but also watching film on network television and the multiple cable channels, some devoted entirely to film, as well as the buying and renting of videos.

Even the Roman Catholic Sacred Heart League now acknowledges that film is "the most powerful medium in the world." "No other medium is as influential." I WANT TO UNDERSCORE THAT THE INFLUENCE OF FILM IS NOT ENTIRELY A NEGATIVE! AND THAT IS NOT EASY TO SAY AS A PROFESSOR OF LITERATURE!

On the other hand, one of the most influential theologians in the world, known to many people here this evening, Jaroslav Pelikan, in his monumental *Jesus Through the Centuries: His Place in the History of Culture* doesn't even make one reference to a film or a filmmaker in his supposedly comprehensive study.

We don't need to go as far as the character Travis in the film *Grand Canyon* who says, "Everything you need to know about life is in the movies." But even Carl Sandburg, one of our great American poets and a biographer of Abraham Lincoln, chastises those who think that the motion pictures Hollywood makes are "merely entertainment," that they have "nothing to do with education.", He says, "those are the darnedest fool fallacies that are current. Anything that brings you to tears by way of drama does something to the deepest roots of our personalities." He goes on to say, "All movies good or bad, are educational, and Hollywood is the foremost educational institution on earth."

We are what we read. We are also what we watch. D. W. Griffith, one of our first and greatest filmmakers who directed *Birth of a Nation* and *Intolerance,* put it simply, "The task I'm trying to achieve is, above all, to make you see." Films can "entertain, reinforce, challenge, and overturn perspectives, assumptions, values" and can enable us to try on "new models, new roles, new theories, new combinations of behavior."

Even C. S. Lewis said, "We want to see with other eyes, to imagine with other imaginations, to feel with other hearts, as well as our own." Martin Scorsese, the great director of such films as *Raging Bull, Goodfellas, The Last Temptation of Christ,* and *Taxi Driver,* said that he wanted to be a priest as a young man but later went into film. He writes, "I don't really see a conflict between the church and the movies, the sacred and the profane. I also see great similarities between a church and a movie house. Both are places for people to come together and share a common experience. And I believe there's a spirituality in film, even if it is not one which can supplant faith. It is as if movies answer an ancient quest for the common unconscious."

In the past few years since my return from Russia, I've approached film from various angles in a variety of presentations, ranging from a series called Sleuthing in Cinema, Sex in Cinema, Science Fiction in Cinema, and even Spirituality in Cinema; I've asked whether you can see the film instead of reading the novel (esp. the long Russian, German, French, or English novels); I've reviewed individual films and given workshops on understanding films to church groups and for college credit. I also teach regularly a seminar on film and literature. And I hope that tonight's brief selections will make you want to see, see again, or see anew, the positives of the movies.

II. AUDIENCES

I stress the word *positives* because I am aware that there are probably a number of different audiences here this evening:

And I am going to try to address all of them. A difficult task! PROBABLY FAR MORE DIFFICULT THAN SOME OF YOU CAN IMAGINE!

A) There are many people here this evening who probably don't think very highly of the movies, who probably don't think they are worth studying or discussing. Movies for some of you are merely entertainment, ephemeral, but hardly weighty. Some may agree with the Shirley MacLaine character in *Steel Magnolias* when she says, "I don't see movies cause they're trash, and they ain't got nothing but naked people in "'em." If that sounds like you, I hope to have you reconsider you viewpoint.

B) Others of you may be somewhat suspicious of movies, especially Hollywood movies, seeing them as a factor in the violence and decay of morals and values in our society—perhaps even sinful. In the 1930s the Catholic League of Decency asked people to boycott certain films, and attendance fell off by forty percent in Philadelphia alone! And you can often read reactions like those in the introduction to the book, *Movies and Morals*, for example, which says movies, "next to liquor, (are) the outstanding menace to Americans and to their world. They are the organ of the devil, the idol of sinners, the sink of infamy, the stumbling block to human progress, the moral cancer of civilization, the number-one enemy of Jesus Christ."

Another writes, "I submit that a frequenter of the theater or movie house cannot at the same time be a spiritual force for good." Even Michael Medved, a rather popular film critic often on television, entitled one chapter "The Attack on Religion" in his book called *Hollywood Versus America*.

On a more personal note: my high school English teacher, Latin teacher, next door neighbor, and the mother of three children who were my best friends growing up in Independence, Ohio,— never went to a movie, a play, or allowed a television set in her home. Yet she also taught me Latin and Shakespeare. For her, cinema was spelled "SINema." And closer by, Kings' College (since closed) required all transfer students to sign a statement that they had not been to a movie since being saved.

C) Still others of you may love film, and believe that many films are worthy of being seen again and again, but are not particularly aware of a spiritual or religious aspect—probably feeling that that has to be "read into the film." For this audience, religion in film may not be at all that evident or expected or even desirable—at least in popular Hollywood films. Someone has said, "The last taboo in cinema is religion or even a whiff of theology." Because of the variety of viewpoints probably present tonight, I've chosen to focus only on mainstream movies made in Hollywood, recent films, box office successes, available on videotape, hoping that that will make my point even more convincing.

III. THE TYPE OF FILM TO BE ANALYZED

A) That is why I am not going to talk about films that are obviously religious or on religious topics like *The Robe, The Ten Commandments, Witness, The Black Robe,* or *The Apostle.* That would be too easy, too obvious—but in later studies, I want to show that there is much more, even in religious films, than meets the eye.

B) Nor am I going to use foreign films, art films, or even science fiction films. Those too are easily mined for the spiritual or religious. The director of such great films as *Amadeus,* Milos Forman, said, "In American films, entertainment comes first and soul-searching comes second, if at all. In foreign films, soul-searching comes first and entertainment comes second, if at all." It certainly would have been easier to point to the sacred in *Babette's Feast* or *The Seventh Seal* or Koslowski's *The Dekalog.*

C) Nor am I going to talk about films in which God appears or speaks (even though rather rare). I will also not talk much about films about Jesus Christ. In fact, I am even going to avoid Christ figures—implicit or explicit. That will be the subject of future presentations. I should make reference here to the three photos on the invitation reprinted here, all of which can be seen as Christ figures, but in some cases, misleading ones. Two I don't think are particularly sacred.

The top photo of James Dean with a rifle over his shoulder and Elizabeth Taylor kneeling before him, is the most misleading—a Christ figure motif doesn't add much to the meaning of the film.

The Jake LaMotta character on the ropes in a boxing ring has some resonance, but the most surprising and most satisfying is the middle photo of the donkey, in one of Robert Bresson's greatest films, truly a Christ figure in every way rich with significance for the film and our understanding of Jesus Christ. A must-see film, though foreign, and thus off-limits tonight.

I've listed some films as an appendix to indicate the riches still to be mined—in films about Jesus alone. I have not listed all of them or even most of them, just those that are indicative of how the subject has fascinated film makers since the very first days of the invention of film.

There is a documentary film, in fact, which covers the first one hundred years of films about Jesus called *Jesus Christ: Movie Star*, made in 1992. Are you aware, by the way, that this year we observe over 110 years of filmmaking! It's hard to imagine how old yet how young this art form is.

An Episcopal minister, Hannibal Goodwin, may in fact have invented the first reel-to-reel photographic film in 1898. And many of the earliest films are religious in nature. Interestingly, even Herbert Booth, the son of the founders of the Salvation Army, made an early film in 1900 called *Soldiers of the Cross*, which depicted Jesus on the cross, the stoning of Stephen, and martyrs burning at the stake, using Salvation Army personnel as actors.

IV. DEFINITIONS

A few definitions are in order: by *sacred*, I simply mean "an experience of the holy," the Other, God, if you will.

One Christian critic even goes so far as to say, "Movies are a window through which God speaks." Something perhaps like what Jacob experienced in the Hebrew Scriptures. Genesis 28:16 says, "Surely the Lord is in this place, and I did not know it." Or in the words of Paul, "to see through a glass darkly" (1 Cor. 13:8, 12). Or even in Luke 24: 13-35, "He interpreted all the Scriptures, the things concerning himself."

Just two provisos, in the words of Christian Metz: "A film is difficult to explain because it is easy to understand." And Sam Goldwyn's "Pictures area for entertainment; messages should be delivered by Western Union."

Probably the two recent and well reviewed films that got me to thinking about the topic for this evening begin and end tonight's presentations: *Magnolia* and *American Beauty*—the latter because, at a national gathering of professors of English we were asked what recent films had we seen that we could recommend to others of our profession (the usual *Shakespeare in Love* and a number of Merchant/Ivory style remakes of Jane Austin and Edith Wharton were mentioned). I suggested *American Beauty*. A number of professors were truly shocked that I would recommend such a "degenerate" film about such dysfunctional people.

I'm not saying *American Beauty* isn't shocking, or that the families depicted in it aren't, for the most part, dysfunctional, but I do think it is an honest portrayal of what is bothering Americans. The film is about beauty and transcendence, but let me get to that later, after we talk about *Magnolia*, which was another real surprise.

Who would ever expect a rain consisting of frogs! Even after the fascinating stories that begin the film. And yet, like the plague of frogs that God and Moses brought down on the Egyptians, the frogs in *Magnolia* were a "sacred surprise," enabling some eleven people to get out of bondage and go on an Exodus to a better life.

A) *Magnolia*, written by Paul Thomas Anderson (who won an Academy Award—as did the theme song, "Save Me" by Aimee Mann, and Tom Cruise as supporting actor), I consider one of the best films of 1999. The eleven characters are enslaved in their own way and freed by the "rain of frogs" (like the frogs in Exodus that freed Israel from the slavery of Pharaoh).

The major characters really don't interact. The movie starts with three bizarre yet true events, including the case of a druggist who was killed by three men whose names put together were coincidently the name of his drugstore: Greenberry Hill. They are meant to show the viewer that life is not always orderly or predictable and readies us for a climax in which frogs fall from the sky like hailstones—an event that actually happens from time to time. But in the movie, in addition, one gets the impression of serendipity or even divine intervention. The frogs fall just at the right time in each person's life to give another chance or to halt a suicide, etc. The film never refers to or shows a church or a clergyman. The only "religious" act is a quick shot of the policeman on his knees praying in his bedroom before he goes on duty.

[A FILM CLIP IS SHOWN HERE.]
(Copyright laws keep me from reprinting film clips.)

B) *Rocky* and *Raging Bull*, of course, are two films about boxing—A PLACE YOU WOULDN'T EXPECT TO SEE TRANSCENDENCE. One fabulously popular and successful, the other seen as one of the great films of the twentieth century—yet together they illustrate some surprising turns in expectations. Do you remember how *Rocky I* opened? I'll bet not, though I would guess that some of you have seen the film a number of times.

Let's go to the video tape. A shot of a Byzantine-style mosaic of an all-powerful Christ with a banner that says "Resurrection AC" under it (probably meaning Resurrection Athletic Club) opens the film, accompanied by trumpets on the sound track. Rocky is somewhat of a Christ figure. He does tell Marie not to be promiscuous; he does rescue a bum; he does get beaten up to redeem the hopes of the common people. But he is more of a secular savior, and his religion is more a civil religion; the ideology is patriotic nationalism. There are George Washington and Uncle Sam costumes. In fact, the film is referencing the 1976 bicentennial of the USA. He is a failed fighter who wants a second chance. Remember, he does not win the fight at the end.

[FILM CLIP]

Raging Bull is somewhat different. It is the true story of Jake LaMotta's rise and fall as a boxer and a man, played by the young Robert de Niro. At the conclusion of the film, Jake is rehearsing the lines of another film, *On the Waterfront,* about a washed-up boxer—Marlon Brando's lines as the fighter Malloy. Jake interprets the punishment he gets from Sugar Ray Robinson as a "self-inflicted penance, a sort of seeking for atonemen,"—a punishment for what he has done wrong. We only see Jake through a mirror, a reflection; as he reflects, so do we. The film closes as he goes out on stage, but as it fades to black, the verses from John 9 are highlighted on the screen, one verse at a time, recounting the meeting of the Pharisees and Jesus Christ:

> So for a second time (the Pharisees)
> summoned the man who had been born blind and said,
> "Speak the truth before God
> We know this fellow is a sinner"
> "Whether or not he is a sinner, I do not know"
> the man replied
> All I know is this:
> "Once I was blind, and now I can see"
> (John 9:24-26 in the Good News Bible)

[FILM CLIP]

What an incredible ending to a violent film!

Raging Bull is at the top of most film critics' lists of one of the finest films ever made and on the AFI's top 100 films of the century. The screen play was written by Paul Schraeder, a Calvinist Christian by background, a product of Calvin College in Michigan. Schraeder also wrote *Taxi Driver*, *The Last Temptation of Christ*, and *American Gigolo*. He says that he was not allowed to go to the movies until he was seventeen.

C) In part C I'd like to focus on values, ethics, and morals. How to live our lives. How then should we live? What do we then do, to quote the film *The Year of Living Dangerously*.

From the earliest theater in ancient Greece, stories ask the essentially religious question: "How should we then live?" Sometimes the answer is rather dubious, but at other times, rather profound. All of these films show people changing for the better—morally and ethically. Not so much by divine intervention—though some of the characters may think so—but certainly by extraordinary experiences.

In *The Year of Living Dangerously*, we are shown the dreadful conditions in Jakarta, Indonesia, through the central character Guy Hamilton (played by Mel Gibson). He is asked by Billy Kwan who is quoting Tolstoy who is quoting Luke 3:10, "'What then must we do?'" Billy tells Guy that Tolstoy sold all that he had to relieve the suffering of the people he had come in contact with in Russia. Guy is obviously not persuaded. If Guy doesn't get the message, the viewer does. It rings in your ears as you leave the theater—Guy bangs it out repeatedly on his typewriter and hangs a banner out of his window to convince Suharto to feed his people. WHAT THEN MUST WE DO?

[FILM CLIP]

Grand Canyon is a Peter Weir film. He also made *The Truman Show* and *The Dead Poets' Society*. He says he has a cartoon on his wall of an old woman banging on a theater ticket window saying, "I want my sense of wonder back."

In *Grand Canyon*, to focus on just one of the characters, Claire senses that there is a reason she found a baby in the bushes. She says, "Something has happened. Some kind of connection has been made, and it has to be played out. What if there are miracles, Mac? Maybe we don't have any experience with miracles, so we're slow to recognize them."

Pulp Fiction depicts a mobster—Jules, played by Samuel L. Jackson—shot at repeatedly at close range and not dying, which convinces him to leave his life as a mobster and to convince others in the film to do likewise (but not John Travolta who thinks the experience is just good luck, but later dies under a similar set of circumstances).

Jules is convinced it is a miracle from "God," and at the end of the film, once again when someone has a gun to his head, recites these words again, and ends up saying, "I'm trying real hard to be a shepherd," which convinces the gunman to spare his life—the second time it happens in the film. You have to pay attention when a miracle happens twice to the same person.

[FILM CLIP]

Jules is always asking, "Have you read your Bible?" And he quotes a long passage he says is from Ezekiel but is not in the Bible, at least in the way he says it.

One of the funniest scenes in modern cinema is the rock group in *Almost Famous*, who are caught in a violent thunder storm in a plane and start confessing their sins to each other aloud because they are sure they are going to die. And it results in a real change and breakthrough for some of them—including the young cub reporter who writes their story for *Rolling Stone* and the leader of the group, who is transformed into someone for whom there is still hope.

By the way, every mother of a teenager who is crazy about music has to see this film.

D) Because of this audience, I do have to indicate three secular films that retell the Jesus story so refreshingly that they almost ask for another look.

The *Matrix* has caught the fancy of a younger generation for its special effects and fast—paced action and engaging music. But also, the story matches in many ways the New Testament understanding of a Messiah, who is to come, The Chosen One, Neo, who recognizes his uniqueness with the help of Trinity and Morpheus and references to Zion, etc. But I have to say that I found very little transcendent in the film. This is the way things are on this earth, and Neo and the others are to change things without the supernatural, without the transcendent, without any reference to a beyond or another realm. Nothing even supernatural about the enemy—computers—in spite of an amazing number of biblical references.

[FILM CLIP]

Quite different is that incredible scene in Spielberg's *Amistad* in the use of the Gustave Dore engravings that so many of us have seen a thousand times and dismissed or ignored or forgotten. One of the black slaves, Jamba, looks through a Bible given to him by one of the Christian abolitionists. He can't read; he is not a Christian, but he looks at the pictures and makes up a story on the basis of the Gustav Dore engravings he sees.

You have probably seen them too. But he sees the pictures of the Hebrew Scriptures and sees how bad things were for them. He then looks at the picture of the Nativity and says, "Then He was born and everything changed. Who is he? I don't know, but everywhere he goes, he is followed by the sun" (a halo). And then he looks at a picture of the Ascension, and says, "This is where we are going when they kill us. It doesn't look too bad." He notices the three crosses on Golgotha, and when they are led out of the courtroom to the prison, he sees the masts of three ships—and he is reminded of the three crosses. There is much more to go in the film, but after this, every viewer knows things can't help but get better.

[FILM CLIP]

As for *Places in the Heart*, I don't think I fully got the ending until I viewed the film again.

I thought at first the Communion scene was to show how a young wife could forgive her husband for adultery, and a community could come together after racism and murder and cheating. But when I saw the film again, I was amazed not only that the hired hand Moses was back after being threatened by the Ku Klux Klan (also present with him in church) and then I noticed Edna (Sally Fields) turns to serve Communion to the "resurrected presence" of her dead husband, and he in turn serves it to the resurrected presence of the man who had accidentally killed him and who in turn was subsequently lynched receiving communion with the living — the last two to receive and the last words of the film are "the peace of the Lord be with you." I've never attended another Communion service with the same attitude again, the living and the dead, the communion of saints.

The next film was a smash box office hit for children and families.

Yes, *Bambi*. I do want to reference something that many of us may have missed as children as we were seeing the film again and again. Bambi's mother tells Bambi about guns and the men who are hunting them. Then young Karus asks, "Will he ever stop hunting us?" The half-grown doe, Marena, says, "They say that sometime he will come to live with us and be as gentle as we are. He'll play with us then, and the whole forest will be happy, and we will be friends with him."(Almost word for word from Isaiah ll:6ff.)

A word about other major faith communities and film: Certainly the *The Thirteenth Warrior* starring Antonio Banderas has received positive comment by the Islamic community as *The Chosen* has by the Jewish community. But these are films on "religious" subjects—and not, by definition, secular—which is the theme of tonight's talk.

Other faith communities will be the subject of a later talk.

E) And I conclude with *American Beauty*, another much discussed film, and I think a truly great film: Lester Burnham, played by Kevin Spacey, is at a low point in his life, looked down on by his wife and daughter and himself. We hear him say at the opening of the film, "I'll be dead in a year. In a way, I'm already dead." And it is a depressing view of American family life, but he is shocked alive by an infatuation with a teenage cheerleader girlfriend of his daughter—he literally wakes up to smell the roses. He brings a perspective to life that can only be understood from the beyond, the other side. What he finds is beauty, "a deeper beauty . . . that conveys a sense of the ultimate worth of life itself, and the mystery that lies behind it." And he is not the only one in the film aware of it. The odd kid next door who is in love with Lester's daughter, tells of videotaping a plastic bag blowing in the wind. He says, "And this bag was just . . . dancing with me. Like a little kid begging me to play with it. For fifteen minutes. That's the day I realized that there was this entire life behind things, and this incredibly benevolent force that wanted me to know there was no reason to be afraid. Ever."

Who could imagine a filmmaker brave enough to film a plastic bag blowing in the wind for fifteen minutes! Match this with the final words of Lester after he has been shot in the last scene of the film with his own voiceover:

> . . . and then I remember to relax, and stop trying to hold on to it, and then it flows through me like rain and I can't feel anything but gratitude for every single moment of my stupid little life . . . . You have no idea what I'm talking about, I'm sure. But don't worry."
> FADE OUT.

[FILM CLIP]

I have to add that some of you may not see any or all of these scenes as at all transcendent, at all sacred, at all holy. But epiphanies, by definition, cannot be forced—I am only pointing to these films to see whether you see the same thing.

V. WHAT DO WE THEN DO?

Go to the movies. View them if you feel you need permission. Continue to go to them if you don't. It's not what goes into a person that corrupts him, but what is within and comes out of him. Watch for recommended films. Believe it or not those nominated for Academy Awards or Golden Globes are usually uplifting, not particularly violent or immoral. The top 100 films of the century put out by the American Film Institute is a good selection.

I would not recommend all of the films we've talked about for general viewing: For the mature, conservative viewer, I'd suggest *Places in the Heart, Bambi, The Matrix, Amistad, Almost Famous, Places in the Heart,* and *Magnolia* if you think you are ready. You can always turn off your video player.

Why? To be inspired? To be uplifted?

To discern the times?

To understand your peers, your children, the rest of the population, the trends, the directions, the possibilities?

To put the films you see in the hopper with everything else you've experienced and know to be true? To be challenged and, educated, —to rethink, retool, redirect?

Usually, people who write, produce, or direct have something they think is important to say—and generally it is not to murder, to rape, to pillage, to rob, to cheat, to steal. Think about it.

I hope, at least, in this brief overview, to have inspired you to take the movies more seriously. To consider what they do, what they can do, and what they have done—and so well.

VI. TO BE CONTINUED

So this is the end of this illustrated lecture, but the approach may be continued in the next film and films you see—and will be for me in further research and presentations like this one. That's why I ask you to share your suggestions (and criticisms and comments).

Life goes on, and not just in the movies.

Early Films About Jesus Christ

The Passion of Christ (1897—just two years after the "invention" of film.) Filmed in France by the Société Lear; all copies are lost; five minutes long.

The Horitz Passion Play (1897) an American production filmed in Bohemia, shown in the U.S. in a limited run.

The Mystery of the Passion Play of Oberammergau (19 min. long, produced in the U.S. in 1898, said to be filmed in Oberammergau, but in reality produced on the roof of the Grand Central Palace Hotel in N.Y.C. in winter.)

The Life and Passion of Jesus Christ (1899) produced in France with a woman director.

Christ Walking on the Waters (1900) only 35 seconds long but with special effects.

Pathé produced three early films: *The Life and Passion of Jesus Christ* (1902: 19 min. long); *Life of Christ* (1907: 5 min. long) and *The Life and Passion of Jesus Christ* (1908) later color-tinted (re-released twice, the last time in 1914).

From the Manger to the Cross (one of the first American feature length films—60 min. long) with some on location shots in Egypt.

Intolerance (1916; D.W. Griffith) 3 1/2 hrs. long.

Restitution (1918) in which Jesus defeats Satan and the Kaiser.

Leaves from Satan's Book (1919; Carl Theodor Dreyer)

I.N.R.I. (1923; Robert Wiene)

The King of Kings (1927; Cecil B. DeMille) filmed in black and white with color for the Resurrection.

Golgotha (French: 1935: was the first sound film on the life of Christ.)

Many films were made based on the novels *Ben Hur, The Last Days of Pompeii* and *Quo Vadis.*

The Robe (1953) in Cinemascope.

The Big Fisherman (1959; Disney)

Barabbas (1962; by Columbia based on Pär Lagerkvist's novel.)

Pontius Pilate (1961) An Italian/French production in which John Drew Barrymore plays both Jesus and Judas.

For more details see Lloyd Baugh's *Imaging the Divine*. Kansas City: Sheed and Ward, 1997.) and W. Barmes Tatum, *Jesus at the Movies*. Santa Rosa, CA: Polebridge, 1997.

Later Significant Films on the Life of Christ:

Musicals on the life of Christ: *Jesus Christ Superstar* and *Godspell* (both 1973); Controversial films: *The Life of Brian* (1979) and *The Last Temptation of Christ* (1988);
Other important films: *The King of Kings* (1927; DeMille and 1961; Ray); *The Greatest Story Ever Told* (Stevens in 1965); *The Messiah* (Rossellini in 1975); *Jesus of Nazareth* (Zeffirelli in 1977); *The Gospel According to Saint Matthew* (Pasolini in 1964); and *Jesus of Montreal* (Arcand in 1989).

Movies in Which God Appears or Speaks are More Rare:

Some interesting examples are: *Two of a Kind* and *The Next Voice You Hear* (in both of which Gene Hackman is the voice of God); Rex Ingram appears as God in *Green Pastures*; Richard Pryor in *In God We Trust*; Charlton Heston in *Almost an Angel*; Alanis Morissette in *Dogma*; and of course, George Burns in the *Oh, God!* series. God is the only character to appear in all three Monty Python films. (See Bryan Stone's *Faith and Film*, St. Louis: Chalice Press, 2000.)

PART III

WHERE I AM NOW

"Now Let Us Sport Us As We May," "At Once Our Time Devour," "And Make Our Time Stand Still"

From Andrew Marvell's "To His Coy Mistress"

CHAPTER SEVEN

BRAZIL THROUGH FOREIGN EYES

"Brazil Though Foreign Eyes" is an interview published on Gringoes.com in 2007. It reflects just some of the highlights of the time I had spent thus far in Brazil, particularly as guest professor at ULBRA, the Lutheran University of Brazil, the largest private university in Brazil with over one hundred thousand students on over twenty campuses. ULBRA, for example, arranged for me to go on the Amazon medical trip, inoculate as many local people as possible, give them physicals, induct men into the armed forces, and teach some necessary skills in hygiene, medicine and agriculture. Among a crew of over ninety—doctors, dentists, and government workers—I was the only foreigner. The interview was not meant to be complete.

I held this guest professorship at ULBRA during a sabbatical from Concordia, New York. When the president of Concordia asked ULBRAs director of foreign affairs how I was doing and what, the email response was very simple: "We are spending the semester making Sluberski happy." They succeeded mightily in that, and also made me fall in love with so many things Brazilian.

{Topics: visas, athletics, ULBRA, Oscar Niemeyer, Amazon, Americus Vespucci, bodybuilding, national anthem.}

THE INTERVIEW

Meet Tom Sluberski, from the USA, who has both worked and traveled in Brazil. Read the following interview where he tells us about some of his most memorable experiences from Brazil and gives some useful advice to newcomers.

1. Tell us a little about yourself: where are you from, what do you do, etc.?

My name is Tom Sluberski, here on a temporary visa to do research and reporting on doping and drugging in athletics for the Associação Brasileira de Estudos e Combate ao Doping (The Brazilian Association to Combat Doping and Drugging in Athletics). This is particularly relevant as the Pan American Games are to be held in Rio de Janeiro this July. I am also on the National Faculty of the United States Sports Academy and have been judging fitness and bodybuilding contests since 1983 in the United States, Russia, and now Brazil. In connection with ULBRA, the huge (over one hundred thousand students on more than twenty campuses) university, I also made some major presentations to Marcosur and Mercosul conferences, ABRALIC (the Brazilian Comparative Literature Association), went on a month long medical/research/governmental ship in the Amazon region (Rio Solomões, Negro, and Amazon), and traveled widely in Brazil. I grew up in Ohio but spent much of my career as a full professor at Concordia University in New York with teaching sabbaticals for example in Russia (St. Petersburg, Siberia, and the Far East); Kuala Lumpur, Malaysia; Hong Kong; Singapore; Austria; Switzerland; Germany; and study and travel in a lot of other places.

2. When did you arrive in Brazil and what brought you here?

My first trip to Brazil was in 2003 and a total revelation! I had led numerous student travel tours to Europe and the Caribbean and had taught in Russia, the Far East, and Germany. Then a student travel company awarded me a free trip to anywhere in the world they had tours since the tour I led for them was a very successful bus trip from Milan to Capri with—forty-one students. I had already visited most of the places on their list except Vietnam and Brazil. I am not sure why I had not visited Brazil before, but within three days after arriving in Rio de Janeiro in June of 2003, I knew Brazil was where I wanted to spend the rest of my life. I went to the airport early in the morning my first week there and bargained for day trips to places like Brasilia, Belo Horizonte, and São Paulo just to be sure my first impressions were accurate. When I got back to the States, I began working on ways to return full time. In 2004, ULBRA (Universidade Luterana do Brasil) offered me a sabbatical position, a free apartment, and a range of incredible experiences. After that, I kept returning on the six month tourist visa. ULBRA tried getting me a guest professorship, but the federal police implied I would be taking a job away from a Brazilian. That led to my asking the most important fitness and bodybuilding association in Brazil to help me get a longer term visa, which they did: "To Research and Report on Doping and Drugging," especially in conjunction with the Pan American Games to be held in Rio de Janeiro.

3. What were you first impressions of Brazil?

The "motto" of ULBRA has become my motto. BRAZIL: WHERE THE FUTURE HAS ALREADY BEGUN! I see Brazil as going in the direction I would like the future to be (politically, religiously, racially, and socially). Oscar Niemeyer's monument to South America in São Paulo (which probably most tourists and residents miss) literally changed my life. He designed a huge topographical map of South America covered with Plexiglas over which you can walk. If you know Niemeyer, he is *not* just an architect! He is a propagandist in the best sense of the word. Half way across the map, I realized: THERE WERE NO BORDERS. There was no way of telling where specific countries were. He did indicate the incredible riches of South America. As a gringo, I realized that *if* South America were united, it would be one of the greatest empires the world has ever known.

4. What do you miss most about home?

After almost two years here, I can honestly say I miss only my family and friends. I don't really like having to be away from Brazil! And I say that even after studying and living in some of the most wonderful places in the United States and the world.

5. What has been your most frustrating experience in Brazil?

Getting a longer term visa has been the most frustrating! I have offered to work for free as a university professor with outstanding credentials and experience, but even though I would not be paid, the federal police believe I would be taking a job away from a Brazilian. At one campus, I was the *only* native English-speaking faculty person with a student body of thirty thousand. The rules are the same. A Brazilian *could* possibly fill the position.

6. What has been your most memorable experience in Brazil (specific incident)?

There are so many, but certainly that trip into the far reaches of the Amazon to document, inoculate, and register countless Brazilians who were in "no man's land" left an indelible impression. I almost wished I had studied medicine. I think I would have stayed on that ship as it plied those almost—uncharted waters in a little-known region of the country.

7. What do you most like about Brazil (in general)?

THE PEOPLE! The Brazilian creation myth is absolutely to the point! There are two different interpretations (one rather self—depreciating from a Brazilian point of view). Mine is more positive. When God set about creating the world, the angels were all looking on. He began by giving Brazil the longest rivers (ten of the twenty longest are in Brazil), the largest rain forests, the best beaches (five thousand miles of them), oil, uranium, precious gems, and no earthquakes, tornadoes, or hurricanes. The angels were more than a little concerned, wondering what was left for all the other nations. Finally, the angel Gabriel asked, "God, what is left for the rest of the world? You have given Brazil the best of what there is?"

God waited only a moment to respond:

"WAIT UNTIL YOU SEE THE PEOPLE!"

They are certainly the *real* treasure of Brazil. The earliest explorers' written records comment on the beauty of the natives (see Americus Vespucci's journal, for example), not the gold or treasure they hoped to find. I was asked to be a judge at a Brazilian national fitness and bodybuilding competition in Goiás (in 2004). As the teenage contestants (beginners) came on stage, I was astonished! I had judged and seen contests like this in many places all over the world, but these were absolutely the most perfect human beings I had ever seen. Was the racial mixture perfecting the human form and figure? Oh yes, fitness routines include music! And the Brazilians generally have rhythm and can dance (not necessarily the case elsewhere—the Olympics for example).

A Brazilian version of the myth is much more self-depreciating, showing their wonderful sense of humor. God has created the Brazilian people to offset the riches he's given the country.

I like both interpretations.

8. What is your favorite restaurant/place to hang out here?

Kilo restaurants anywhere in Brazil!

9. Do you have any funny stories/incidents to tell about your time in Brazil?

The smaller ferries on the larger upper rivers of the Amazon are completely enclosed. I had no sooner asked why they would do that in such a glorious environment than a tropical storm hit, almost completely engulfing the ship in wave after wave of water. The captain just smiled and continued steering the ship toward Codejas. I did not care much about the scenery in the midst of that storm.

10. What difference between your homeland and Brazil do you find most striking?

The upbeat, positive, almost joyful way Brazilians live their daily lives, sometimes in circumstances that are far from ideal. What a contrast between the barefoot, laughing, singing children playing football in the favelas of Rio and often those in the slums of New York or Cleveland or Detroit!

11. How is your Portuguese coming along? What words do you find most difficult to pronounce/remember, or are there any words that you regularly confuse?

DIFFICULT! I lived in Geneva, Germany, Russia, Malaysia—and none of those languages seemed this hard to master!

12. What advice do you have for newcomers to Brazil?

Try to spend time in a variety of places Brazilians live, study, work, and enjoy! Spend time on a university campus, live with a family, participate in a samba school, take part in athletics, attend a candomblé ceremony and worship in one of the newer Pentecostal or charismatic churches.

13. What are some things that you would recommend for a visitor to do in São Paulo (or anywhere else in Brazil)?

See and experience as much of the country as you can! Be sure to include the historic, natural, and architectural wonders of Brazil. I would hope that, at a minimum, visitors should absorb as much of Rio, São Paulo, Brasília, Porto Alegre, Forteleza, Recife/Olinda, Natal, and Iguaçu as their time permits, knowing there is more, so much more! Try to be part of a samba school in carnival. Take a tour of a favela (or better yet, work with a group involved with them). Be part of a birthday celebration, a wedding, even a funeral if you know a member of the deceased family, or a football match. Try to attend a fitness and bodybuilding competition. Luis Henrique, Marlene, and Fabio Norte hold annual Monarch of the Beach contests in February in Vitoria, Espírito Santo. They are *free,* and often a beach rock concert follows with a great chance to mingle with absolutely gorgeous and wonderful people! BRAZIL: WHERE THE FUTURE HAS ALREADY BEGUN! I am only sorry that I waited so long to visit and now live in this glorious country. To quote some lines from their national anthem (by the way, one of the best in the world):

Brazil, a dream sublime. Thy future mirrors this, thy greatness.
MORE LIFE IS TO BE FOUND IN THY GROVES.
MORE LOVE IN OUR LIVES IN THY EMBRACE.
Beloved homeland, Brazil! *Patria Amada, Brasil!*

CHAPTER EIGHT

HOW TO RESIST AMERICANIZATION: IDEAS FOR MERCOSUL/MERCOSUR COUNTRIES

"Resisting Americanization" (2004) is an ironic title because, as an American, I was giving advice to Mercosul/Mercosur nations (Brazil, Argentina, Chile, Uruguay) on how to resist American influence, which is quite pervasive and increasing in South America. The entire presentation was simultaneously translated into Portuguese.

{Topics: national anthems, Fulbright, Jose Ignezio Rodo, Oscar Niemeyer, Dom Bosco, MALBA Museum in Argentina, *Sabado Gigante*, Napoleon, Americo Vespuccio, El Dorado, intermarriage, candomblé, Templo da Boa Vontade, extraterrestrial}

"Can the inroads, influence, and encroachments of American (USA) advertising, film, and public relations be resisted or even transformed by a mercosul/mercosur mentality?" (November 2004)

I.   Why I Feel I Can Add Some Insights to This Important Issue
II. The Problem

   A) The McWorld, Wal-World Phenomena

   • The pervasive influence of US advertising, film, and public relations

- The parody of the Brazilian National Anthem

B) Not All of This "Americanization" Is Good—Some Awful, Some Shallow

- Why then do so many Brazilian/Mercosur/Mercosul "buy into it" and want to live in America?

III. Possible Solutions

A) The "Latinization" of the United States
B) The USA Fulbright "Antidote"
C) "One" South America
D) Jose Ignezio Rodo

IV. My Own "Take" and Suggestions

A) The Brazilian "Myth of Creation"
B) Oscar Niemeyer's "Monument to Latin America" in Sao Paolo
C) Dom Bosco's "Prophecy"

V. Evidences of the transforming power of Mercosul/Mercosur/ Brasil—"where the future has already begun"

A) Intermarriage
B) Intermingling of Religions
C) Sexuality
D) "The Enjoyment of Life"

- The "Real" Brazilian National Anthem (in Portuguese and English)
- The French National Anthem in English
- The USA National Anthem in English

A Dedication

I would like to dedicate this presentation to ULBRA and to Brazil. I thought I had seen and done it all (or most of it)—traveling and living and teaching in so many places all over the world, always with an eye out for what might be the ideal place to live. It had often been New York City and maybe St. Petersburg, Russia, for a time, until I came to Brazil and ULBRA (near Porto Alegre, a truly "Happy Harbor"—the English translation of *Porto Alegre*).

I owe special thanks to Dr. Johannes Gedrat, director of foreign relations at ULBRA. He is the one who invited me to a place I had never been and knew almost nothing about. He made the simply amazing six months I spent at ULBRA possible, including convincing Rector Ruben Becker to have me stay and observe. It seems more like six lifetimes than just six months. When I returned to the States and to Concordia, which had sponsored the guest professorship, I looked at the file of reports on my stay in Brazil. When the president of Concordia asked, "What is Tom doing at ULBRA, Brazil?" ULBRA's reply: "We have been spending the last six months making Sluberski happy." They not only did that but changed the course and direction of my life.

I.   Why I Feel I Can Add Some Insights To This Important Issue

Many US professors teach only twelve hours a week, get twenty weeks a year "off," and get every seventh year with half pay or a half year off with full pay. I personally have used almost all of this "free" time to study, travel, and live abroad—enabling me to see and experience many places.

In the USA, I am a tenured full professor in the Concordia University System (in New York). I lived for four years in Germany, one in Switzerland, a summer in Austria, and taught for two and a half years in Russia. I also taught a summer in Singapore, Hong Kong, and Malaysia and had extensive stays in almost all of Europe, Asia, North Africa, and the Caribbean. This is not said to brag—in fact, I am rather humbled when I see how hard my colleagues here at ULBRA Canoas work—but it is said to underscore that I could not help noticing everywhere I have lived and visited the almost overwhelming influence of the United States in almost every aspect of life, culture, and politics. And in most places, it is meeting almost no effective resistance. Some call it the McWorld or Wal-World effect.

II.   *O Problema*

As early as 1901, William Stead wrote a book entitled *The Americanization of the World*. It is certain that the 1999 elections in Argentina were heavily influenced by Americans. Dick Morris and James

---

Carvelle (the two men who helped get Bill Clinton elected) were hired to manage the political marketing (USA style) of the candidates with some rather hilarious results. And certainly, the elections of Alejandro Toledo in Peru, Vicente Fox in Mexico, Andres Fox in Columbia, Ricardo Lagos in Chile, and perhaps even Hugo Chavez in Venezuela all used US political marketing techniques, changing the way campaigning is done in South America. Perhaps the best illustration of this in Brazil has been circulating on the Internet for months. It is a parody of the Brazilian national anthem. It was written by Adriano Siri of Os Melhores do Mundo (The World's Best). More than ten thousand people heard it for the first time in a parody show called *Politica* in Brasilia in 2002.

Num Posto da Ipiranga, às margens plácidas,	On the placid banks of an Ipiranga gas station
De um Volvo heróico Brahma retumbante	From a heroic Volvo resounding Brahma
Skol da liberdade em Rider fúlgido	Skol of Liberty in glittery Rider
Brilhou no Shell da Pátria nesse instante	Shone in the Shell of Fatherland this moment
Se o Knorr dessa igualdade	If Knorr of this equality
Conseguimos conquistar com braço Ford	We were able to conquer with arm Ford
Em teu Seiko, ó liberdade	In your Seiko, o Freedom
Desafio nosso peito à Microsoft	Defies our breast Microsoft
Ó Parmalat, Mastercard, Sharp, Sharp	O Parmalat, Mastercard, Sharp, Sharp
Amil um sonho intenso, um rádio Philips	Amil an intense dream, a Philips radio
De amor e Lufthansa à terra desce	Of love and Lufthansa it goes down to land
Intel formoso céu risonho Olympikus	Intel pretty laughing sky Olympikus
A imagem do Bradesco resplandesce	Bradesco's image shines
Gillete pela própria natureza	Gillete by nature
Éis belo Escort impávido colosso	Behold a pretty Escort fearless colossus
E o teu futuro espelha essa Grendene	And your future mirrors this Grendene
Cerpa gelada!	Icy cold Cerpa!
Entre outras mil és Suvinil,	Among thousands you're Suvinil,
Compaq amada.	Beloved Compaq.
Do Philco deste Sollo és mãe Doril	From Philco of this Sollo you're Mom Doril,
Coca Cola, Bombril!	Coca-Cola, Bombril!

Please see the "real" translation of the Brazilian national anthem at the end of this essay. This satiric version emphasizes the corporate changes in Brazil; advertising logos are substituted for words in their national anthem.

If you laughed, you get the point. Homogenous and corporate style Americanization is pervasive and not particularly salutary, even here in Brazil. Some is simply second rate or even awful.

The MALBA Museum in Buenos Aires mounted an amazing show on "The Uses of the Image: Photography, Film, and Video in the Jumex Collection" from September 29 to November 22, 2004. The first section of the exhibit is a prologue and shows how the commercialized image "has been transformed into an icon of its own superficiality." Almost a perfect commentary on much Americanization.

Why then do so many people in Brazil and Mercosur/Mercosul countries sometimes "buy" into it and sometimes want to live in America? I don't think there is a US citizen who has visited anywhere in South America who has not heard over and over again "I Want To Live in America" (a song, by the way, in Bernstein's musical *West Side Story*).

Let me give two really heartbreaking and completely incomprehensible (to a US citizen, at least) examples. Both are connected to Porto Alegre, by the way. I've got even better ones from elsewhere if you want to hear them.

A young, obviously successful Federal University graduate—already a bank manager in his twenties, really bright and so helpful when it came to international banking—pulled me aside one day in the bank and in a hush-hush voice said, "I'm going to the United States."

I asked as a matter of course, "How did you get a visa?" knowing that they are almost impossible to get for talented young South Americans. He said, "Oh no. I don't have one. I'm going illegally." I was dumbfounded and said, "Look what you are leaving behind! You will never have this standard of living unless you turn to crime or start selling illegal drugs in the United States. You'll be mowing lawns or washing floors at night for $5 an hour!" His answer was typical—and so much more heartbreaking because he was so smart yet believed what he was saying and doing. "Oh no. I am going to get rich there." (Evidently no concerns about never getting a legal job or a pension in the USA and possibly getting arrested and deported.) Worse is a Brazilian young mother and father with three beautiful children, a new home, new furniture, the latest TV, computer, a car, and all the rest: private schools for all three children, weekly private foreign language lessons (in guess which language) for all three children, and a maid two days a week!

Even if they get legal status in the USA, there is almost no way they will ever equal this quality of life they have here. For example, no one at my university in New York has anything even remotely close to this quality of life, even with both husband and wife working full time. Yet this Brazilian family wants to live in the USA.

III. Some Possible Solutions

A) The "Latinization" of the United States

The "press" to be Americanized may be offset by the increasing Latin influence in the USA. The Hispanic population has already surpassed the Afro American in the USA. In fact, the State of New Mexico may be as much as 40 percent Latino, Texas is approaching 25 percent, and California's Latino population is burgeoning—so much so that it is now called Mexico's reclaiming of lost territory. The main Hispanic television networks in the US (Telemundo and Univision) have huge South American audiences. *Sabado Gigante* has the largest TV audience in South America. Christina Saralegui is the Hispanic Oprah Winfrey and broadcasts from Miami. There are more than fifty million Spanish-speaking people in the USA, probably already equaling the entire population of Spain! Some wonder then whether these two cultures can mix there and form a new type of American civilization. However, often these Hispanics are seen as second-class citizens, often without a good education or special skills. It is doubtful, in my mind, whether anything like equality will be attained in my lifetime at least, nor will it stop the Americanization of the rest of the world (including South America).

Yet even the name "Latin" is strange. It was evidently "invented" in France to connect its culture to the great civilizations of Rome and Greece. The term Latin America was in use before 1860 but was used increasingly again in France (including by Napoleon) because the United States was claiming for itself the word "America" (and still does). A good friend, Edward Bergman, a professor of geography, shed some light on this. He points out that there is some justification for the term Latin America. It suggests that some important cultural themes spring from ancient Rome (Latium). Spanish and Portuguese are rooted in Latin, yet Italy is not important in the history of Latin America. What seems to have happened is that during the conflict of the US Civil War, Napoleon III considered occupying Mexico. He used the pretext that since France was also a Latin nation, it would be "defending Latin honor." So on July 3, 1852 Napoleon the III had a letter published in a French newspaper (La Moniteur) which may have introduced the term "Latin America" to justify France's invasion.

Thus the term "Latin America" was born, but think about it. The words "Latin America" do not include the native Indians or Africans in South America. And what about the pre-Columbus past? The term, in fact, strongly implies the colonization of South America. Even the term "America" named after Americo Vespuccio implies his "discovery" of the new world. The words "Latin America" seem to enable the West (Europe) to claim dominion over South America.

There are some very interesting developments, however. Cowan finds that developing countries still yearn for music composed at home: in India, 96 percent of the market; in Egypt, 81 percent; and in Brazil, 73 percent. Even the world's most popular movie star is not Julia Roberts or Ben Affleck but Amitabh Bachchan, an Indian film star. What is more, Charles Paul Freund, in *Reason* magazine, notes that in 2001 more than 70 percent of all TV shows in sixty different countries were locally produced; and the *Guardian* noted that top-grossing films in 2002 in Japan, Germany, Spain, France, and India were domestic! That still does not counteract, however, the overwhelming Americanization of the rest of the world's culture, politics, and advertising.

B) The Fulbright "Antidote"

When I got my first scholarship to Germany as a student, Fulbright and the Institute of International Education required us to take their ship to Europe and take classes on board every morning and evening—for obvious reasons. They knew that most of us would be overwhelmed by the "advanced" civilizations in which we would be studying: Germany, France, Spain, and England. So they scheduled a host of lectures to teach us the strengths of American culture and politics: our great writers, artists, thinkers, the qualities of our political system—a lot of which most of us did not know much about. I am still grateful for what I learned on that ship about my country's culture. It certainly helped all of us deal with the frequent put downs of America by the Germans, French, and English. Something like that could be thought about in South American schools and institutions of higher learning. Many, if not most, South American students are unfamiliar even with the most famous artists, writers, thinkers of South America (nor am I, of course).

Interestingly, many students here at ULBRA did not know what and why they were celebrating a particular national holiday. I knew and had to tell them, only because I had been so impressed by Petropolis and the wonderful guides there. Anyway, something like studying the history and culture of South America might help temper some of the South American enthusiasm for often a second-rate American (US) culture.

C) "One" South America

What about "one" South America? Oscar Niemeyer's "Monument to South America" in Sao Paolo changed my life! Honest! He is quite a propagandist as well as architect, in case you don't know it (and many Brazilian students apparently don't). What he did in one part of the complex is have a huge topographical map of South America constructed on the floor with all the great rivers, mountains, cities, and archeological sites in three dimensions. Then he put the whole thing under a sheet of Plexiglas over which you can walk.

In doing so, you realize that there are no borders, no indication of where Brazil begins and Argentina lets off, or even that there is a country called Brazil! I was floored! What if this entire continent of South America were one entity like the European Common Union? It would be one of the greatest powers the world has ever known. And I—as a US citizen, supposedly at this time the greatest power in the world—was more than a little shaken. Even though I never say "never" to my students, some of you know "it ain't gonna happen." There are too many ancient and current rivalries, let alone no one common race, religion, language, or culture in South America for it to unite into one region, let alone one country. There is no "one" South America except as a geographical entity! But Oscar Niemeyer had me thinking about the possibility for a long, long time; and in fact, that monument is one of the reasons I am in Brazil right now!

IV. My Own "Take" and Suggestions

I almost think the following myth is a footnote if not a separate chapter in all Brazilian bibles. It is said that when God was creating the world, the angel Gabriel and all the other angels were looking on with great interest. He began by giving Brazil ten of the twenty longest rivers in the world; the largest rain forest; the longest stretch of great beaches; no natural disasters like hurricanes, earthquakes, and tornadoes; plus gold and silver and uranium in abundance. Finally, the angel Gabriel could keep quiet no longer. He said, "God you have given all the best things to Brazil, what is there finally left for the rest of the world still to be created?" God paused only a moment before replying: "Wait till you see the people I give Brazil!" And that is what I think many of the early explorers overlooked. They were looking for gold and silver and material treasures in Brazil and South America, but the *real* treasures of Brazil are its people. There is a wonderful early text describing the first encounters of the explorers with the Indians, and the comments were primarily about how beautiful the Indians were! The people of South America are the real El Dorado. Some Brazilians have a rather self-deprecating interpretation: that true, Brazil has all these riches, but they are offset by the less-than-worthy Brazilian people. It does show they are able to laugh and make jokes about themselves. I like both interpretations.

In addition to Oscar Niemeyer's "Monument to South America," something else changed my life, and that is the prophecy of Dom Bosco (depicted in part on the doors of the beautiful church erected in his honor in Brasilia). Dom Bosco was a Salesian priest in Turin, Italy, who had a prophetic vision in 1883 of a great civilization that would "resurrect itself" in the twentieth century in South America between the 15th and 20th parallels, and the capitol of that civilization would be built between the 15th and 16th parallels—precisely where Brasilia is built (perhaps purposely, in my opinion). I am not a Roman Catholic. I am not a mystic. I am not given to believing in prophecies, and I have to say that, probably, Dom Bosco and I do not always agree with or even approve of these evidences increasingly evident of that new civilization "resurrecting itself" in Brazil. But consider the following.

V. Evidences of the Transforming Power of Mercosul/Mercosur/Brazil: "Where The Future Has Already Begun" (ULBRA's Motto)

I am fairly certain that Dom Bosco did not have a clear picture of the civilization that he thought would "resurrect itself" in the twentieth century between the 15th and 20th parallels. In fact, I am fairly certain that he and lots of others would have some difficulties with what is actually happening in that "new" civilization that is beginning to transform the world starting in Brazil.

But who am I or, for that matter, who is Dom Bosco to stand against the inevitability of history or the course of events or the wave of the future?

All I can do is only look on in *awe* and *wonder* at what I am seeing here! Let me outline at least four things that sociologists and scientists have noted that are happening in Brazil and Mercosul/Mercosur that are unique, unusual, progressive, convincing, and certainly of importance to the rest of the world. In fact, Braszil/Mercosur/Mercosul seems to be the place where the future has already begun. Much of this may not seem so striking or unusual or shocking to a Brazilian audience, but if I gave this presentation in the United States or Germany or Russia, there would be constant gasps throughout what follows.

A) Intermarriage

The evidence seems to be that the intermingling of races has been salutary in a number of ways in Brazil, but nothing like it is happening anywhere else in the world! Ever since the first explorers first landed in South America, they had children with the local peoples as did the Spanish, the Dutch, the English, and the Africans; and this continues today with later waves of Italians, Germans, Poles, Japanese, and Russians. And this is happening faster and most obviously in Brazil, and almost nowhere else in the world. In my country, much of the time, white is white, black is black, Latino is Latino, and Indian is Indian; and seldom do they ever intermarry, let alone have children. And if they do, they are often discriminated against. What is and has been happening in Brazil is something new for the issue of racism alone. I think there is less racism in Brazil than in any other country in the world, partly because you never know what race someone's parents or grandparents are. Many states in the USA until comparatively recently had laws against whites marrying blacks. Even the extremely popular and influential Brazilian soap operas take pains to depict not just interracial dating but also interracial couples and children.

What is more, the mix is apparently producing more perfect human beings. I was asked to judge the most important fitness and bodybuilding contest in Brazil at the beginning of October 2004 in Goiania. There were 150 contestants from 21 of the 26 States of Brazil competing, approximately five men and women from each State. I was astounded at the perfect symmetry, form, beauty, skin tone, and health of the contestants!

I have judged and seen similar contests all over the world, and I was the representative of the International Federation of Bodybuilders and the only foreign judge, but this Brazilian contest had the finest specimens of human beings I have ever seen anywhere! Are the weaknesses of one race being transformed by strengths of the others in Brazil, offsetting inbreeding? Is this just one evidence of the new civilization "resurrecting itself" between the 15th and 20th parallels?

B) The Intermingling of Religions

I have time only to make reference to what is happening in two of your capitals: Salvador and your current capital, Brasilia. By the way, Americans would be very uncomfortable and ill at ease in either place. Both are "over the top" for most of us. This is something not only amazing but also shocking to most visitors to Brazil. Many Brazilians seem to belong to or at least pay allegiance to a variety of religions.

I spent an astonishing week in Salvador and attended a candomblé service for hours on the Monday night after your national elections. A lot of important politicians in suits and ties (and not all Afro-Brazilians) were there and prostrated themselves on the floor before the "mother." And, of course, the goings-on in the crowd were equally interesting with people going into trances, getting possessed, barking like dogs, or hissing like snakes (a little like some of our charismatic services in the US). That, however, is not the end of the story.

On the following Tuesday night, I attended the historic Roman Catholic black slave church in Pelourinho. The same kind of drumming and percussion instruments were used—to different melodies and words, of course, but no organ or piano at all. And the singing was led by women, yet it was a high Roman Catholic mass: the correct vestments, incense, order of service, yet some of the same people who had attended the *candomblé* on Monday night were there also with seemingly no disconnect!

The next day, I went to Bonfim—a beloved Salvadorian church where, every year, the Roman Catholic priests, along with the "mothers" of candomblé, wash the steps together in harmony! In the United States, those priests would most probably be defrocked immediately. Is this another way you are about to transform the way the world worships? And, of course, there is Brasilia, your capital! The Temple of Good Will (Templo da Boa Vontade) is really new age. Not only does it have the world's largest crystal in its dome, but it has an Egyptian meditation room and, of course, it is dedicated to the unity of all faiths.

About forty-five kilometers east of Brasilia is the Valley of the Dawn where Egyptian, Greek, Aztec, Indian, Gypsy, Inca, Trojan, African, and Brazilian rituals are regularly observed! In the center is a large Star of David.

They really "cover the waterfront." And one hundred kilometers west of Brasilia is the "Eclectic" City, which hopes to unify all religions. Brasilia itself has a Holistic University, which is to help educate a new generation with new mental attitudes. I don't need to mention all the extraterrestrial cults in the region to prove my point. Is this the religious future of the world? Eclectic? Interreligious? New Age? Dom Bosco might not have approved, but . . . .

C) Sexuality and Sensuality

This section may be censored, and I will totally understand if it is because it has shocked me as it has and is shocking the rest of the world! Just watch Carnival on TV with Western or Eastern eyes! Let alone the beaches and clubs of Rio de Janeiro! Brazilians seem to be among the most sexual, sensual people in the world—so much so that the evidence seems to be pointing to an increasing fluidity of sexuality here, probably much more so than in any other nation in the world.

"Drag" is popular and seemingly accepted, especially during Carnival and even on nationally televised programs.

The fluidity of female sexuality in Brazil is also very evident. Just observe a show with the incredibly popular Ivete Sangalo—watched by millions on television, and her videos are owned by even more. She is the equivalent of a Brazilian Madonna or Cher. The concert I saw was an MTV special with Gilberto Gil! But even Madonna and Cher could not get away with what she did in that televised concert. Not only passionate female to female kissing, but celebrating Black/White, Indian/White, and probably Indian/Black sex! Is this yet another way Brazil is transforming the world, the way we look at sexuality? Again, I am not sure Dom Bosco would approve.

Sao Paolo has the largest gay pride parade in the world, and other Brazilian cities have such well attended events. Recently a Brazilian volleyball star was "outed" during a game with some heckling, but in the next professional game in which he played, he was cheered, and the crowd evidenced their support of his choice.

D) Enjoyment of Life

Just one more point—and I have lots more, but we don't have world enough or time. You might think that enjoyment of life is taken for granted by all people everywhere, but remember, even our American (sorry, US)

Constitution only promises "life, liberty, and the *pursuit of happiness*." In the USA, for example, the average vacation time allowed per worker is only three weeks a year! In Rio, Salvador, Manaus, the Amazon, and lots of other regions of Brazil, that almost seems the required *work* time per year! People in Brazil tend to take more time for vacation, holidays, celebrations, dancing, music, meals, and sex (except for ULBRA Canoas, of course). But think about it. When people from other countries visit Brazil, they often return to their home countries wishing their countries were more like Brazil. Maybe they should be! Maybe they could be! Why does such a wealthy nation as the USA or Japan, for example, only allow three weeks vacation time to its workers? Is this yet another way Brazil/Mercosur/Mercosul is transforming the way we look at life and live it? I don't think you even have to bother with *resisting* Americanization.

Dom Bosco's prophecy was certainly at least a good guess, if not an inspired prophecy—prescient, if not prophetic!

Aren't you glad you are the place "where the future has already begun?"
Aren't you glad you are not a "has-been" nation?
Aren't you glad you are not a "been there" nation?
Aren't you glad you are not a "done that" nation?

Brazil/Mercosur/Mercosul is beginning to transform the world rather than be transformed by it!

Brazil/Mercosur/Merosul is beginning to lead the world rather than follow it!

Brazil/Mercosur/Mercosul is beginning to influence the world rather than be influenced by it!

brazil/mercosur/mercosul is beginning to inspire the world rather than being inspired by it!

I want to conclude with some words from your national anthem (the real one), which you probably take for granted!

more life—mais vida
more love—mais amores
peace in the future glory in the past—paz no futuro e gloria no passado

all hail! all hail!—salve! salve!
beloved land, brasil—patria amada, brasil

where the future has already begun

Brazilian National Anthem (In English)

The placid banks of Ipiranga heard
the resounding cry of a heroic people
and brilliant beams from the sun of liberty
shone in our homeland's skies at that very moment.

If we have fulfilled the promise
of equality by our mighty arms,
in thy blossom, O freedom,
our brave breast shall defy death itself!

O beloved,
idolized homeland,
Hail, hail!

Brazil, an intense dream, a vivid ray
of love and hope descends to earth
if in thy lovely, smiling and clear skies
the image of the (Southern) Cross shines resplendently.

A giant by thine own nature,
thou art a beautiful, strong and intrepid colossus,
and thy future mirrors thy greatness.

Beloved Land
amongst a thousand others
art thou, Brazil,
O beloved homeland!

To the sons of this land
thou art a gentle mother,
beloved homeland,
Brazil!

Eternally lying in a splendid cradle,
by the sound of the sea and the light of the deep sky,
thou shinest, O Brazil, garland of America,
illuminated by the sun of the New World!

Thy smiling, our prairies have more flowers
than the most elegant land abroad,
"Our meadows have more life,"
"our life" in thy bosom "more love."

O beloved,
idolized homeland,
Hail, hail!

Brazil, let the star-spangled banner thou showest forth
be the symbol of eternal love,
and let the laurel-green of thy pennant proclaim
'Peace in the future and glory in the past.'

But if thou raisest the strong gavel of Justice,
thou wilt see that a son of thine flees not from battle,
nor does he who loves thee fear death itself.

Beloved Land,
amongst a thousand others
art thou, Brazil,
O beloved homeland!

To the sons of this land
thou art a gentle mother,
beloved homeland,
Brazil!

Contrast "*La Marseillaise*"—the French national anthem—which is warlike and bloody in comparison to Brazil's almost utopian, peaceful anthem.

Composed by Claude-Joseph Rouget de Lisle in 1792, it was declared the French national anthem in 1795.

Let's go children of the fatherland,
The day of glory has arrived!
Against us tyranny's
Bloody flag is raised! (repeat)

In the countryside, do you hear
The roaring of these fierce soldiers?
They come right to our arms
To slit the throats of our sons, our friends!

Grab your weapons, citizens!
Train your batallions!
Let us march! Let us march!
May impure blood
Water our fields!

This horde of slaves, traitors, plotting kings,
What do they want?
For whom these vile shackles,
These long-prepared irons?
Frenchmen, for us, oh! what an insult!
What emotions that must excite!
It is us that they dare to consider
Returning to ancient slavery!

What! These foreign troops
Would make laws in our home!
What! These mercenary phalanxes
Would bring down our proud warriors!
Good Lord! By chained hands
Our brows would bend beneath the yoke!
Vile despots would become
The masters of our fate!

Tremble, tyrants! and you, traitors,
The disgrace of all groups,
Tremble! Your parricidal plans
Will finally pay the price!
Everyone is a soldier to fight you,

If they fall, our young heroes,
France will make more,
Ready to battle you!

Frenchmen, as magnanimous warriors,
Bear or hold back your blows!
Spare these sad victims,
Regretfully arming against us. (repeat)
But not these bloodthirsty despots,
But not these accomplices of Bouillé,
All of these animals who, without pity,
Tear their mother's breast to pieces.

Sacred love of France,
Lead, support our avenging arms!
Liberty, beloved Liberty,
Fight with your defenders!
Under our flags, let victory
Hasten to your manly tones!
May your dying enemies
See your triumph and our glory!

We will enter the pit
When our elders are no longer there;
There, we will find their dust
And the traces of their virtues.
Much less eager to outlive them
Than to share their casket,
We will have the sublime pride
Of avenging them or following them!

Contrast also **"The Star Spangled Banner" (US national anthem)**

Oh, say can you see, by the dawn's early light,
What so proudly we hailed at the twilight's last gleaming?
Whose broad stripes and bright stars, through the perilous fight,
O'er the ramparts we watched, were so gallantly streaming?
And the rockets' red glare, the bombs bursting in air,
Gave proof through the night that our flag was still there.

O say, does that star-spangled banner yet wave
Over the land of the free and the home of the brave?

And where is that band who so vauntingly swore
That the havoc of war and the battle's confusion
A home and a country should leave us no more?
Their blood has wiped out their foul footstep's pollution.
No refuge could save the hireling and slave
From the terror of flight, or the gloom of the grave:
And the star-spangled banner in triumph doth wave
Over the land of the free and the home of the brave.

CHAPTER NINE

BRAZIL AND *BROKEBACK MOUNTAIN*

For the Brazilian Comparative Literature Association

(ABRALIC)

"Brazil and *Brokeback Mountain*," a presentation to the Brazilian Comparative Literature Association (ABRALIC) held in 2006 in Rio de Janeiro (Universidade do Estado, UERJ), which connected the popularity of the film around the world and in Brazil to various genres of literature, short story, fiction, screenwriting, and feminism, as well as showing how the film is perceived differently outside the United States, especially in Brazil (simultaneously translated into Portuguese).

{Topics: E.Annie Proulx, cowboys, the American West, James Fenimoe Cooper, D. H. Lawrence, Point of View, Abraham Maslow, the Closet, Gustavo Santolalla, Matthew Shepard, Mary Renault, Patricia Highsmith}

OUTLINE: INTRODUCTION
                BACKGROUND
                GENRE
                GENDER
                SETTING
                FILM AND LITERATURE

CONCLUSION: THE MEANING OF THE TITLE

{The presentation concludes with a short coda of film clips accompanied by excerpts of the music.}

BRAZIL AND *BROKEBACK MOUNTAIN*

A PERFECT SCENARIO FOR THE THEME OF THIS YEAR'S ABRALIC SYMPOSIUM:

Participants were asked to focus on "emerging identities versus expectations and the new challenges of comparativism," new technologies (screenplay and film), and emergent identities ("straight" men portrayed as sexually drawn to each other)

Identity, gender, and sexuality (Married cowboys with children and their sexual relationships; the author and one of the screenwriters are females writing in a genre often reserved for men.)

* * * * * *

Brokeback Mountain: short story into screenplay into film, interpreted by critics (popular and scholarly), and now read and seen by the general public around the world.

To quote one of Bette Davis's famous lines from another film, *All About Eve*, "Fasten your seatbelts! We are in for a bumpy ride!" But since *Brokeback Mountain* is a Western film, we should say, "Fasten your saddles!"

BACKGROUND

The short story "Brokeback Mountain" by Pulitzer Prize winner E. Annie Proulx (then in her sixties) was first published in the *New Yorker* magazine in 1997 after years of rejection slips by other publishers. It is now seen as one of her best short stories ever published in that magazine.

The screenplay by well-known authors Larry McMurtry and Diana Ossana was also rejected by a number of directors. No one seemed to think it would succeed with a general audience. In fact, most people were surprised that such a short story (thirty-five pages) could be made into a feature-length film. Larry McMurtry has said that he seldom even reads short stories for that reason. The film—directed by Ang Lee, a

Taiwanese—went on to win general acclaim and box office success and was nominated for and won a number of prestigious awards (the Venice Film Festival, the Golden Globes, the Academy Awards). It opened in Brazil on February 3, 2006, topping all the charts. It has earned over ninety million dollars in the United States and over eighty million around the world. It is already the fifth highest-grossing Western movie in history. Yet, and here *secure your saddles*, the critical reviews generally and often the general public in particular often misunderstood (sometimes completely) the story, the screenplay, and the film! Sometimes reversing, in fact, the original intent and meaning. That is the reason I wanted to present this paper at this symposium in Brazil!

This symposium in focusing precisely on new technologies, emergent identities versus expectations, and the new challenges of comparativism, which might possibly clarify how and why so much literature and film around the world is misunderstood and misinterpreted. In fact, this may be more evident in the case of *Brokeback Mountain* in Brazil than in the United States!

Yes, I know there are cowboys and even rodeos in Brazil; some of the best rodeo riders in the world are from Brazil. (I even know one of them personally who now lives in Vitoria, Espírito Santo.) I know about and like Forró. I also lived in Rio Grande do Sul for a year, the home of the Gaucho. But I do not think most Brazilians or people outside the United States can feel or think or understand or react to this story or this film the way a North American does! The West, the cowboy, the wide open spaces are central to the way we North Americans think of ourselves and our country. It is our central "myth." We are steeped in it from childhood by television, comic books, magazines, literature, theater, music, film, costumes, games (Daniel Boone, Wyatt Earp, Kit Carson, Wild Bill Hickock, the Lone Ranger, Shane, the Dallas Cowboys, country and western music, Levi's, the Marlboro Man, and the musicals *Annie Get Your Gun*, *Oklahoma*, etc.). Increasingly, though, a number of major literary critics have noticed that there is more to that myth than most of us realize. Leslie Fiedler, in his important and seminal work *Love and Death in the American Novel*, asserts that the friendship between the early American pioneer Natty Bumppo and the native Indian Chingachgook in the novels of James Fenimore Cooper is an archetypal relationship which haunts the American psyche . . . two lonely men bend together over a carefully guarded fire in the virginheart of the American wilderness . . . . They have forsaken all others for the sake of the austere almost inarticulate, but unquestioned love that binds them to each other and to the world of nature, which they have preferred to civilization (1959).

In another book, *The Return of the Vanishing American*, Fiedler says that Cooper's . . . peculiar brand of sentimentality . . . underlies all genuinely mythicdescriptions of the West, all true westerns—a kind of Higher MasculineSentimentality utterly remote from all fables whose Happy Endis Marriage (l968, Madison Books).

In l923, D. H. Lawrence, from an English standpoint, was even more specific. In an essay on James Fenimore Cooper and the *Leatherstocking* novels, he writes that

When you are actually in America, America hurts, because it has a powerful disintegrative influence . . . America is tense with latent violence and resistance. The very common sense of white Americans has a tinge of helplessness in it, and deep fear of what might be if they were not commonsensical.

Lawrence then describes Cooper's prototype, but one not nearly as radical as that depicted in *Brokeback Mountain*:

> What did Cooper dream beyond democracy? . . . he dreamed a new human relationship. A stark, stripped human relationshipof two men, deeper than the deeps of sex. Deeper than property,deeper than fatherhood, deeper than marriage, deeper than love. So deep that it is loveless. The stark loveless, wordless unisonof two men who have come to the bottom of themselves . . . . Then it finds a great release into a new world, a new moral,a new landscape. (D. H. Lawrence, *Studies in Classical American Literature.* Chapter 5;New York: T. Seltzer, 1923).

In my opinion, Annie Proulx goes much farther and much deeper, depicting what happens when two men come to "the bottom of themselves," "stark, wordless"—but *not* "loveless." *Brokeback Mountain* (short story, screenplay, and film) intentionally and radically subverts our American myth, turning it upside-down shockingly, completely, and convincingly. I don't think many people who aren't reared and educated in the United States can have any idea of how disturbing and disorienting "these emerging identities versus expectations" in *Brokeback Mountain* are to us as Americans. I even doubt that James Fenimore Cooper, Leslie Fiedler, or D. H. Lawrence could ever imagine anyone treating our archetypal myth in this way, especially a female writer! Not only is the surface text of the story often misread, but often, the rather evident subtext and contexts are ignored. Perhaps, in part, this happened because of the genre in which it is written (the Western or cowboy story, so traditional in the United States) or even because the author is a woman (gender). The story also has multiple important ramifications: social, political, psychological, economic, and historical (setting).

GENRE

The story, screenplay, and film have often been understood and interpreted using outdated models and comparing it to other stories with completely divergent expectations. The short story and film seem to be purposely leading the reader and viewer into expecting a typical Western or cowboy story, so central to the American myth and self-identity. All the traditional features are there: location, the great outdoors, the West, horses, dogs, tents, campfires, rodeos, rifles, even a bear and a can of beans!

Of course a close reader or viewer would notice at once that they are NOT herding cattle but sheep! considered by real cowboys as less challenging. Only two shots are fired (and only at animals), only three fistfights, and no murders except in two flashbacks. What kind of Western is that? That may be why so many readers and viewers are unable or unwilling to begin to understand even the surface text of the story because of the expectations and traditional depictions of the West and cowboys. Even Ennis and Jack are always depicted as manly, macho, masculine, able and willing to ride and shoot and fight.

GENDER

The author of the original short story as well as one of the authors of the screenplay is a woman. Women ARE important to this story, often not the case in other Westerns, and even more important in the film. In fact the major additions to the short story in the film are meant to flesh out the unsatisfactory family lives of these two men. Women and family life are usually in the background of the Western story.

Both men are married, both have children. The women characters are all portrayed positively in both short story and film, although often as helpless victims (wives, a waitress, and a daughter).

GENDER AND JACK AND ENNIS

The point of view of the story is Ennis's, so we can't completely know what the other characters are thinking, but in the story and the film both men are obviously taken by surprise at what happens on Brokeback Mountain a few days after they get there. They have gotten to know each other. Ennis has probably talked more than he ever has before, and even thinks that "he'd never had such a good time." One night a few days after they get there, Ennis gets too drunk, and it is too late to go down the mountain to the sheep. It is cold, and they share a bedroll in the tent and "deepened their intimacy considerably." The story has many more erotic details than the film, but it is obvious from both that that they have sex, and it continues that whole summer, first only by night, then by day. They don't talk about it except once Ennis says, "I'm not no queer," and Jack replies, "Me neither. One-shot thing. Nobody's business but ours." When they part after the summer, they make no plans to meet in the future. In fact Ennis says again he is going to get married that December, but after Jack drives off, Ennis "felt like someone was pulling his guts out hand over hand . . . tried to puke but nothing came up. He felt as bad as he ever had." Ennis had evidently not had that kind of relationship until he met Jack. As he puts it, "You may be a sinner, but I have not had the opportunity." Neither man is the predator. Both obviously enjoy immensely their relationship and the sexual act, the greatest passion either has ever known. That scene ends the only summer they will ever spend on Brokeback Mountain (truly a "mountain top experience"), but four years later, Jack writes to Ennis and says he is coming that way. Ennis writes back at once, "You bet." Ennis takes the day off, paces the floor, waiting for Jack. When he arrives, they keep hugging and kissing each other "mightily." Ennis's wife sees it, but Ennis explains it away, saying that they have not seen each other in four years. They spend the night in a motel in town with the excuse that they can get drunk. Jack says, "I didn't know we were going a get into this again—yeah, I did. Why am I here?" He calls Ennis "friend" repeatedly and endearingly throughout the story and film. They are not only friends, but lovers. Ennis tries to put a name on what they are doing and says things like "I know I ain't. I mean, here we both have wives and kids, right? I like doing it with women . . . but ain't nothing like this." In the short story he says he has never done it with another guy, but has masturbated often thinking of Jack. Jack in the story has evidently continued to seek out sexual relationships with other men. Basically the word "homosexual" denotes an orientation or a specific sexual act; "gay" denotes the attitude (usually positive) toward that orientation. Both are definitely not "gay" or "queer" in the usual sense of those words. Homoeroticism may be evident in many Western stories, but seldom so overtly! Andy Warhol is one of the few ever to depict a "gay" cowboy. Regret is a major feature of the story and film. Ennis realizes already in the motel room that he should have never let Jack leave. But it was "Too late then by a long long while." He thinks there is nothing they can do. Both are married. Ennis fears what others might think and do if they were caught together. Jack suggests they could move to his family's farm together. Ennis says he is stuck, caught, and tells the story of what his father showed his brother and him when he was about nine: a man who had ranched together with another man in a ditch beaten with a tire iron and dragged by his penis until it was pulled off. That experience has stayed in his mind ever since. That is why he thinks they can only get together once in a while "way the hell out in the back a no-where." Ennis concludes, "If you can't fix it, you got to stand it" (a continual theme of the story). They go on so called fishing trips once or twice a year, but that is it. Ennis's wife divorces him, and he is forced to pay child support. For years (until 1983), they get together a few times a year in a variety of wilderness locations but never return to Brokeback Mountain. In May of 1983 they get together again. Jack summarizes his own situation saying nothing has ever worked the way he wanted it too. The short story adds, "One thing never changed: the brilliant charge of their infrequent couplings . . . darkened by the sense of time flying, never enough time, never enough." Ennis then tells him that their next get-together can't be until November. Jack, again calling him "friend," responds by saying what an unsatisfactory situation this is. Ennis asks if he has a better idea; Jack replies, "I did once" (farming together). He lashes out at how few times they'd been together in twenty years and ends by saying, "I wish I knew how to quit you." The short story is wonderful here with added undercurrents of what is left unsaid which the film can't relate, and Ennis falls to the ground in anguish. But it comes to nothing: "Nothing ended, nothing begun, nothing resolved." Jack is always the romantic, the optimist; Ennis the realist, the pessimist. Jack remembers again that distant summer on Brokeback Mountain when Ennis held him close and shared a sexless hunger. That was in his memory "the single moment of artless, charmed happiness in their separate and difficult lives." They were really *only* happy when they were together, and *only* in the wilderness, in nature. "Doing what comes naturally," to quote one of the great musicals about the American West—embodying the "archetypal relationship," to use Fiedler's words. That same year Ennis gets a postcard saying that Jack had died (age thirty-nine) supposedly killed by an exploding tire. Ennis of course thinks the same thing happened to Jack as to that rancher his father had shown him when he was nine. That is *not* confirmed in either the short story or film. Jack had expressed a wish to be buried on Brokeback Mountain, "his place." So Ennis goes to Jack's parent's ranch to scatter Jack's ashes on Brokeback Mountain, "his place" in the words of Jack's wife, and receives a cold welcome from the father who says the ashes will be put in the family plot. Jack's mother invites Ennis to see Jack's old room where he discovers that Jack had kept an old shirt of his inside (embracing) one of his own, "one inside the other." Both the short story and the film are rich in imagery and symbolism. When he gets back, he buys a postcard of Brokeback Mountain which he pins up on the *closet* in his trailer and below it a nail on which he hung the two old shirts. (In the movie, this time, Ennis's shirt is on the *outside* embracing Jack's shirt inside, a touch supposedly suggested by Heath Ledger.) His last words in the story and film are, "Jack, I swear . . ." which are left unfinished as are many things in the story and film. The reader and viewer are invited to add their own interpretations. The story has a detail the film does not show and that was Jack's appearing in Ennis's dreams after that. "And he would wake sometimes in grief, sometimes with the old sense of joy and release; the pillow wet, sometimes the sheets." (This was obviously from tears and wet dreams). There is no question that they do love each other! An overwhelmingly powerful love in both the story and film. And the emotions, the characters, the situation, and the setting are so realistic that readers or viewers will be able to empathize with them and identify with them with regards to the importance of love and relationships in general, and even feel a sense of tragedy at what society and public opinion has done to them.

SETTING

Both the story and film have multiple ramifications: personal, psychological, social, political, economic, historical. The era is indicated (1963-1983) but almost ignored except for a reference to the draft, {I should add here that I was about the same age as the characters were supposed to be when the story takes place.} The mystique of the "Great West," the "Westward Migration, that Great Vanguard of Civilization and Liberty, essentially ended in 1805 when Clark (of Lewis & Clark) wrote in his journal 'Ocian {sic} in view! O! the joy.' . . . . Everything beyond that date . . . is anticlimax for the American West. Predictable, heroic, heart-breaking, horrible, hopeful, and Homeric. The sea stopped us . . . . years of westward migration ended at the sea. We lost our drive, our ambition, our destiny, our Manifest Destiny when Clark saw the sea." It has just taken generations for that reality to become evident. True poverty is seldom portrayed realistically in the Western story. If it is, it is treated as quaint, or rustic, or out-of-date, seldom the reality it was and is! These two, like so many others at that time, are going nowhere. Ennis doesn't even have a tenth grade education. They have few options. Both have fathers of no value, Ennis an orphan; and Jack's never gave his son any advice or help or even watched his son perform in a rodeo, his own profession. Abraham Maslow in his hierarchy of human needs (1954) has a vivid illustration of the social, psychological, and economic, triangle to illustrate what this means. Human beings need to have their basic needs met (food, shelter, clothing, income, safety) before they can ever think of the higher kinds of happiness, love, self-esteem, self-fulfillment, let alone have the interior strength to go against society's norms. Jack and Ennis have little awareness of the larger world or possibilities. The Kinsey report has already been issued, but probably these two had never even heard the name, let alone made aware of the range of sexuality he discovered.

FILM AND LITERATURE

I wish there were more time to talk about this. I have taught a course for years on "film and literature" as the holder of an endowed chair in the subject at my university in New York. The film includes just about the entire short story word for word but doubles its length to 100 pages by a few additions (like portrayals of the unsatisfactory family lives of the men, the daughter of Ennis, and a waitress he meets— to underscore their situation and put it in stark contrast to everything else in their lives). Otherwise both story and film are focused almost entirely on the relationship between these two men.

The film works marvelously at expanding and opening up the story itself because the setting is so important The American West! Cowboy country! Words cannot express what images and visuals can, at least in the same way. The cinematography by a Mexican American justly won an Academy Award. The actors, of course, not only flesh out the written descriptions but add the visual and the aural. Heath Ledger brings to life Ennis—a difficult character to portray—surprisingly well, especially if you have seen him in other films. The author has said that she was amazed how well the actors interpreted her descriptions, but she added that Heath Ledger did even more. He inhabited the character! Part of the power of film is its ability to show people's reactions to what is being said and done to one another. Here the film is brilliant, especially in portraying the women's responses to what they surmise and what they see. (The wives of Ennis and Jack and Jack's mother are particularly evocative.)

The film also tries to imitate the passage of time, the twenty years that this relationship continues. That is harder to do, but the director has slowed the pace enough to let the viewer know time has passed. There are few references though to current events to let the viewer locate when this all took place. The film leaves out a lot of the erotic from the story, it leaves out, for example, the dreams that Ennis had after Jack dies.

The film begins and ends in trailers (different ones), but with a similar idea. The film and story end with two extremely dramatic *closet scenes* (one in Jack's old bedroom and the other in Ennis's trailer). The screenwriters and film director (more than the author of the short story) seem to be trying to underscore the internalized and external homophobia back then and now.

In this film, especially, *music* adds another dimension. The composer, an Argentinean, Gustavo Santaolalla, justifiably won an Academy Award and a Golden Globe for it. The words are astonishingly appropriate. It is hard to believe that an Argentinean wrote music so evocative of American country and western music and words to match so closely what is happening in the film. Imagine a Taiwanese director, a Mexican-American cinematographer, and an Argentinean composer having so much to do with enabling this film to embody the Western film genre.

Adding the Bob Dylan/Willie Nelson song, "He was a Friend of Mine" was a perfect choice to end the film, as was including Rufus Wainwright's "The Maker Makes." Otherwise Santaolalla's words and music ARE the film. It is worth quoting a few lines from some of the songs. This is one film where it is important to pay attention to the words and music.

This section of excerpts from the songs is used as a short Coda, accompanied by film clips.

*Willie Nelson sings:
"He was a friend of mine/ Every time I think of him/ I just can't keep from crying! He died on the road/ Never reaped what he could sow."

*Rufus Wainwright's "Maker Makes":
"One more chain I break/ to get me closer to you. One more chain does the maker make/ to keep me from bustin' through. Oh, Lord, how I know/Oh, Lord how I see, That only can the maker make a happy man of me."

*But it is Gustavo Santaolalla's words and music that undergird and parallel the film's meanings so well, like "A Love That Will Never Grow Old" (which won a Golden Globe award):
"Just lay back in my arms for one more night/ I've this crazy notion that calls me sometimes/ Saying this one's the love of our lives/ Lean on me, let our hearts beat in time/ In a world that may say that we're wrong."

Or "I don't want you to Say Goodbye":
"All I want to do is live with you/ Don't you know that's where our hearts belong?"

Or "I Will Never Let You Go":
"When I feel that lonesome prairie wind/ I let my soul get back to you again. Even though this wasn't meant to be/ I will never let you go."

THE TITLE (MY TAKE)

The story and the film present the reader and viewer with options, places to put personal responses and reactions and leaving them open forcing the reader and viewer to become personally involved. The viewer is left, for example, to finish Ennis's concluding words in the story and film, "Jack, I swear . . ." Some think he was ready to say "I love you" (words never mentioned either in the film or the story). What about adding something like the words, "If I knew then, what I know now! What a difference that would have made" to finish Ennis's concluding exclamation? Of course the saddest words are those "it might have been."

My reading is that Jack's death has changed Ennis—too late, of course, but for the better. Ready to reach out and touch and be touched, more ready to open up. The film tries to give this take, but both the film and the story leave us all overwhelmed with sadness for so much gone wrong. Tragic in the way that everyone involved is hurt, but heroic in a sense that they both keep on loving and coming back although the outcome seems doubtful and dubious. Some viewers have even felt that the film gives people permission to love again: If these two poor, uneducated, '60s Western cowboys found it, it might be possible for anyone. In fact, in an interview, the director, Ang Lee, says that this film healed and enabled him "to love" films again.

The title? *Brokeback Mountain?* On one level, I think it refers to the poverty so evident throughout the film and story—always dignified but always so pervasive and overwhelming. Poverty like this keeps both men from having many choices. Negative. Broke all the time (so unlike the traditional Western story).

But I am wondering also if it might refer to that American saying: "the straw that broke the camel's back." Was it the family, the social, the psychological, the economic, the political surroundings, AMERICA ITSELF, that finally broke them? The internal and external judgments about such relationships? The pervasive poverty and lack of options? Society's negative judgments on such relationships? Only a year after the story was written, in 1998, a young man, Matthew Shepard, a young gay male, was hung on a fence to die outside Laramie, Wyoming, the home of the Univ. of Wyoming, probably the most enlightened region in the state!

How true D. H. Lawrence's words sound after reading the story and seeing the film: "America hurts, because it has a powerful disintegrative influence . . . tense with latent violence and resistance." And is Annie Proulx in some way tapping into and fulfilling James Fenimore Cooper's dream beyond democracy . . . of a new human relationship?" And will it, in the words of D. H. Lawrence find release into a "new world, a new moral, a new landscape"?

Could this film be a watershed in the way Americans think of themselves and gender and sexuality?

The film and the story, however, never try to step back and give the reader or viewer a message. We make our own conclusions, and I think both story and film can affect people differently depending on what the reader or viewer brings to it! That is why I think viewers reared and educated in the United States will read this story and see this film so differently than anyone else. Not better perhaps or more aware, but certainly having the American myth, the American dream, the American West, American hopes and dreams, disturbed and rethought—subverting the Western story and the American myth about ourselves to show the harsh contemporary reality! This is NOT a Western story about Roy Rogers and Dale Evans or John Wayne or the OK Corral! Those depicted unreality, romantic fiction—myths that we wanted to believe about ourselves. The story and film reverse our expectations, allowing new possible identities to emerge, possibly even (using D. H. Lawrence's words) "finding release in a new world, a new moral and a new landscape." A lot to expect, to be sure, from a short story and a film; but perhaps it is a start in the right direction.

This is one of the few times that a work of literature has been so faithfully adapted into a screenplay and film. It "works" as a short story, as a screenplay, and as a film. Read it, and see it on its own merit.

ENDNOTE

One answer to some of these perplexing reactions may lie precisely in the fact that *women* are so involved, as authors and characters. In fact, mention must be made of the parallel phenomenon that probably some of the best contemporary fiction written about male homosexuals is written by women. So many could be mentioned, but among the best known are Mary Renault who wrote a series of excellent novels about homosexuality, often in the ancient or classical world: *The King Must Die, The Bull from the Sea, The Praise Singer, The Last of the Wine, The Mask of Apollo, Fire from Heaven, The Persian Boy,* and *Funeral Games.*

Of course, there is the even more controversial, frequently filmed, and popular work of Patricia Highsmith (who also wrote using the name Claire Morgan): *Strangers on a Train* (filmed by Alfred Hitchcock), *The Talented Mr. Ripley* (one film version starred Alain Delon and another Matt Damon), and *The American Friend* (starring Dennis Hopper). Some are inspired by Ripley: *Ripley Underground, Ripley's Game* (also made into a very popular film with John Malkovich), *The Boy Who Followed Ripley, Ripley Under Water*, and others. Just as interesting is the fact that Patricia Highsmith also wrote lesbian novels under her pseudonym (Claire Morgan): *The Price of Salt, Small G, A Summer Idyll,* and others. Significantly, there have been few male authors of good fiction about lesbians.

The answers to this last question are often complex and go beyond one obvious conclusion: women are better able to perceive and even evoke the feminine side of the male and appreciate the masculine side. But why did and do so many critics and so much of the public have difficulty even deciding if the story and film are a love story, a gay love story, or really something else and more significant?

CHAPTER TEN

SPORTS JOURNALISM: WRITING ABOUT PLAYING

"Sports Journalism" was the introduction to a new student journal, *Clipnotes* (1995), at Concordia, New York, for which I was the advisor. I had been appointed to the national faculty of the United States Sports Academy in connection with a series of very popular lectures on a similar topic, delivered prior to the Goodwill Games in St. Petersburg (Russia) in 1994. I also taught the subject in Kuala Lumpur, Malaysia, Hong Kong and Singapore, to groups including members of the Olympic and Commonwealth Games Committees. I had never specifically taught "sports" journalism or marketing before that experience. This was a "byway" in my life that turned into a "highway" or, at least, an "interchange."

(What I did not say was where sports led me: into important circles in Russia, Hong Kong, Singapore, Malaysia and Brazil, and to places I might never have gone—Tyumen, Lake Baikal, Irkutsk, Vitória, Goiás, Rio de Janeiro, São Paolo, João Pessoa, and so many others. Sports was almost totally off my radar screen until 1983.)

> Dictionary definition of *sidelines*: "the side limits of a playing field, usually occupied by spectators."

As many as one third of Concordia's students are involved in athletics on campus, in anything from varsity sports to intramurals. This student journal aims to focus on that side of Concordia and to provide opportunities to write about sports—an important aspect of athletics often forgotten.

Athletics needs interpretation, needs spectators, needs reporting. As David Shaw writes in the *Los Angeles Times*, "The times—and the nation's sports pages—they are a-changing, and it is now no longer sufficient to write sports stories by the numbers or by the clichés."

The salaries of top-ranking athletes are often in the news, the salaries of top-ranking journalists not as often, even though journalists like Louis Rukeyser (host of public television's *Wall Street Week*), Marshall Loeb (editor-at-large of *Fortune* magazine), and Lou Dobbs (lead anchor of CNN's business news) all earn over $1 million a year. Others earning over $250,000 are Jane Bryant Quinn (*Daily News* columnist), Stuart Varney (CNN anchor), James Michaels (*Forbes* editor), Dan Dorfman (*USA Today* columnist), Irving Levine (NBC economics correspondent), Ray Brady (CBS business correspondent), Paul Steiger (*Wall Street Journal* managing editor) and Dan Shepherd (CNBC anchor). Journalism is also one route to public relations, particularly in sports. This past summer I was involved in the Goodwill Games in St. Petersburg, Russia, primarily because of a series of seminars I held on sports writing. This led me to train volunteers for the Goodwill Games Press Corps, lead press conferences in conjunction with the Russian/American Press and Information Center, meet high-ranking officials and dignitaries, and be part of all the "hoopla" that surrounds an international event like this. On my return, I was named to the national faculty of the United States Sports Academy (and all without athletic prowess). Students should not overlook this avenue to involvement in athletics. *Clipnotes* is not taking the place of a general interest student newspaper at Concordia, but perhaps this generation of students is more interested in and will profit more from publications with a narrower focus, such as this one. I'm impressed with the enthusiasm, the range of interests, the professional abilities, and the journalistic skills of this year's staff, and I'm proud to serve as faculty advisor. (Of course, I hope to have all of them in my journalism class this fall, which will have as its special focus "sports journalism.") In reporting, motivation is the name of the game—just as in athletics and academics.

CLIPNOTES

Spring 1995   Vol. 1, No.1

Inside

Clippers conquer foes in Fla.

by Kerry Guydir

One of the biggest disadvantages baseball and softball programs from the Northeast face is late starting dates due to the winter. Many programs try to raise enough money to send their teams down south, so they can get out of the gym and onto the warm ball fields of Florida. This was the decision of Concordia's varsity baseball and softball teams. Both undertook the daunting task of funding very expensive travel and hotel costs so their respective teams could overcome the shortcomings of playing in snow-covered New York.

Not Since Hurricane Andrew

The baseball team took Florida by storm. From a statistical standpoint — a 9-0 record, .353 team batting average, and 1.53 earned run average — the Clippers overwhelmed the competition. "It was important for us to go out and get our feet wet before league play," explained senior captain Joel Perez. "It showed the other teams in the league that we're not going to be laughed at like last year. Last year, we didn't go on a trip, and we were crushed in our first series against Adelphi." Senior captain and shortstop Mike Roig had an outstanding trip. Roig, a native of Eastchester, led the team in most offensive categories including an eye-popping .550 batting average. "He carried us," says Perez. Captains Joe Smith and Sean Lytle also contributed to Concordia's offensive explosion and lent stability to the middle of the batting order. Sophomore leftfielder Scott

Kerulainen solidified his spot in the three hole of the order while knocking in 12 runs. The pitching staff was equally as effective. Rookies Rob Cerasi and Paul Stremel combined to limit the opposition to an earned run average of 1.65. The highlight of the trip included a scrimmage with the Atlanta Braves rookie team. "They were awesome," says Kerulainen, "and it was a good experience to see people who would someday play in the Majors."

No "I" in Team

The women's softball team didn't dominate opponents as the men had, but don't let the 2-6 record fool you. The improvement of the team during the trip was very evident according to coach Kathy Laoutaris. "There was a dramatic increase in the level of play from the first day," the coach explains. "It was very important to get the kinks out before we came back to New York for league play." What improved Coach Laoutaris was the strength the Lady Clippers displayed *up the middle*. With co-captain Heather MacColloch on the mound, co-captain Allison Eckhart in leftfield and impressive freshman Patricia Northrup behind the plate, Concordia had the core players needed to be competitive in the NYCAC this season. Just like the baseball team, coach Laoutaris sees the need for going to Florida: "Yes, we had to fund it ourselves, but it was well worth it. We needed to get out of the gym and do what the other programs were doing — going down south." Also, the Lady Clippers grew as a team according to the coach.

Learning about and rooming with your teammates is something that extends beyond the field. "If there is one huge asset of going on one of these trips, it is that your team grows together," asserts Laoutaris.

3 *Just another coach?*
A look at new volleyball coach Ivan Marquez.

4 *From the sidelines*
Dr. Sluberski's look at sports, journalism, marketing and this publication.

6 *From gridiron to Dean of Students*
A talk with John Bahr.

8 *Out of date? Never!*
A retrospect on fall sports

CLIPPNOTES
Special
Senior Tribute

CHAPTER ELEVEN

BODYBUILDING IN RUSSIA

"Bodybuilding in Russia" is one of the many articles I wrote for the *St. Petersburg* (Russia) *Times* (1991-1994) as a guest professor of journalism and culture at St. Petersburg University, Alexander von Herzen University, the Universities of Omsk, Khabarovsk, and Vladivostok, and the Russian Merchant Marine Academy. I judged three Mr. Russia contests (Omsk, St. Petersburg, and Moscow), served as an advisor for the Shaping Federation, and was on the board of and taught at the Ben Weider College of Bodybuilding—hosting Ben Weider and his wife in Tyumen, Siberia, followed by a "side trip" (camping on Lake Baikal and Irkutz). Arnold Schwartzenegger did not come to Russia while I was there, but the Russian Federation of Bodybuilders chairman, Vladimir Dubinen, did attend some Arnold Classics in Ohio. I worked with the RFBB and Russkoi Film Video, one of the foremost film companies of Russia, to produce a film on Russian bodybuilding. Russkoi Film Video also later cooperated in a film entitled *Bridges*, about the volunteers in St. Petersburg from the LCMS, in part because of that previous collaboration.

Schwarzenegger in St. Petersburg? Could be. He's been officially invited (1992) and is seriously considering the request, says a source close to him. Why? Because bodybuilding is fast becoming one of Russia's most popular sports.

St. Petersburg is a center of this once-banned personal art form. The St. Petersburg Bodybuilding Championships—known as the St. Petersburg Cup—will be held here May 20-21. Preliminaries take place March 24-27 at the Military Physical Training Institute on Karl Marx Street.

The All-Russia Championships, or "Mr. Russia," are scheduled for May 26-30 in Krasnoyarsk. And for the first time, the European championships will be held in Russia—in the city of Tyumen—in June. (Evidently, Western Siberia is considered by bodybuilders part of Europe—and who's to argue with them?)

As part of this muscular exchange, Ben Weider—a publisher and entrepreneur known as the "father of modern bodybuilding"—has invited fourteen Russians to the Arnold Classic in Ohio this month, and is paying their way. Schwarzenegger, for the third year in a row, has personally summoned his friend and St. Petersburg bodybuilding giant Vladimir Dubinen to attend. Dubinen is a gold medal laureate in bodybuilding and a member of the Russian Olympic Committee. And he's almost as big as Arnold—in Russia, anyway.

In a little-known distinction, St. Petersburg is home to the world's only college of bodybuilding. Opened in November 1992, the academy is named after—you guessed it—Ben Weider. More than fifty students are enrolled and are to be its first class of graduates this summer. The president of the college is a woman: Dr. Elena Maslakova.

A film on bodybuilding (a sort of Russian *Pumping Iron,* a classic in which Arnold made his cinematic debut) was produced in St. Petersburg and released for television last fall. To cement the St. Petersburg connection, both the president (Mr. Dubinen) and vice president (Sasha Nazarenko) of the RFBB are from the city.

Despite substandard workout equipment and a shortage of bodybuilder foods (such as tuna fish and chicken breasts), Russian bodybuilders are poised to become major competitors on the world stage.

St. Petersburg's Alexander Vishnevsky, the current Mr. Russia, competed this year in South Korea and Spain, and has a good chance of placing high in the European championships. His posters are sold all over the city, alongside those of Schwarzenegger and Van Damme. Aficionados call his posing routine world class.

How does Russian bodybuilding differ from the American or European variety? First, most athletes train in private gyms set up by enthusiasts in basements and storefronts. There are a few commercial gyms, like the one in the Lenin Sports Stadium (run by Mr. Dubinen), which cost more to join but have better equipment.

Although lacking the range of equipment Western bodybuilders take for granted, Russian bodybuilders have enough for thorough training. As a judge since 1983, both here and in the United States, I can say that Russia's best bodybuilders are neither inferior to nor less thoroughly trained than their Western fellow athletes.

As for Arnold, stay tuned. He's been invited to at least three major events this summer (two in St Petersburg): graduation day at the College of Bodybuilding (of which he is the honorary first graduate), the European championships, and the Goodwill Games. Vladimir Dubinen says he's likely to come.

Dr. Thomas R. Sluberski is a guest professor of journalism at the University of St. Petersburg and Alexandre von Herzen University while on sabbatical from Concordia University in New York.

PART IV

WHAT'S NEXT?

"Time's winged chariot," "Eternity," "The grave"

From Andrew Marvell's "To His Coy Mistress"

CHAPTER TWELVE

THE FURNITURE OF HEAVEN AND THE TEMPERATURE OF HELL

Eschatology Traced from Thomas Aquinas through Later Orthodoxy

"The Furniture of Heaven and the Temperature of Hell" indicates how seminary students of my era were encouraged to "test the doctrines," to consider the background, context, and reasons for the church's confessing the doctrines she does. The study was not meant for publication, so it remains a set of student notes: a rough, tentative survey of current scholarly thinking on the subject, with no attempts to interject criticism or counterpoint. These fragments do show how we were encouraged not simply to accept doctrinal stances, in blind faith, but to address them with hardnosed inquiry. They also reveal how earnest an aspiring scholar (or how hardcore a nerd?) I was at the time—who else would think to *footnote* jottings of this kind?

The inquiry I thought I had exhausted in this essay I saw, on completion, left numerous issues and problems to be addressed. I undertook to tackle these in the piece that follows as chapter 15—and even "borrowed" some of the material from this essay.

Note: The views surveyed in chapters 12 and 13 are not necessarily orthodox or traditional but represent current scholarly thinking on the issues which will need to be reconciled with the Lutheran Confessions in the Book of Concord.

Revisiting them both after more than forty years, I was struck by how fitting
a conclusion they make to a volume entitled "Having World Enough and
Time."

ARGUMENT

Eschatology traced through: Thomas Aquinas,
Martin Luther
pre-confessional statements,
Eck's *404 Theses*,
The Book of Concord
the Council of Trent,
later Orthodoxy,
centering on the Augsburg Confession,
Article XVII.

I)   Preliminary considerations

    a)   death
    b)   eschatological awareness of the times
    c)   realized eschatology

II)   The Last Judgment
III) Resurrection
IV) Eternal Life
V)   Hell
VI) Universalism
VII) Millennium
VIII) Purgatory
IX) Intermediate State

THE FURNITURE OF HEAVEN AND THE
TEMPERATURE OF HELL

Reinhold Niebuhr once said that he became a little suspicious of anyone
who knew too much about "the furniture of heaven and the temperature
of hell." There is also a danger in erring the other way—knowing too little.
Tracing the fluctuating understanding of what happens after death, especially
the doctrines of heaven, hell, and the intermediate state, from Aquinas and

Luther through the pre-confessional, confessional, Catholic reactions, to later orthodoxy is the aim of this study. The unifying focal point will be Article XVII of the Augsburg Confession, itself the *Grundbekenntnis* of the Lutheran church. Of necessity, brief mention has to be made of other doctrines that interrelate with the study's main theme. (Chapter 15 adds preparatory studies in the Old and New Testaments, the early and medieval church, up to and including later Lutheran orthodoxy.) To my knowledge. no such study has been made, especially in interrelating any of the areas under discussion, nor any study concentrating on either Luther's or the theologians of orthodoxy's doctrine of the last things to show the doctrine's development.

Briefly, the procedure to be followed is to analyze the doctrines under discussion topically, treating each as they occur in the various periods and interspersing the discussion with evaluations of the development.

I)   It is necessary to give at least preliminary attention to the concept of **DEATH**, the ESCHATOLOGICAL AWARENESS of the times, and "REALIZED ESCHATOLOGY."

Although Thomas Aquinas is not to be seen as *the* primary influence either upon Luther or the other confessors, his doctrinal viewpoints are important for the subsequent Catholic doctrine of eschatology and for a comparison with later orthodoxy.

Aquinas built his eschatological system on a dualistic concept of death as the separation of the soul from the body. He recognized two kinds of death: the death of the body—the separation of it from the soul; the death of the soul—its separation from God. Interconnected with this dual death is, therefore, a dual resurrection. The resurrection of the body occurs when the soul rejoins the body, and the resurrection of the soul occurs when the soul is reunited to God (*Comp. Theol.* 239).

The Lutheran confessions speak of *three* kinds of death: spiritual, physical, and eternal. Physical death is not dealt with at any length or thoroughness (cf. Ap. IV, 302; XII 153). Luther, likewise, seems not to have been much concerned with the whys and wherefores of this kind of death. However, in his Large Catechism (I, iv 137) he states that evil people rarely die a proper or a timely death, by which observation he approximates an Old Testament stance toward mortality.

Until later orthodoxy, it would appear that death was not analyzed in any detail, and even then the modern concern with the mechanics of death is ignored or dealt with only incidentally. Baier (354), Gerhard (XVII, 149), Quenstedt (IV, 535) agree with Aquinas in seeing the essence of death as the separation of "the soul from the body." Baier, further, observes that death is a consequence of the fall (354). Hollazius seems to approximate the Hebrew concept of death when he says, "The death of the body formally consists in the deprivation of natural life "(1225). Gerhard elaborates on his basic definition. "Death is the release of the soul from the body" (XVII 51). "Death is nothing else than the taking off of this garment (the body)." He quotes Aristotle for proof, and approximates Aquinas's view (628).

Another preliminary consideration is the eschatological character of 16th century. This emphasis is not so evident in Aquinas, but Luther's *Confession of 1528* affirms that all his doctrine will be judged in the light of the last judgment, and so, even "teachings" take on an eschatological character.[1] Luther deemed eschatology the chief end of Christian teachings.

> Whatever we teach, appoint, or establish is done to the end
> that the pious may look forward to the coming of their
> Saviour on the last day (Erl. Ed. xxii, 12).

Connected with his understanding of the last times as "now," Luther's interpretation of the political, cosmological, and ecclesiastical situations of the sixteenth century led him to connect scripture's portrayal of the last times with current phenomena (*Tischr.* 4979, 5130, 5239, 5488, 6984). When an astronomer predicted a great flood for 1524, Luther hoped that this was a sign of the second coming.[2] In the beginning of the *Church Postils*, Luther interpreted the conjunction of the planets scheduled to occur in 1524 as another sign of the last day, but still warns against a too-precise reckoning.

A fascinating bit of Luther lore appears in his *Supputatio Annorum Mundi.*`Luther, there, calculated the timing of the end of the world by asserting that the year 1540 A.D. corresponded to the year 5550 after the creation. Luther therefrom posited, by patristic logic, that as there were six days of creation and a seventh of rest, these days being each a thousand years, in the year 6000 after creation (or about 2000 A D.), God would bring creation to an end (again). This work was printed in 1541 and reissued in 1545. An arithmetically inclined reader might ask whether Luther did not realize he was more than half a millennium off. Luther, faced with such caviling, would surely reply that the Lord promised to shorten the days for the sake of the elect, and so the end of days could come at any time.

For material on the signs of His coming, Luther looked to Daniel and the book of Revelation. In the former, the end of the fourth world kingdom Luther interprets to mean the end of the Roman Empire. The Antichrist, in the latter, Luther equates with the Turk, destined to overthrow the third of the ten horns (rulers) of that Empire (Erl. Ed xli 233, 243sqq; xxxi 83ff.).

The thousand years mentioned in Revelation he counts either from the date of the book itself or from the birth of Christ. It is not necessary to be minute, Luther maintains, but he sees Gog and Magog, too, as possibly being the Turk. (The Ottoman Empire was a very real threat in Luther's time.) Luxury and the signs in the heavens are signs of that day (Jena iv 741). In connection with his thoughts on signs of the last day, Luther hoped for the general conversion of the Jews (Erl. Ed. x 231ff), but later in his writings we find no such references but rather disillusionment with and antipathy toward the "chosen people."

The confessions take their cue from Luther and assert that "the last times, they are now" (Ap XII, 126; AC XXIII, 14; Ap XXIII 53). These "last times" are not only to be affirmed in view of the eschatological announcements that continually break into the life of a Christian through the forgiveness of sins, excommunication, the Sacraments, preaching, and death; the confessions also note signs of the last times. "Sins and vices are not decreasing but increasing daily" (Ap. xxiii, 53). "We see that these are the last times, and just as an old man is weaker than a young man, so the whole world and nature is in its last stage and fading" (Ap XXIII, 53). The church is also in a poor state. The Smalcald Articles end with the prayer, "O dear Lord Jesus Christ, invoke a council yourself and deliver your servants through your glorious advent."

Luther often invoked the second coming he did in his Confession,

> This is our faith, doctrine and confession in which we are
> also willing, by God's grace, to appear with intrepid hearts,
> before the judgment seat of Christ and give an account of
> it. S.D. VII 31, 29, 40 (Cf. Melanchthon's *Erster Entwurf
> fuer den Beschluss* and AP XXVIII 5; Ap. XI 124).

With their usual thoroughness, the orthodox theologians divide the signs of the times into five categories: (1) the multiplication of heresies, (2) seditions, (3) the persecution of the godly, (4) careless security, and (5) the universal preaching of the gospel (Gerhard XIX 246). It is to be noted that the dogmaticians do not list the general conversion of the Jews which Luther affirmed early in his career. In fact Hollazius (1263) and others explicitly reject it. There is no time setting, and there is an unusual silence (for the dogmaticians) on signs of the times.

Finally, the last preliminary consideration is the Johannine understanding of "realized eschatology." "In the resurrection, the eternal life *already begun in us* will be brought to completion in our glorified body" (LC II, ii 57; Ap VI 56).

> The Gospel (which is preached in the church) brings not merely the shadow of eternal things, but the eternal things themselves . . . . But every true Christian is even *here* upon earth a partaker of eternal blessings, even of eternal comfort, *of eternal life*, and of the Holy Spirit and righteousness which is from God until he will be completely saved in the world to come (Ap. VII 15).

II) **THE LAST JUDGMENT**, a theme that has caught the interest of poets and painters of all generations, has likewise drawn major attention from the theologians. Aquinas starts from the premise that judgment occurs after a man has "run his course." Until then no final judgment can be made. Men live on a) in the memories of others and in their reputations for good or ill; b) in offspring who are a part of them; c) in the results of actions; d) in the body, which eventually crumbles into dust; e) in the projects in which they have set their hearts; and finally f) in their souls. All of the above are submitted to the final judgment and are taken into consideration "when everything whatsoever about a man will be manifestly known" (*Summa. Theol.* 3 a, lix 5). Christ will judge us in His human nature, for to gaze on divinity is a reward! There is also a certain amount of poetic justice in this mode, for He who was unjustly punished is lifted up to judge the living and the dead (*Compendium Theologiae* 141).

Luther and the pre-confessional statements reaffirm the creedal statements on judgment. In his sermons and writings Luther described the last judgment with biblical expressions (the last trumpet, Christ coming in the clouds), but he adds, "These are only allegorical words . . . as we have to picture it for children and simple folk" (WA 10 I, 2, 93-120 and Erl Ed.

xix, 153ff; xviii 342ff). The believers will meet the Lord in the air "and unite with Him in passing judgment on the wicked" (Erl Ed XXX 372; xix 345). We will look upon the naked Godhead, no longer enshrouded with words (Erl Ed xxxii 307). Note the contradiction between Aquinas and Luther in this last statement. One might see the reason for this in Luther's understanding of "the hidden God" in contrast to the "naked Godhead" which would be pure wrath and judgment.

In addition to the creedal affirmations on the last judgment and the eschatological judgment impinging on the believer daily, the confessions see all history as pointing to *the* judgment. The purpose for which Christ will come will be to judge the living and the dead (AC III and XVII). There will then be a division between those who have done good and those who have done evil. It would seem that this statement contradicts Ap. IV, but see paragraph 278. Only faith justifies, and heaven is not gained by works (Ap. IV, 195), but a living faith shows forth fruits. All faith will have works to show and these will be evaluated in the last judgment. In this connection both the Solid Declaration (XI 13) and the Apology (XII 157) delineate Christ as the book of life in which Christians are written. He guarantees our salvation. The judgment occurs after the resurrection as the Small Catechism states,

> And at the last day he (the Holy Spirit) will raise up me and all the dead, and will give to me and all believers in Christ eternal life, that I might be his own and live under him in his kingdom and serve him in everlasting righteousness and blessedness even as he is risen from the dead and lives and reigns to all eternity.

Later orthodoxy expands these elementary affirmations on the part of Luther and the confessions. At the final judgment, all the men who are alive will not experience death, for the living are unified in body and soul. (Death is the separation of soul and body.) Instead, the living will be transformed. The precise time of His coming is not known, but it is known that Christ will judge and that all will see Him. All men will be judged according to the norm of revelation which is given them on earth (Schmid, p. 643).

Gerhard, in his usual thoroughness, lists five reasons for a universal judgment (particular judgments have already taken place): (1) "the manifestation of divine glory," (2) "the glorification of Christ," (3) "the exaltation of the godly," (4) "the completion of rewards and punishments," and (5) "the continued consideration of good and evil works." Finally, as a practical formality Hafenreffer (682) asserts that the dead will rise before the living are transformed. (The dogmaticians neatly tie together all loose ends.) Gerhard also deals with such questions as whether the return will be local, why He is coming in the clouds, and in what form He will be seen.

The last judgment is presented in all its grand simplicity by both the confessions and Luther, but Aquinas and the dogmaticians of orthodoxy attempt to answer questions on the details of that coming. As will be noted many times in this paper, dogmatics tends to be cyclical. There is a periodic reaction to over-involvement with minutiae, but in response there evolves a similar situation in comparison of the scholastics and the dogmaticians.

III.) Aquinas duly proves the **RESURRECTION** of the body. (In turn, he condemns those who feel that the soul can have no function apart from the body in *Disputations De Anima 14)*. Our present body will rise, and this doctrine is supported by "sound reasons." The human soul is immortal, but without the body it is an unnatural condition and what is unnatural can "not go on forever." "The soul's immortality, therefore, seems to demand the eventual resurrection of the body." Another "proof" for the resurrection inheres in the natural human drive toward happiness, which is "man's ultimate completion":

Everything made to be perfect desires to be perfect, and a disembodied soul is to that extent incomplete; it is a part out of its whole.

We will not find final perfection until our soul quickens our body. In this life perfect happiness is impossible; therefore, "human completion requires the resurrection of the body" (III *Contra Gentes* 79).

Finally, Thomas argues from the justice of the universe, wrongdoers *must* be punished and well doers must be rewarded. Because the people who performed these acts were flesh and blood, the reward or punishment must also affect bodily as well as spiritual life. Seldom do the scales balance in this life, and it is right and proper that humans be "fitly punished and rewarded" (III *Contra Gentes*, 79).

The *Compendium Theologiae* (151) adds other "proofs" of the resurrection. "Our wills cannot be quite at peace until our natural appetites are altogether satisfied." The soul has a natural desire to be reunited with the body and to be ultimately fulfilled the soul must be complete. "Therefore, it must be combined with the body." "What is adventitious and unnatural is not perpetual."

Thomas insists that the humans who rise are identical to those who lived before, "though their vital processes are performed in a different way." However, we are not to understand the resurrection as designed to perpetuate the human species, "for this could be accomplished by "interminable generation." The purpose of the resurrection is rather to perpetuate the individual! (*Comp. Theol.* 155)

To cover every possibility (and answer every conceivable question) Aquinas posits that "even though men were to die again after the resurrection, they would still not remain forever without their bodies." The bodies would rise again and die, and rise again and so forth, so necessary is the doctrine of the resurrection. Thus Thomas is fairly certain that the more reasonable premise is that the "first resurrection is final" (*Comp. Theol.* 155).

The bodies we assume are not a heavenly or ghostly kind of body; the material is not altered. Their immortality comes from a divine strength that "enables the soul so to dominate the body that corruption cannot enter" (*Comp. Theol.* 155). Because the soul is the "substantial form of body and its active moving principle," it is the soul that gives the body its "substantial reality," and it is the "principle of the proper characteristics that follow from its union with the body" (*Comp. Theol.* 168).

The resurrection is not specifically mentioned in the Schwabach Articles, but it is included in the *AC*. It is Christ's resurrection that guarantees ours. It is the Holy Spirit who raises us (according to the Large Catechism) but other statements (i.e. the *AC*, and Athan. Creed) seem to predicate the resurrection of humanity by Jesus Christ. This is not so serious a contradiction if we see Christ working through the Spirit and the same God working all in all.

In the resurrection, the sinful aspects of the flesh will be destroyed and the flesh will come forth in perfect holiness in a new and eternal life (LC III, 57). In the Large Catechism Luther criticizes the term "resurrection of the flesh," yet the bodily resurrection is not denied. Schlink notes that although all the dead will rise, only the believers have bodies predicated of them. It is hard to say exactly why he asserts this, or whether it was purposeful or not. Death destroys the original sin in our nature (Epitome I, 10). We will then be completely renewed (Ap XII 153). Thus the "substance of our flesh, but without sin shall arise, and . . . in eternal life we shall have and keep precisely this soul, although without sin" (FC, SD I 45ff).

We should not, however, be misled by the mention of the resurrection, salvation, and destruction of "souls" (Tract 52:3 and SA *Vorrede* 490). *Soul* as defined by Luther (in his explanation of Psalm 16:10 in the Torgau Sermon, which is referred to in Article XX of the SD),

> according to the scriptural use of the term, (soul) does not mean, as we usually think, a separated essence in distinction to the body, but the entire man, as it is called by the saints of God.

The dogmaticians propose a somewhat different conception of the soul from either Luther's or the Confessions'. Baier maintained that the "soul . . . survives and performs its operations separately outside of the body; for example those things which pertain formally to the intellect and will" (368). Quenstedt (like Aquinas) proves the immortality of the soul from such arguments as,

> From the opposition of the soul and body, from the original creation of the soul. The souls of the brutes were produced from the same material as their bodies, whence when their bodies perish the souls themselves likewise perish (Gen. 1:20). But unto man he breathed a soul (Gen. 2:7).

Gerhard adds the concept that the difference between our immortality and God's is that "He is essentially and independently immortal." Our immortality is given to us (631). Gerhard finds numerous natural proofs, metaphysical, teleological, cosmically, plurality, analogical, moral, and ethical, arguments to the Juridicum, empirical, traditional (which includes the consensus gentium of Homer, Virgil and others) and finally from the New Testament and history (631).

Quenstedt has a rather representative concept of resurrection.

> The subject of the resurrection is the entire man as had previously died and been reduced to ashes. The subject from which, is the body, the same in number and essence as we have borne in this life, and as had perished through death, yet clothed with new and spiritual qualities (IV 588).

Thus the body that will rise will be spiritual in quality and endowments, but not substance. Hollazius notes the difference between our present bodies and our resurrection bodies lies in duration, outward form, vigor, activity, and endurance (1243).

In transition from the resurrection aspects of eschatology to the eternal life aspects Gerhard delineates certain principles. In the resurrection, the wicked and godly will have incorruptibility and immortality in common, but the godly alone will have glorified, glorious bodies which are powerful, spiritual, heavenly, like the angels'. The wicked will not be impassible, but will be foul and ignominious (XIX 38).

The development of understanding of the resurrection has come full circle. The dogmaticians agree with Aquinas on the duality of body and soul. Luther would disagree, and the confessions make no dogmatic stand one way or the other. As a logical outcome of this scholasticism, the rational proofs for the immortality of the soul and resurrection proceed. Thus Aquinas and the later dogmaticians (especially Gerhard) agree in the listing of rational proofs for the resurrection and immortality of the soul. The confessions and Luther tend to stress the miraculous and the power of the Gospel in this connection.

IV.) **ETERNAL LIFE** is contingent on the resurrection in Aquinas, but both have logical outcomes that would only be true in connection with the immortality of the soul. This is his first premise. When the body is entirely possessed by the soul, it will be fine and spirited. The body will then be noble, beautiful, invulnerable, lissome, agile, radiant, and will be entirely like an instrument "in the hands of a skilled player." He quotes 1 Corinthians 15 verses 42-44 to prove most of the above (Comp. Theol.168). It is a logical outcome of his basic premise.

In Christ's transfiguration body, we have a type of the resurrected body (Phil iii, 22). The "light-footedness" as when He walked on the waves, the "delicacy" as when He did not break open the virgin's womb, the "invulnerability" as when He escaped unhurt from the Jews who wished to stone Him are also types of the soul and body after the resurrection (Summa Theol. 3 a XLV i, AD 3).

The resurrected humans will live in a new heaven and earth in a city "that lieth foursquare." "Whatsoever can make us joyful, it is there in heaven and superabundantly" (honor, knowledge, security, companionship, Job 22:26 in the Exposition on the Apostle's Creed). There seems to be little difference between the "immortal" life of humans before or after the resurrection except that there will be a new heaven and earth.

The angels, also, can be compared to the resurrected human beings. "With respect to God's love and grace and glory, some angels will be mightier than human beings, and some human beings will be enthroned above the angels." (Summa Theol. I a XX 4, Ad 2).

The creeds affirm a "life everlasting" and this would appear to be reflected both in Luther and the confessions. Eck's theses accuse Luther of equating Abraham's bosom with the "Word of God" (Thesis 151). Though this exact statement could not be located in Luther's works, it would not be unlikely that he did state it. It matches almost exactly his statement that Abraham's bosom means that the dead were asleep in faith and are embraced and preserved in the Word of God (Erl Ed xiii, 10; xviii, 266 and vi 116). Parallel this statement with others such as "Paradise is a condition, not a place (Erl Ed i, 110ff)." The hell of Dives was an evil conscience (Erl Ed xiii, 11; xviii 267).

The concepts of heaven and hell as places become reality after the resurrection. It is after the resurrection that we are exempted from places and times (Erl Ed xxi 199). Our bodies will remain bodies, even though they will not have limitations. For example, the distinctions between the sexes will be perpetuated, but the form of the body will be transformed and made beautiful, healthy, not weary, perfect (Erl Ed xix 133f; iv 2, 411; xviii 346). Our bodies will then be able to pass quickly from place to place. Our eyes will be able to look through mountains, and our ears will be able to hear from one end of the earth to the other. We will then travel like a flash (Erl Ed iv 2ff; xix 135; li 183). Our resurrection is attested to by Christ's. And then we will not have disease and pain, limitations, and will not be perishable and changeable.

The whole world will be transformed by fire, and the sun will then shine seven times more brightly than it does now. Everything will be more beautiful; the moon will then be as bright as the sun is now. "Now heaven and earth wear their working clothes, but then they will be in their Sunday clothes" (to his son Hans, Brief June 19, 1530). There will even be "new animals" with gold hair (Erl Ed x 74; xxxix 35; li 243; lx 106; Tischr. lv 239ff). We will live on the earth (Lii; 270; xxxix 37ff).

Luther's concern with "the furniture of heaven" appears to be primarily pastoral. He has not bothered to work out a "system," a "map" of the place, much less dissect scriptural allusions to heaven for hints on what it will be like there. Here, Luther is following scriptural example. The only thing told us about what we will do in heaven is negative. There will no marriage or giving in marriage there.

An historical study of the "descent into hell" and the "ascent into heaven" could show that Christ did not "necessarily" descend into a "place" hell or heaven. The heaven into which Christ ascended was not spatial but into the skies, the right hand of God.

The confessions assert that after the resurrection, the eternal life already begun in us will be brought to completion in our glorified body (LC II ii 57; Ap. vi 56). There, we will have a new will (Ep. II I). There, the law and Gospel will no longer be necessary (LC II 57). This is one reason why the Pelagians, Schwenkfelder's and Papists are condemned. They believe that man does not have to wait for Christ's return but can already be perfect (Ep. 5). There the means of grace will also be dispensed with (SD VIII 44). We will there be made perfect and preserved (LC II iii 162). We will be peaceful (Ap. XXIV 60) and eternally rich (LC I iv 164). All our doctrinal and theological problems will be solved (Ep. IX 4). There will be distinctions of glory among the saints in light (Ap. IV 355). The confessions have very little to say in reference to heaven (reflecting the scriptural silence).

The orthodox theologians maintain a relative degree of silence, but manage to ramify what we do know into a fairly thorough system.

Melanchthon viewed heaven as an academy wherein he hoped to converse with the apostles, prophets, and church fathers about pure doctrine (CR 7, 319). Hollazius, however, stressed the chief aim of heaven. "Our eternal and highest blessedness consists in the perfect sight and enjoyment of God" (456). Quenstedt divided the blessings of heaven into privative and positive blessings. Privative blessings are absence of sin and its causes (death), and the positive blessings consist of internal and external blessings. The internal blessings are further divided into those benefiting the soul and the body. For the soul, there will be: (1) the perfect enlightenment of the intellect, (2) the complete righteousness of will and appetite, (3) the highest security. There will be, for the body: (1) spirituality, (2) invisibility, (3) impalpability, (4) illocality, (5) subtlety, (6) agility, (7) impassibility, (8) immortality and incorruptibility, (9) strength and soundness (I 553).

Some of the irksome questions are also answered with some degree of assurance.

> Infants departing without baptism either believe or do not believe. If the former, they are in the grace of God, and obtain the remission of their sins; if the latter they remain children of wrath under condemnation, exiled from the heavenly Jerusalem and are cast into the lake of fire (Gerhard XVII 189ff).

Our joy won't be marred by seeing these infants, our friends or relatives in hell being tortured. Then, we will have perfect wisdom and know that God is just, even by his torture of sinners in hell. We will, likewise, recognize one another in heaven (Hafr. 699).

The practical significance of heaven is that in considering the joys of eternal life every day we may keep closely to the way leading thither, and carefully avoid all that can cause delay or recall us from entrance into life eternal (Ger XX 528).

In heaven, the godly "will enjoy according to the degree of their godliness the highest and completely undisturbed happiness in beholding the face of God" (Holl 978). Thus there will be degrees of heaven.

The Lutheran theologians from Luther through orthodoxy seem to be unanimous in stressing the value of the "last things" for the here and now. They all stress the ethical thrust of the doctrine. Most have exercised a restraint when dealing with this the Christian's terminus.

V.) Eck lists two statements in his theses on what he thought the Lutherans believed about **HELL** Eck may misquote some of these sources.

Christ descended *ad infernos non* to a *limbus patrum*, a term unknown in the Holy Scriptures, but truly to hell, in order to see all places full of despair (Bugenhagen). Thesis 149.

That the Fathers in the Old Testament descended to hell is fictitious (Haller). Thesis 150.

The Schwabach Articles, which influenced the Augsburg Confession, assert that Christ will "punish the unbelieving and godless, and to condemn them eternally, with the devil in hell."

Luther's comforting words on heaven should not mislead anyone to believe that he offers anything of the kind on hell. As early as 1523, he disagreed with those who thought that hell was too harsh a doctrine. He does, however, say that God is even in hell, and the ungodly are punished only by their own consciences, but he warns against further prying (*Brief* ii 453ff; Erl Ed xxx 372; Jena iv 482; xxxiv 207; Erl Ed v 179; xxxiv 207). Their greatest "pain consists in the feeling of God's wrath and the knowledge of being separated from Him" (Tischr. 6982). In his Latin Commentary on Genesis Luther will not take a position or express a positive opinion as to whether the torments of hell begin at once after death or after the judgment. (He says this should be left to God in Erl. Ed xlii 22; vi 122, 124; x 208, 213).

The confessions, evangelically, assert that damnation cannot be of interest in its own right or divorced from the Gospel. Augustana 17 affirms that punishment is everlasting. God desires that no one should perish, but that all should be saved (SD II 49). God is not the cause of damnation, sin is. Inherited sin brings about this condemnation (SD XI 81; SD V 23: AC II).

The punishments of hell are variously described. It is a perishing (SD II 58). It is eternal wrath and death (AP IV 161). It is misfortune and heartache (LC I 140). It is eternal wrath and condemnation (LC II iii 66). It is like paying God the penalty for a crime (Tract 82). It is an eternal burden on their (the damned) shoulder (SC *Vorrede* 4). It is a destruction of souls (Tract 48). It is being held in the jaws of hell (Ep IX 4). It is hellfire (SD V 20). It is an eternal fire (*Quinqunque vult*). It is hell's vengeance (LC II ii 30). However, hell is nowhere explicitly defined. Rather it is viewed as a state of eternal sufferings from which there is no hope of relief. Even the devil cannot escape (A CXVII; LC II ii 30). They cannot repent there (SD II 22 AC XX).

In spite of the exposition to the Lord's Prayer, which seems to indicate that hell will someday be destroyed,

> We pray in the Lord's Prayer that the devil's kingdom may be overthrown, and he may have no right or power over us, until finally the devil's kingdom shall be utterly *destroyed* and sin, death, and hell *exterminated*, that we may live forever . . . .

the confessors made it clear that hell is eternal! It would take considerable eisegesis to prove otherwise. The critique of the Prussian theologians requested that eternal damnation be especially mentioned that "people would know that original sin merits not temporal but also eternal death and damnation" (SD). The symbols nowhere consider those who have not heard the Gospel in relation to hell. However, the heathen, the Turks, the Jews, the false Christians, and the hypocrites stay in eternal anger and condemnation (LC II iii 66).

The "damnamus" clauses would appear not immediately relevant to the question of eternal damnation but only ultimately in that if a person continues in false doctrine he will then be damned.

Later orthodoxy treats the doctrine of hell quite similarly to the doctrine of heaven. The ungodly suffer in hell "according to the degree of their ungodliness, in bodily and spiritual pains for their sins eternally" (Holl 978, 990). Thus there are also degrees of hell. Quenstedt divided the sufferings of hell into privative and positive punishments with the devils (Quen I 565; see also Hfr 691). Gerhard delineates two kinds of hell; the internal and the external, the objective and the local hell (which is the real hell XX 175). He goes into detail on the tortures of hell:

1). There will be every kind of torture there because, in hell, there is the presence of all evil and the absence of all good.
2). The torture will be most "exquisite," like the pains criminals experience.
3). They will feel the anguish of belonging to those who feel the "pains of childbirth."
4). They are burned not lightly and superficially, but in the midst of flames penetrating *ad medullas.*
5). They are not given a drop of water to cool their body, "much less the least consolation for their soul."
6). They are able to see the elect in glory, "and hence, from envy, are seized with horror and indignation."
7). Their sorrow is increased by remembering former good things.
8). They will know that their punishment is eternal.
9). They will be tortured by seeing the pains of their relatives.
10). They will resist and contend against God, and this is the gnashing of teeth mentioned in Matthew 13.

Although the evil men will not receive the full measure of their pain immediately after death, the experience is begun right after death (Gerhard XVIII 21). The theologians of orthodoxy have thus delineated all attributes of hell but temperature.

Obviously, in the wake of excessive medieval emphasis on hell and its tortures, Luther attempted to de-emphasize the doctrine and concentrate on the Gospel. Nor did he use hell for motivation (to enter the ministry or any other salutary act of a Christian). This is not to say that he denied the doctrine. He affirms it and even suggests a "demythologized" interpretation of it, i.e., the evil are punished by their own consciences. It would make an worthy study to sort out the demythologizing statements of Luther and the confessions, especially since Lutheranism in the twentieth century has been the most fertile ground for theologians of that "bent." Perhaps, Lutheranism's attitude and stance over against Scripture ultimately enables such a position. (Elert has already studied the relativity aspect of Lutheranism in regards to worldview.)

Quite in contrast, is orthodoxy's fragmented view of hell. One might even note a return to medieval doctrine in their attitude toward it.

VI.) Closely connected with the doctrine of "hell" and eternal punishment is the first of the antitheses of Article XVII of Augustana: **UNIVERSALISM**. This was quite an issue in the early church fathers, but by Aquinas's time the issue had died down somewhat. It was reasserted by some of the Anabaptists. Hans Denck was the most important champion of universalism in the Anabaptist movement. He made reference to it in chapters 16, 17, and 28 of *Wer die Wahrheit wahrlich lieb hat, Vom Gezetz Gotes,* and in *Ordnung Gottes und der Kreaturen Werk* (1527) 8ff. Because God is love and mercy, He can not be angry forever. The *Mennonite Enclopedia* asserts that the Augsburg Confession wrongly attributes universalism to all Anabaptists of the time. It was never really accepted in those circles. In fact, "it is found nowhere else except perhaps in Jakob Kautz and Hans Hut" (Vol IV p. 783). In fact Denck won Hans Hut to the "cause." Urban Rhegius was his chief opponent. Melchior Rink (1494-1546) appears not to have been involved in universalism (despite the *Bekenntnisschrifte* footnote) although J. Menius in his book *Der Widdertaufer Lehre und Geheimnis* (1530) attributed this doctrine to him.

Luther's 1528 Confession includes his attitude toward universalism.

> I believe in the resurrection of the dead, both the good and the evil, at the last day, when each shall receive in his body what he deserves; the righteous eternal life with Christ, and the wicked eternal death with the devil and his angels, for I do not agree with those who teach that finally even the devils will be saved.

The confessions take up this antithesis and are explicit that only those who are elected called, and justified will be saved (SD XI 22; see also SD XI 5, Ep XI 9). Statements in the confessions (previously mentioned) which could be interpreted that the evil men are annihilated, must be interpreted in the light of the whole. Hell is eternal. The dogmaticians obviously would also deny this possibility (either of universalism or annihilationism).

> VII.) It would appear that Aquinas did not deal with the possibility of a **MILLENNIUM** although many fathers of the church posited this doctrine.

Luther expressed varying views on the subject, but none approximated Chiliastic or Jewish hopes. He said, for example, that the one thousand years mentioned in Revelation represented the thousand years in which the Church was comparatively free of heresies. Satan was then released in the form of the Antichrist, the pope, and the nations of Gog and Magog, and the Turk. (*Brief*, March 7, 1529 to W. Link; Oct. 26, 1529, to N. Hausmann; Nov. 10, 1529, to J. Probst). The new world is to be brought about by the action of Christ, at any rate, and not by human development or force. We will continue to have strife and wars until Christ's final return (Erl Ed XI 85; xlv 110sq). Even though he firmly believed that the sixteenth century was "the last age," he did not succumb to the Anabaptist excesses. Luther developed few distinctive eschatological ideas and his principle achievement in this area seems to be his rejection of purgatory and his level headed attitude to the doctrine of the last things.

Chiliasm is the concern of the second antithesis of Augustana XVII. Schlink notes that only crass millennialism is to be disavowed and perversions forsaken. Chiliasm was rampant among the Anabaptists. (Incited by Hans Hut and some Jews in Worms, Melchior Rinck predicted that the millennium would be ushered in during Easter, 1530—just a few months, by the way, before the presentation of the Augsburg Confession.) Hans Hut, a most colorful figure, preached the imminent coming of Christ. In addition he saw in the Turks a sign of the return of Christ, and asserted that the Lord had given three and a half years more for repentance as shown in Rev 13 and Daniel 12. Those that repented would rule the earth. The *Variata* of 1540 condemns the Originists by name. Charles the Fifth was interested in the article merely as a matter of government because the Anabaptists were often anarchists.

Luther's early speculation that all the Jews would be saved, or that all the world would hear the gospel before Christ came again, are omitted either as affirmation or denial. (It would make a valuable study to see whether the confessors used any concept employed by the writer of Revelation, without verification by another book of scripture, as doctrinal proof.)

The dogmaticians likewise deny chiliasm a place in their writings. The general resurrection and the final judgment follow one another with no time interval (Quenstedt, IV 649). However, the dogmaticians make a distinction between gross and subtle chiliasm:

> The former estimates the millennium as happy because of the illicit pleasure of the flesh; the latter, because of the lawful and honorable delights of the body and soul. Both are rejected (Holl, 1256; Grh. XX, 109).

The various views are elaborated upon and rejected. Gerhard's explanation of the thousand years of Revelation is that they begin in the empire of Constantine, and the Antichrist is thus the Turk. Hollazius argues that the millennium can be explained away by the allegorical and quasi-enigmatical character of the Apocalypse (1259). Lutherans continue the same attitude that the medieval church had toward the millennium.

VIII).Naturally, **PURGATORY** was taken for granted in the Middle Ages, and Thomas is a child of his time. Interesting, is a practical ramification of the doctrine. "We should also come to the assistance of our friends in purgatory." He then stresses the great difference in pains between this world and the next. The three ways to bring relief to those souls in purgatory are: masses, prayers, and alms. (In *The Exposition to the Apostle's Creed*, a fourth is added: fasting, which interconnects with the others,)

Luther's early view of purgatory is explicated in his confession of 1528,

> As Scripture mentions nothing about the matter, I do not regard it a sin to pray for the dead, as our devotion may direct, either as follows or in some similar fashion: Dear God, if the soul be in such a state that it may be helped, be gracious to it. And when this has been done once or twice, let that suffice. For the vigils and masses for souls and annual requiems are useless and the very devil's auction. Neither is there anything in Scripture concerning purgatory, and it has been originated by the hobgoblins, so I hold that it is not necessary to believe anything concerning it, even though all things are possible to God and, if He wished, He could

rack the souls after they have left the body, but as He has caused
nothing to be told or written concerning it. He does not wish
to have it believed. I know indeed of another sort of purgatory,
but this is not a subject for teaching in the congregation nor will
pious endowments and vigils avail against it.[40]

(Luther in that last sentence probably is referring to the sufferings of this
life.)

Eck has found a few "anti-purgatory" statements in the pre-confessional
writings.

37: Purgatory cannot be proved from the canonical Scriptures
(Luther)
39: Soul's in purgatory sin without intermission, as long as they seek
rest and dread punishments.
40: Souls delivered from purgatory by the intercession of the living have
less happiness than if they had made satisfaction of themselves

He adds a comment of his own to the controversy,

59: After this life there is a purgatorial fire.

Probably, Eck has correctly quoted his sources.
Luther rejects purgatory as it was commonly understood, because it
conflicted with the doctrine of justification by faith alone. His "doctrine" of
the intermediate state (which will be discussed at length later in this chapter
and the next) can be seen to have originated in the discarded doctrine of
purgatory. Decisive in any discussion of purgatory was the statement, "The
final decision on salvation has already been made." It is true that similar to
the *1528 Confession* Luther could say,

I have never yet denied that there is a purgatory and I still hold
that there is, as I have many times written and confessed, though
I have no way of proving it incontrovertibly, either by scripture
or reason. I find in the scriptures, indeed, that Christ, Abraham,
Jacob, Moses, Job, David, Hezekiah, and many others tasted hell
in this life. This I think to be purgatory, and it is not incredible
that some of the dead suffer in like manner. Tauler had much to

say about it, and in a word, I have decided for myself that there
is a purgatory, but cannot force any others to the same decision
(*Brief* Jan. 13, 1529 to Amsdorf).

Although he could not countenance a view that understood purgatory to
be a place of development (as though salvation through Christ was not
enough), he could possibly think that it might be a place of purgation for
those saved by grace. Note here, again, however, that Luther takes the first
step toward demythologization in his "realized purgation."

Luther was driven to this mediating position by the problem of those
who died without faith. God could save them after death, but does He?
(WA 10, II 325, 3). At any rate, Luther hoped God would be gracious to
Cicero (*Tisch.* 3925). Naturally masses, good works, and prayers meant to
influence the fate of the dead are rejected, but he does allow a short prayer
of intercession for them.

The confessions take up Luther's later position. They do not object
to purgatory as an intermediate state, but rather because it contradicts
the central doctrine. Just as the 39 *Articles* (Episcopal) reject the "Romish
doctrine of purgatory," so also the confessions reject the Roman doctrine
of purgatory. As the Smalcald Articles put it, "Purgatory is contrary to
the fundamental article that Christ alone, and not the work of man, can
help souls, Besides nothing has been commanded or enjoined upon us
concerning the dead" (SAIII, 12). It "may" consequently be discarded,
"apart entirely from the fact that it is an error and idolatry" (SA II, ii, 13;
see also Ap. XII, 13ff, 134ff; XXIV, 90ff; SA II, 11, 13).

The Council of Trent took exception to the stand of Luther and the
confessions and thus devoted a few paragraphs to anathematizing the
Lutherans.

Canon 30: If anyone says that after the reception of the grace
of justification the guilt is so remitted and the debt of eternal
punishment so blotted out to every repentant sinner, that no
debt of temporal punishment remains to be discharged either
in this world or in purgatory before the gates of heaven can be
opened, let him be anathema.[5]

Session 25. Those who say the mass ought not to be offered for
the living and the dead . . . let him be anathema.[6]

There is a purgation and that the souls there detained are aided by the suffrages of the faithful and chiefly by the acceptable sacrifice of the altar . . . .

The more difficult and subtle questions, however, and those that do not make for edification and from which there is for the most part no increase in piety, are to be excluded from popular instructions to uneducated people.

Likewise, things that are uncertain or that have the appearance of falsehood, they (the bishops) shall not permit to be made known publicly and discussed.[7]

The split between Rome and Augustana is explicit, and adding the statements of the dogmaticians would contribute nothing to the discussion; they approximate Luther and the confession's point of view.

IX.) The **INTERMEDIATE STATE** Aquinas discounted, in view of his unusually strict delineation of heaven and hell, which come immediately after death (as does purgatory, *limbus infantum*, and *limbus patrum*).

Eck found a statement of Luther's that, if accurate, presents a doctrine of the intermediate state,

Since the ascension of Christ no one has gone to heaven or will go until the end of the world. (Thesis 123).

Statements like this are to be found elsewhere in Luther. Though holy scriptures make a great many references to the last times, Luther notes that there were almost none referring to the time between the death of the individual and the last day.[8] He views the intermediate state as a kind of sleep in which actual consciousness has ceased. The dead rest in peace and comfort, and will not know that they have passed through death, but will think they "have been asleep only an hour." Although the dead do not have consciousness of "life" or "faculties," they "gain, view, and hear conversations of the angels and of God, in Whose presence they live." In other words the sleep will be like a trance (Cf WA 17:11 w 35 17ff;.36, 252, 10; 37, 149-151; 43, 359ff; 480f; and the Erl. Ed. Vi, 116-124, 329;

also x, 75; xi 141ff; xli 373; xiv, 315). (He espouses these views also in his Latin commentary on Genesis.)

On the locality of this intermediate state, Luther only states that,

> The soul goes to its place, whatever kind of a place that might be, for it cannot be corporeal; it is a sort of sepulcher of the soul, outside of this world.

In the same vein he writes,

> What paradise is, I do not know. It is enough for us to believe that God has a place where he perhaps preserves also the angels. Things are not as they are here (Erl. Ed. XXI 193ff; xxxiii, 156).

Both these statements (and for that matter most of Luther's eschatological remarks) have rich overtones of Old Testament theology. He took such Old Testament ideas seriously, and is thus able to describe sheol in his *Ennarratio* of Psalm XVI of 1530 as, "Everything that there is in the existence upon which we enter after life" (which includes the fire of the rich man and the "bosom of Abraham") Erl Ed xvii, 125ff; xli, 378; x 206ff). Strongly reminiscent of the Old Testament are such statements as the "grave of souls" and the "promises in which we fall asleep" (Erl Ed x 208; xi 302; vi 121). It would appear, then, that after death the good and the evil enter a state perhaps like sheol of the Old Testament which includes paradise, the bosom of Abraham, and hades of the New Testament and awaits the judgment day, after which heaven (or better, eternal life) and hell take on their existence.

Luther posits that the "majority of the dead" are in the intermediate state, but does not venture to regard this sleep as universal.[9] Because holy scripture presents varying views and attitudes on death and the life thereafter, Luther is constrained to do likewise.

It is, in view of these opinions, strange that the confessions say nothing about an intermediate state, though Luther seems to have affirmed such a doctrine to his dying day. Likewise, the further purgation of the Christian dead is not mentioned, although Luther suggested the possibility. The dead are spoken of as in the grave and in heaven (SA II ii 25). The Formula mentions that Christ "ascended into heaven, not just like some other saint" which appears to favor the idea that when a person dies his soul goes to heaven, leaving his body to rot in the dust (SD VIII 27). Peter, Paul, and all the saints are in heaven (SDVIII 77). Mary prays for the church (APXXI 27). It would thus be the position of the confessors that the dead have an active existence (but this would not exclude such an existence from the grave as in the Old Testament grave-sheol-shades concept). The dead may not understand our prayers (Ap XXI 12), but the saints pray for the church in general (Ap XXI 8). They may even pray for individuals (SA II ii 25). We are not, however, to pray *to* them, have celebrations for them, or masses in their honor (SA II ii 25), since there is no example of it in scripture, and a prayer to Christ is a thousand times better (See SA II ii 24: Ap VII 23; and SA II ii 21).

It would seem, therefore, that the confessions allow either position, but the very placement of the resurrection (before the mention of eternal life or punishment) in article 17 of the Augsburg Confession might support an intermediate state. In this way, however, they may also be reflecting the placing of doctrinal word order in the ancient creeds.

The dogmaticians, however, take a position on the whole unfavorable to an intermediate state (or soul sleep). Many of them posit the immediate entry of the soul after death into either heaven or hell. It must, therefore, be remembered in discussing heaven and hell that these exist for the orthodox dogmaticians both before and after the resurrection.

Metempsychosis is entirely rejected (Grh XVII 171), as are the papists' division of the afterlife into five receptacles for the soul (hell, purgatory, *limbus puerorum, limbus patrium,* and heaven). The dogmaticians recognize only two places for the dead: heaven and hell, and categorically deny the intermediate state:

> Neither after death do the souls of the godly live in a cool and tranquil place, and possess only a foretaste of heavenly happiness, but they enjoy full and essential happiness. Neither after death do the souls of the wicked feel only the beginnings of tortures, but perfect and complete damnation (Quen IV 538).

Baier is just as explicit:

> Yea, we believe that the souls of the godly attain essential blessedness immediately after they have been separated from the body, but that the wicked undergo their damnation (364).

HAVING WORLD ENOUGH AND TIME   171

Gerhard, also says that after the death of the body, the soul,

> returns to God, to whose judgment it is committed from which
> it is either borne by holy angels into heaven, or is delivered to
> evil spirits to be cast into hell (Gerhard XVII 149).

It is to be asked, then, what is left for the resurrection of the body? Does
the resurrection mean nothing or is it only a difference in degree? If the
souls enjoy "full and essential happiness" why do they have to rise unless we
turn to Aquinas's logical reasons for the resurrection. Cullman's theory of a
difference in time between God and us may be a more satisfactory solution
to the dilemma than the dogmaticians of orthodoxy put forth.

Statements in the orthodox fathers make it appear the dogmaticians
leave a loophole for an intermediate state. For example, Gerhard says that
the soul

> is preserved *somewhere* (pou) until, on the appointed day of the
> general resurrection, the body raised up by divine power will be
> joined to the body again (Gerhard XVII 149).

The only adequate interpretation of this statement is that this somewhere
is either heaven or hell. Quenstedt's doctrine is similar and therefore when
he says,

> Following death is the judgment, whose forerunner is the general
> resurrection of all men, and whose following attendant is the
> end of the world (IV534).

Even Gerhard says that after death comes the "resurrection, the judgment,
and finally the eternal state in heaven or hell" (XVII 8), which would be
perfect in a Cullman understanding or a Luther understanding, but Gerhard
has merely neglected to mention the hell or heaven before the resurrection.

Hutter, however, (and perhaps only because his other writings have not
been fully examined) makes a statement more in harmony with the Old
Testament, New Testament, and Luther,

> The souls of the godly are in the hand of God awaiting there
> the glorious resurrection of the body, and the full enjoyment of
> eternal blessedness (Loc Th. 297).

172 THOMAS RICHARD SLUBERSKI

With reservations only on the body/soul dualism, most modern scholars could agree with this statement. Contrast this statement of Hutter's with a statement of Gerhard which comes much closer to describing the "temperature of hell" than any of the attitudes expressed above with the possible exception of St. Thomas Aquinas,

> Of receptacles and habitations Scripture by a general appellation, speaks of a place. Not that it is a corporeal and physical place properly so called but because it is a "where" *pou* into which souls separated from the body are brought together . . . . Scripture enumerates only two such receptacles, one of which, prepared for the godly, is called by the most ordinary appellation, heaven, and the other intended for the souls of the wicked is called hell. (Ger XVII 178; however, see the IDB for the use of heaven in the Old and New Testaments.)

Luther, as have many others in the intervening centuries, came close to being called "heretic" by the theologians of the church in which he did his confessing. Gerhard, who in his critique of psychopannichists held a doctrine somewhat similar to that of Luther (and many others, including the modern Greek Orthodox Church), comes in for damning criticism by Quistorp, the Calvinist theologian (damning from the Lutheran point of view):

> It is especially typical for the development of Protestant eschatology that the great architect of Lutheran orthodoxy, John Gerhard, in his doctrine of the state after death, represents not the standpoint of Luther but that of Calvin.[10]

His arguments follow a definition of the psychopannichist's position:

1). The dead are said to sleep. Answer: As sleep holds only the members and outward senses while the soul exercises its inner operations, as is inferred from dreams; so in death the body alone perishes, while the soul of the godly are transferred to Abraham's bosom, and enjoys consolation.
2). The dead shall not praise thee. Answer: these passages refer to the proclamation and propagation of true doctrine, and the celebration

of divine blessings through which, in this life, others may be invited to true conversion and the glorification of the divine name.

3). (Posits a general and a particular judgment).

4). The rest of the souls must be understood with respect to the *terminus a quo*, i.e., they rest from labors and troubles . . . but not with respect to the *terminus ad quem*, as though the souls of the godly rest after death in the stupor of sleep (Gerhard XVIII 24ff).

As to the knowledge of the dead of the earth, in the place cited, Gerhard makes some general assertions:

> It is a pious and good thought to hold that the dead have a general knowledge of what is occurring to the church militant here on earth, and therefore they beseech Christ with whom they are present in heavenly glory, for some good for the church . . . . Meanwhile, it must not be inferred from this, that they have in full view the individual circumstances or calamities to the godly.

Thus, we may see a definite development from Luther through the dogmaticians of orthodoxy. In the doctrine of the intermediate state this development is perhaps most pronounced. The confessions take a mediating position and always stay away from controversial areas (even where Luther himself held an opinion). This is wise, even though today, some would have liked a closer approximation of Luther's doctrine of the intermediate state, because perhaps along with this enlightened view might have also come his view on the conversion of the Jews or some other opinion not completely in accord with the Catholic faith. This chaste and circumspect attitude of the confessions toward eschatology is felicitous for twentieth-century Lutherans in the midst of the struggle between exegesis and systematics, between form criticism and the tradition of the church. History provides guidelines for today, and also to some extent anticipates the problems of the future. The Lutheran churches of the world are in the beginnings of a reaction to the rigid dogmatism of the past and to some extent the divisions match up with those between Luther and the dogmaticians of orthodoxy. The middle ground, then, and now, appears to be the confessions; it is on the confessions that the church of the Augsburg Confession takes her stand. Article XVII stifles none of the richness of revelation the Lord has given to his church either in the Old or New Testament, yet takes a position on the essentials:. The six essentials are, as follows: (1) Our Lord Jesus Christ will return on the last day for judgment, (2) and will raise up all the dead, (3) to give eternal life and everlasting joy to believers and the elect, (4) but to condemn ungodly men and the devil to hell and eternal punishment, (5) rejected, therefore, are those that deny eternal punishment, and (6) chiliasm. And in the light of the Lutheran-Roman Catholic dialogue, the Confutation's acceptance of the article is doubly significant.

NOTES TOWARD A CONCLUSION

According to plan, the paper should be easily summarized by analysis of Augustana 17. Obviously, there will be rough edges and extra material that will not fit, but it is hoped that these others are supporting arguments rather than irrelevant data.

Augsburg 17 can be divided into four affirmations and two denials.

1. Jesus Christ will return on the last day (the Parousia). The Old Testament in its doctrine of the day of Yahweh, the Apocalyptic books Yahweh or Messiah centered, and the New Testament (Synoptic, Pauline and the rest) all affirm and enrich this affirmation of Augsburg. With the varying opinions, word pictures, symbolic, and even enigmatic language of holy scripture, not to mention the conceptions of the early and medieval church, Luther and later orthodoxy's embroidery on the basic theme of the parousia, Augustana's simplicity allows room for many embellishments as long as they do not contradict scripture. It is also to be noted that throughout the history of the church, this basic affirmation of Christ's coming again has not suffered perversion to any great extent.

2. The second affirmation is that Christ will come for judgment. Much the same argumentation can be used under this heading as under the first.

3. He will raise up all the dead. Note that Augsburg 17 takes a position on who will rise. *All* the dead rise. Nothing is said about an intermediate state. It is Christ who does the raising, but this does not mean the Holy Spirit's work need be slighted. Admittedly, some passages would seem to favor a degree of universalism, but the confessors agreed that the majority do not, nor do the majority of interpreters. Perhaps it was omitted in the light of the controversy

over the form and matter of the resurrection body and other such trivia. Because there might have been honest disagreement, and scripture itself gives only general guidelines, the confessors remain silent on the subject. As to the fact that the Old Testament does not seem to teach clearly a resurrection from the dead, progressive revelation might be invoked. We are not bound only to the Old Testament view. The Augsburg Confession confesses in the light of the New Testament and creedal formulations.

4. He will give eternal life and everlasting joy to the believers and elect but will condemn ungodly men and the devil to hell and eternal punishment. (The Latin has the plural of devil, and the German alone says hell specifically.) Augsburg takes a position on heaven and hell and would seem to place them after the resurrection. Note also that election, faith (believers), and works (ungodly) all play in to the decision, thus reflecting the fullness of revelation and solving the seeming contradiction of Article 4 of AC and Ap. with the Athanasian Creed. Also the punishment will be eternal, but nothing is said about the nature of the torment. The confessors cannot be faulted for knowing too much about the "furniture of heaven and the temperature of hell."

5. Universalism is condemned (and also annihilationism, if rightly understood).

6. Chiliasm is rejected, and it seems to be crass chiliasm that is specifically pointed out in the light of the Anabaptist and Jewish ideas. It would seem that a type of millennialism could be maintained in the church of the Augsburg Confession, especially in view of Revelation chapter 20, rightly interpreted. This would seem to be stretching a point, but it is open.

Perhaps mainly because of the chaste way in which eschatology is handled in Augsburg 17, but also because of the stand that is made on essentials, the Lutheran Church has been kept from extremes in eschatology (even by the later dogmaticians), but it could be wished that they were more explicit about more things to keep certain opinions out of current dogmatics' textbooks. However, too many dogmatic pronouncements would stifle the fullness of the revelation the Spirit has given to his Church until the fullness of time has come when "we will know, even as we are known" (from 1 Corinthians 13:12, the Epistle for Quinquagesima Sunday in which this chapter was completed).

NOTES

1) Collection of Sources of the Augsburg Confession, Concordia Seminary Print Shop, p. 24.

2) Kramm, H.H. *The Theology of Martin Luther*, London, pp. 103-104.

3) Collection of Sources, p. 43.

4) *Ibid,* 30.

5) Schroeder, H.J. *The Canons and Decrees of the Council of Trent*, p. 46.

6) *Ibid,* p. 149.

7) *Ibid.,* p. 214.

8) Kramm, *op. cit.* pp, 103, 104.

9) Köstlin, Julius. *The Theology of Luther*, Vol II, Phil., p. 471.

10) Quistorp, Heinrich. *Calvin's Doctrine of the Last Things.* trans. by Knight, p. 193.

BIBLIOGRAPHY

Althaus, Paul.   *Die Letzten Dinge.* Gutersloh: Bertelsmann, 1949.

Aquinas, Thomas   *Complete Works*

Burtness, James.   "Immortality and/or Resurrection," *Dialogue*, Easter 1962. *Collection of Sources. Augsburg Confession.* Concordia Seminary Print Shop.

Cullman, Oscar.   *Immortality of the Soul or Resurrection of the Dead.* London, 1958.

Elert, Werner.   *The Structure of Lutheranism.* St. Louis: CPH

Guy, H.A.   *The New Testament Doctrine of the Last Things.* London: Oxford Press, 1948.

Hall, George.   "Luther's Eschatology," in *Aug. Quart.* Vol 23, 1943, Rock Island: Aug, Book Concern. pp. 13=21.

Interpreter's Dictionary of the Bible. Various articles.

Jacob, H. E.   *Theology of the Old Testament.*

          "Eck's 404 Theses" Papers of A.S.C.H., Putnam, N.Y

Kelly, J.N.D.   *Early Christian Doctrines.* pp. 459==49.

Köstlin, Julius   *The Theology of Luther.* Philadelphia: Lutheran Publishing Society, 1897.

Kramm, H. H.   *The Theology of Martin Luther.* London,: Clarke, 1947

Muenscher, W.   *Elements of Dogmatic History.* New Haven, Conn:1830.

Pieper, Charles. — *The Eschatology of the Lutheran Confessions.* An STM Thesis. Concordia Seminary, St. Louis.

Quistorp, Heinrich — *Calvin's Doctrine of the Last Things.* trans by Knight, Richmond: John Knox, 1955.

Rupp, Gordon. — *The Righteousness of God.* London: Hodder and Stoughton, 1953.

Shlink, Edmund — *The Theology of the Lutheran Confessions.*

Schmid, Heinrich. — *The Doctrinal Theology of the Evangelical Lutheran Church.* Minneapolis: Augsburg, 1875.

Schroeder — *The Canons and Decrees of the Council of Trent.*

Smith, Ryder — *The Bible's Doctrine of the Last Things.*

Smits, Edmund. — "Blessed Immortality, a Study in Gerhard." *Dialogue*, Easter 1962, pp.

Tappert, T. — *The Book of Concord*

Von Rad, Gerhard — *Theology of the Old Testament*

Watson, Philip — *Let God be God*

CHAPTER THIRTEEN

ESCHATOLOGY: THE END TIMES

This chapter on "Eschatology" began as a series of background papers on the studies included in "The Furniture of Heaven and the Temperature of Hell." I aimed, at the time, to be a systematician, integrating exegesis, church history, philosophy, and contextual studies. The studies I set out to organize here amounted to a "trial run" at one doctrine: eschatology. The (still) incipient article extends the studies laid out in the previous chapter with a survey of the Old Testament, New Testament, apocrypha, the early church, the medieval church, and the writings of Thomas Aquinas, and on up to Lutheran orthodoxy of the 17th century. Together, as I observed in the preamble to that chapter, they strike me as a fitting—and fittingly unfinished—conclusion to a collection on the general topics of "World Enough and Time."

ESCHATOLOGY

I must again cite the remark of the great theologian Reinhold Niebuhr—on his suspicion of anyone who knew too much "about "the furniture of heaven or the temperature of hell"—and my addendum to it: there is also danger in erring the other way. Disregard for heaven and hell indeed appears to be a modern malady; we observe even a de-eschatologicalization of the church and her message.

In rummaging for research materials on the subject, I came up with blanks or near blanks on the eschatology of Later Orthodoxy, Luther, and the comparisons to earlier eras of the church. The paper underway is thus of necessity distended (and in places disjointed). My consideration began as an investigation of the where, when, what, and how of heaven and hell; these aspects had further ramifications in beliefs about death, the soul, judgment, resurrection, and the intermediate state. So, I have taken Article 17 of the Augsburg Confession and traced its emphases through history, from the Old Testament (where they can be found) through the apocalyptic era, and finally into the New Testament. From there, the doctrines are rapidly sketched in as they progressed through the early, medieval, and pre-confessional eras of the church, especially in Luther. To round out the study, I move to the Roman Catholic reaction and the developments in Lutheran orthodoxy, I hope preparing the way for later, more in-depth studies of what happened to eschatology in the contemporary church. Reaching part four of this draft, I still saw hope of accomplishing at least a tentative theory, but this was soon forgotten in the glories of later orthodoxy's eisegesis. It is hoped that the combination of exegetical (only the Old Testament survey approaches what I consider to be a good overview) and historical (finding references to original sources is still a problem even in Luther) research into a systematic whole will approach what Schlink proposes in the closing of his *Theology of the Lutheran Confessions*, a constructive approach to doctrine.

No attempt has been made to make relevant the results of research. This can be done only from a solid footing, which I cannot claim to have gained through this modest bit of research. There remain too many problems, too many places in which I have had to rely on the word of another to "leap" as it were from the footnote to the factory.

Note: The views surveyed in chapters 12 and 13 are not necessarily orthodox or traditional but represent current scholarly thinking on the issues which will need to be reconciled with the Lutheran Confessions in the Book of Concord.

The effort has, all the same, attained its primary goal: to enable *me* to confess the confession of eschatology with the confessors.

Argument

I.   Eschatology in the Old Testament and Apocalyptic Writings

    A) Death
    B) Sheol
    C) Other concepts
    D) A Note on Development

II. Eschatology in the New Testament

    A) The Synoptics and Jesus Christ
    B) Abraham's Bosom
    C) Hades
    D) Gehenna
    E) Paradise
    F) Parousia
    G) The Millennium
    H) The Resurrection
    I) Universalism

III. Eschatology of the Early Church

    A) The Resurrection
    B) Heaven
    C) Hell
    D) The Millennium
    E) Purgatory
    F) The Intermediate State

IV. Eschatology of the Medieval Church (Thomas Aquinas)

    A) Death
    B) Purgatory
    C) Judgment
    D) Resurrection
    E) Heaven and Hell

V. Luther's Eschatology

    A) Intermediate State
    B) Purgatory
    C) The Last Times
    D) Millennium
    E) The Last Judgment
    F) Heaven and Hell
    G) Universalism

VI. Eschatology in Pre-Confessional Documents

    A) *The Schwabach Articles*
    B) *The Marburg Articles*
    C) *Luther's Confession of 1528*
    D) *Eck's 404 Theses*

VII. The Eschatology of the Lutheran Confessions

    A) Death
    B) Realized Eschatology
    C) The Creedal Affirmations
    D) Article XVII

        1. Judgment
        2. Resurrection
        3. Eternal life
        4. Hell
        5. Universalism
        6. Millennium
        7. Purgatory
        8. The Intermediate State

    E) An Abbreviated Critical Study of Article XVII
    F) The Antitheses

VIII. The Eschatology of the Councils of Trent

IX. The Eschatology of Later Orthodoxy

    A) Death
    B) Judgment
    C) Resurrection
    D) Heaven
    E) Hell
    F) Universalism and Annihilationism
    G) Millennium
    H) Purgatory
    I) Intermediate State

I

ESCHATOLOGY IN THE OLD TESTAMENT

Tormenting to the mindset of a contemporary theologian of the twentieth-first century is the dearth of systematic attitude toward eschatology in the Old Testament. Instead, we find tentative, emergent answers, along with what might best be labeled a lack of concern.

A) In any discussion of death in the Old Testament it must be affirmed that "life" was emphasized far more. In fact the O.T. may be read as a life-centered book with a life-centered theology. Man would have lived forever had he not fallen in the paradise given him in Eden. Death therefore takes on a largely negative characteristic: lack of life. Death does not seem to be a gateway to bliss or to liberation. There are passages, all the same, that stress the destructive, punitive character of death. A premature death was considered a punishment for sins. (Gen 38:7; 7:4; 19:24; II Sam 6:7). Death can contrastingly be viewed as a normal occurrence after a long life (Job 5:26; Gen 15:15; 6:3). This is especially the case in the priestly documents. The good lived long lives (Gen 5:6-31). In the O.T., only two men, Enoch and Elijah, escaped death (explicitly, at least).

It would appear that death is *not* the soul's separation from the body (however, see Gen. 35:18). Rather, the Hebrew mind-set evidently conceived of death as the "falling apart," a dissolution (II S. 14:14) of the various components of the body, i.e., the nephesh went to sheol, the body returned to the dust (Ec 12:7), and the breath and spirit returned to reside in the tomb, which usually was dug into the ground. Nephesh does not seem to occur in any other Semitic language. The LXX usually translates the word with "Hades."

B) As to just "where" sheol was located there is no universal agreement; usually Sheol was considered to lie beneath the earth (in a three-storied universe—Dt 32:22; Is 14: 9; Pr 15:24). This meaning is supported by those passages that describe "descending" into sheol (Gen 37:35; 42:38; 44:29, 31; Is 14:11). Lest anyone become too dogmatic (or systematic), however, about the concept, Job 26:6,7 and Jonah 2:3,6 picture sheol under the mountains and seas. Enoch places it in the west, where the sun goes down (En. 22:1-5). There are also those passages that describe sheol as barred (Jb 17:16) and gated (Ps 107:16 and Jonah 2:6). H. E. Jacob, in his *Theology of the Old Testament,* puts forth a fascinating explanation for the sheol imagery. The reason Sheol appears so often connected with "down" is that the tombs of ancient Israel were usually in pits or wells. In addition the graves were family graves and, when one was reunited with one's fathers (Gen 35:29), death and descent signified a local reuniting; the fathers lay, literally, in the grave with you. Sheol thus may have originally meant the grave, the continued existence in an individual grave. Later, the concept became more generalized and corporate.

Sheol is conceived of as a place of darkness (Job 10:21-22, 17:13; Ps 143:3), silence (Ps 115:17, 94:17), and sleep (Is 14:10, Job 3:14-19 and many others).

Sheol is a place of forgetfulness, inactivity, lack of knowledge (Ps 88:12-13; Ec 9:5-6,10; Jer 31:15-17); however, see Lev 19:31 and 20:6, and Is 19:3—"the knowing ones" and the connections with necromancy). These references might be harmonized with an understanding that the dead never have a knowledge superior to that they had in life. Other O.T. passages that may be enlightening in regard to this question of the consultation of the dead: Ex 22:17; Lev 19:31; 20:6, 27; I Sam 28:3, 9-13; Is 8:19; 19:3; 29:4.

Sheol is a place of separation from the living and from God (Ps 6:5). There is no praise of God in sheol (Is 38:18; Ps 115:17; Is 36:18f; Ps 30:9; 84:4f). The dead are out of history, but Yahweh is able to do anything. God can raise the dead, but this is not the usual thing (II Kings 2:1-18; Ez 37:1-14 [the valley of dry bones]). To the very latest of O.T. periods, God leaves sheol and the dead alone, for that is seemingly his purpose, but God is still in control (Job 26:6; Ps 139:8).

The inhabitants of Sheol, termed "rephaim" are described as weary (the word may derive from *raphah,* to sink down, relax, but more likely from *rapha,* to heal, with further meaning of "to mend"; the later etymology emphasizes the community aspects of death's denizens (Job 3:17). The dead suffer constant thirst (Is 5:13), and there may be an aristocracy of the dead, who retain their ranks (Is 14:9 and 26:14; Ez 32:21, 24). Usually, those who entered the realm of the dead enter to stay (Job 16:22). However, "elohim" is used of the dead, for those who could be evoked (Is 8:19; 29:4).

C) Sheol and the "existence" after death have borne the brunt of many other concepts of well-meaning eisegetes. There seems in the Old Testament to be neither punishment nor blessedness (rewards) after death. Rather good and evil men exist in death together (Jb 3:13-19; Numbers 16:30ff; Ps 14:16). The Mosaic system of rewards and retributions are awarded this side of the grave in most of the Old Testament writings. (Death itself may be part of the retribution.) The resurrection of the body is apparently mentioned only twice in the O.T.: Is 26:19 and Dan 12:2 and both of these are post exilic (*i.e.*, very late). Many scholars see only the latter passage as referring to the resurrection and only to that of the Jews (worthy and unworthy). Death was usually considered eternal (Jer 51:39,57) or the question was left unraised.

Important for later chapters of this paper is the relationship between the Valley of Hinnon and Gehenna. The concept does not seem to be connected in the O.T. with sheol (see II Kings 23:10 and Is 66:24). Perpetual fire or punishment is foreign to the Hebrew concept of Sheol (Jb 26:5; Pr 15:11; Ps 88:10,12). But see part 6 below, "Day of the Lord."

Analysis of the reasons and the nature of the development of these Hebrew conceptions presupposes a brief listing of the other synonyms for death and the abode of the dead:

1. "*Bor,*" the pit occurs sixty-eight times (Gen 37:20-9; Ps 28:1).
2. "*Shachath,*" the ditch, (RSV "pit") occurs twenty-three times (Ps 9:15, Ez 19:4 Jb 33:18; Ps 16:10).
3. "*Muth,*" the "house" or "realm of death" (Jb 28:22; 30:23; 38:17 In Ps 22:15), "the dust of death";
4. "*Eretz,* "the earth" or "the nethermost earth" (Ez 31:14 Jonah 2:6) corresponds to the Akkadian concept of the lowest of three areas of the earth in which the dead dwelt.
5. "*Abaddon*" was not used until after the exile and is used six times (Jb 26:6; Ps 88:11; Pr 15:11). It means to "perish" or "be lost." In rabbinic literature, Abaddon comes to mean the place of damnation, situated in the third lowest stratum of the earth and reserved for the wicked (see Rev 9:11).

6. The coming of Yahweh is another concept that can put a stumbling block in the path of one steeped in New Testament lore, and seems to be the central concept in O.T. eschatology. Just as Yahweh brought his people out of Egypt so He will deliver them again (Gen 15:7, 18; Num 23-24; Gen 49; Is 10:24; 27). In that time, in that day of the lord, Yahweh will save, and He will punish (Ex 20:5-6; Is 6:3,5). His coming will be cosmic (Is 24:1), affecting not only the historical realm (Is 10:24-27), the foreign gods, and heathen nations (Zeph 2:11; Jer 25:15ff) but also the Israelites (Hos 4:1,2; Mic 6:1ff). His coming will consist in a return to the conditions of paradise (Is 51:3; Hos 2:20) with abundance (Joel 3:18f), with peace among animals (Is 11:6-8), with a return to the good old days of Moses and David. In other words the day of Yahweh is seen primarily in restorative terms. Yahweh is the shepherd and king, David *redivivus*. This concept generally only included Israel.

It would be well here (in preparation for part 2) to note individual books' and specific authors' additions to this concept. Amos is preponderantly a prophet of doom (7:1-8). He stresses the destruction of other nations, although Israel, too gets mention. The day of the Lord is darkness and not light (5:18-20). The northern kingdom will be deported and there will be earthquakes and death. Positive prophecies of salvation are found only in 9:11-15. King David will rise again, but the "last judgment", "the end of the world," or the "renewal of the world" remains lacking.

In Hosea the promises of salvation come through more strongly. As yet there is no universal salvation or messiah.

Isaiah seems to be the first to include foreign nations (14:26, 27) and offers a well-developed plan of salvation, which centers on Mt. Zion and a kingdom of peace (5:19; 14:24; 30:1). The judgment is a refining and will take place in the near future. As in Amos, the remnant motif appears. (Micah is similar in his treatment of that day.)

Zephaniah foretells that the earth itself is to be consumed by fire. The remnant (which means the poor of the land) will be saved on that day of world catastrophe. All nations will have a share in the salutary change. (Jeremiah, Nahum, and Habakkuk add little to these themes.)

Of the exilic and post-exilic prophets, Ezekiel is concerned largely with Israel and individual retribution. There will be a chance to return to a country much like the Garden of Eden. David will rule and there will be a new temple with a living stream.

Deutero-Isaiah presents a pure eschatology of salvation. The people are rewarded not by merit but by mercy. Yahweh is the king of Zion, and there is universal hope of salvation. The servant of Yahweh (49:6) appears, and Deutero-Isaiah sees these things already in the process of accomplishment. He expects the heathen to turn to God along with a new creation (42:9; 43:18, 19).

D) By including the later prophets one can make certain comments on the development of eschatology taking place in Israel. Universalistic features were becoming more common. The creation of a new heaven and a new earth were not as cosmologically anchored as the apocalyptic books present them. Naturally, Israel is the center of this Day of Yahweh, and there is more emphasis on the universal judgment than on salvation. A late addition is the outpourings of the spirit and the portents in heaven and on earth, which are to accompany and precede that day. The Isaiah Apocalypse makes mention of the resurrection of the dead (24-27). However it should be made clear that it would be a misconception to see in the day of Yahweh anything like the parousia, in which the dead are raised (in most of the Old Testament). The day of Yahweh is for the living. Also here it can be noted that the silence of the prophets on life after death (and for that matter the relative silence on the subject by of all writers of the Old Testament) is not proof that the people of the Old Testament expected nothing after death other than the sheol described above. They were definitely, however, more concerned with this life, going by what is reflected in their writings.

A word on the development of doctrine and the apocalyptic period will enable the reader to understand the New Testament doctrine of the last things. The material for this section relies heavily upon the *Interpreter's Dictionary of the Bible* and follows the three suggested areas of development 1) in the concept of sheol, 2) of the resurrection, 3) and of the judgment. Two sentences of introduction: The Hebrew writers, and people, may have borrowed from many sources. Because Job and Ecclesiastes (and for that matter the rest of the sacred writers) apparently could not answer the vexing question of why the righteous die (and suffer) and why the evil go unpunished, an afterlife, a time of retribution and rewards became necessities. As Renan phrased it, "The martyrs were the real creators of the belief in an afterlife."

1. The possibility of a distinction to be made in sheol between the good and the wicked became possible in the second century BC. When the King of Babylon is said to have been thrown into the *depths* of sheol (Is 14), one can posit that the dead of Israel perhaps occupied a place not quite so deep in sheol. In Ez 32, the Gentiles are said to occupy one side of sheol, or at least this interpretation can be made. However, even in the early Hellenistic period, ordinarily, sheol contained both good and evil, and neither punishment nor reward is predicated of existence there (Ecclus. 14:16; 22:11; 28:21; 30:17; 41:4; Bar 2:17; 3:3; Tob 3:6; 14:10).

Punishment first appears in the Book of Enoch (10:2). The innovation may be traced to Persian influences. Enoch then posits three separate zones of hell. One has a spring of water (which ties in with the concept of the *Rephaim* as continually thirsty) for those who will ultimately be resurrected. The second part of sheol is reserved for those (the wicked) who died without suffering for their sins. In the resurrection this will be accomplished. The third part contains those wicked who received adequate punishment while alive. Note that Enoch, therefore, views sheol as an intermediate place for the souls of *all* the dead. At times (Ps Sol 14:6-7; II Macc 7:9) Sheol is seen as the intermediate place only of the righteous. Later the doctrine seemed to develop that when the righteous were raised (a particular resurrection) sheol remained as a place of punishment.

Whereas the Old Testament mentions explicitly only Enoch and Elijah as escaping sheol, the Apocalypse of Moses 33:4 has Adam taken to paradise (the third of seven heavens). Wicked Elihu in the Testament of Job was cast down to a lower world when he died, but Job was taken by angels into heaven. Baruch and Ezra (II Bar 21:23ff, IV Ezra 7:95) believe that the righteous souls go to heavenly chambers to await the resurrection whereas the wicked descend to sheol.

2. In this period, the resurrection was viewed in diverse ways. Antecedents of the developed doctrine of the resurrection seem to be the three resurrections in Kings (I Kings 17:17ff; II Kings 4:29 and 13:21) connected with Elijah, Elisha, and the bones. Yahweh himself called the people back to life. Some say the New Year festival contributed to the idea, which was intertwined with the dying and rising of Baal. Some have thus seen a David *redivivus* (Ez 34:23; 37:24) as preceding the idea of a more general resurrection. The

most common belief was that all will be summoned to judgment but that only the righteous will be resurrected (Ps Sol 3:16; II Bar 30; Adam and Eve 13) while the wicked are punished with a second death (Ps Sol 13:9; II Bar 50:1). We cannot be sure whether the resurrection is ever conceived of in this period as universal. There was also a difference of opinion as to whether the resurrection would be spiritual or corporal. See Enoch 1-36 in contrast to chapters 91-94. The Sadducees were known to have denied the resurrection, and the Pharisees affirmed it. Judaism followed the Pharisees. They believed in the immortality of the soul and the resurrection of the body. Philo was responsible for the widespread belief in the body/soul dualism. The soul is good and the body bad. A resurrection is unthinkable to him as is the final judgment (cf. Wisd of Sol.)

From the simple faith in Yahweh who is the God of the living, the Hebrew people developed more explicit beliefs in the resurrection, which prevailed until the New Testament period. There is some tension between a general or an individual resurrection. Not much is said about the resurrection body. The Sibylline Oracles (IV.179) do stress that the resurrection body will be just like the body that was buried. Maimed bodies of martyrs will be restored (II Macc 7:11). II Bar 50 says that after the resurrection the bodies will undergo changes. The righteous will have their bodies glorified, to become like angels and the stars, and then become even more glorious than even these. When the wicked see this transformation, their bodies will waste away.

3.) The day of Yahweh developed in this framework of apocalypticism. Dan 7:9-11, Enoch 47:3; 90:2-27 and IV Ezra 7:33 set the key note with the "ancient of days" seated on his throne pronouncing judgment from the books which will then be opened. Thus the judgment is automatic. The people are judged by their deeds, as they are written in the books. The Test. Benj 10:6-8 states that the Jews will be judged first and then the Gentiles. Enoch 10:6 and other places add the concept of fallen angels, who are to be judged along with men. Although God is usually recognized as the judge, Enoch 45:3 says that the heavenly messiah will be the one to sit on the throne and pronounce judgment. Philo of course posits no final judgment, and the Wisdom of Solomon agrees. IV Maccabees stresses the eternity of punishment *by fire* (9:9; 12:12), which the wicked will suffer.

Thus, the Apocalyptic books bring us up to and include the New Testament era. This provides the framework for New Testament eschatology, and serves as an important link between the doctrines of the old covenant and those of the new.

II

ESCHATOLOGY IN THE NEW TESTAMENT

[This section must of necessity be brief, sketchy, and incomplete—because of the wealth of available information, and will be handled somewhat differently from the first because of the nature of its material. The New Testament is not a unified doctrinal whole, so to present any "one" doctrine would be dishonest to the texts. The material presented draws heavily upon H.A. Guy's *The New Testament Doctrine of the Last Things* and the *IDB*.]

Some characters in the New Testament's eschatology are thoroughly Hebraic-Jewish. All the Egyptian and Persian contributions to eschatology had been already absorbed into Jewish apocalypticism before the Christian era. Even Paul and John did not draw very much from outside this framework.

The Synoptics and Jesus: Central to their eschatology is the concept of the kingdom of God. It is at once a present reality and a future expectation (Mk 1:14-15; Lk 7:22 (Q) Luke 4:18ff (L) and Matt 4:23(M). It is now at work. "The Kingdom of God is in the midst of you" Lk 17:21. It "is to come" Mk 13:32; Lk 10:12 (Q). Christ is the one who will bring about and has brought about this reality. He is the mediator of the new kingdom (Mk 8:31-33 10:35-45). The twelve were to be the prophetic remnant to bring about the new people of God. The Son of Man has its background in Is 53 and His function as mediator of the kingdom. Some think that Jesus specified that the day of Yahweh would come during His lifetime (Mk 9:1; 13:26 14:62), but these passages are capable of other interpretations. It ignores the fact that Jesus worked so hard to train His disciples. More likely, Jesus never concerned Himself with the times and the seasons (Mk 13:32-37; Lk 12:39-40; Mat 24:43,4; (Q) Lk 21:35-36). The end would come suddenly without warning. The little apocalypse (Mk 13:1-31) really refutes the expectations of those who are hoping for signs.

Luke seems to tone down Mark's eschatology by omissions and alterations. (See Huck's Synopsis on Mark 8:38; 9:1; 13:4, 14). The eschatological event has been treated historically. For example the Fall of Jerusalem is already past. However, Matthew has the opposite tendency. (See the parallel passages). He is more definite, plainer, adds the parousia, and the consummation of the age. These last ideas are his favorite keynotes.

This makes many things look like the final events of the age. The ascending order of eschatological awareness is Luke, Q, Mark, Matthew. Guy feels that much of the eschatological significance of Jesus' words has been added. The earliest traditions (see Dibélius) do not emphasize this aspect of the teachings.

Christ emphasized the universal character of the kingdom in contrast to much Jewish teachings of the time (Mk 7:26ff; Lk 7:2; Matt 8: 43). He often pointed out the difference between this age and the age to come, as did the Jews of His time (Mk 10:30). He referred to the judgment (Mat 12:36) and assumed a resurrection from the dead (Mk 12:25f). He emphasizes the possibility of reward after this life (Mk 10:21; Lk 6:23) as well as loss (Matt 25:41-46). The passages on everlasting punishment all occur in Matthew (3:29; 5:26; 9:48). There appears even to be the possibility of universalism (Matt 5:26), though it seems unlikely.

In the coming judgment everything will be made clear (Matt 10:26-33; Lk 12:2,12 see also Paul I Cor. 3:13). Only a few will be saved (Lk 13:22ff), and these are the elect (Mk 13:22), the righteous (Matt 25:34). There seems to be a contradiction, some say, between the twelve thrones of the apostles (Matt 19:28; Lk 22:28) and Mark 10:35-45 where Jesus says he cannot assign places of honor.

Abraham's bosom can be defined as "the place the good go at the moment of death" (IDB), where a preliminary judgment occurs. It is the opposite of sheol (Hades) in the parable of the rich man and Lazarus (Lk 16:22ff). This concept of a divided Hades developed just prior to the New Testament era (Enoch) "Rabbinic Judaism sometimes spoke of a rest in Abraham's bosom in relation to the meal of the blessed in the world to come" (IDB, p. 22). Compare Luther, who came to a similar conclusion without Strack, Billerbeck. This connection stresses fellowship with the faithful.

Hades, in the New Testament, is invariably the abode of the dead. Only in the Lazarus story does someone suffer therein. Usually suffering takes place elsewhere. Hades is the N.T.'s counterpart to sheol and its name the LXX uses to translate that Hebrew word.

Gehenna is the Greek and Latin form of the Valley of Hinnom, where children were burnt as offerings to idols (see II Chr. 28:3 et al.). Later, it meant a place of "fiery torment," either after death or after the last judgment. The Iranian concept of a fiery hell begins to influence the Jewish concept of the afterlife in the Greco-Roman period, but nowhere in the Apocrypha is this place called Gehenna. That name first appears in the New Testament. There, Gehenna is identical with the lake of fire into which Hades will be cast on the last day (Revel. 20:14). (Matt 5:22, 29; 10:28; 18:9; 23:15, 33; Mk 9:43, 45, 45,; Li 12:5 Jas 3:6).

Paradise occurs three times in the New Testament and means "the Garden of Eden and the abode of the righteous after death" (Lk 23:43; II Cor. 12:3; Rev 2:7). The LXX had used it. It correspondes to Gehenna, and had three meanings: a) the Garden of Eden in Genesis, b) the abode of the dead prior to resurrection, c) the eternal home of the righteous. Note also the use of a tree in connection with Gehenna's appearance in Rev 2:7. Perhaps Jesus or Luke assumed entrance of the righteous into the paradise in Lazarus's story. Intriguing, too, is the use in Paul (II Cor 2:1-4). This passage seems to assume all the righteous are with the Lord in paradise. In this connection see II Cor. 5:8 and Phil 1:23), but at an earlier stage, Paul seemed to believe the dead would not be united with the Lord until the parousia. Rev 2:7 uses the word in such a way as to suggest it comes into existence at the resurrection. However 6:9-11 and 7:9-17 appear to assume some of dead at least are in a heavenly abode before the resurrection. Thus it seems that beliefs were still in transition in the New Testament period. Much of the language is of course symbolic; one thing, however, is sure: the life after death will be with Christ (Jn 12:26; 14:2,3; 18ff; 16:16ff; Acts 7:59; Rom 6:8-11; 8:17ff; II Cor. 4:14 5:8; Phil 1:21ff; I Jn 2:28; 3:2; Rev 7:17; 20:4; 21:23ff; 22:3ff).

The second coming does not seem to occur in Scripture, but *parousia* does. It became the continuation of the Old Testament hope in the Day of Yahweh. (See in this connection the many references to day of the Lord). Even the use of "revelation" is eschatological in seven of the eighteen instances in which it appears in the New Testament. Likewise "epiphany" (II Thess. 2:8; I Tim 6:14). The N.T. writers in general expected an imminent return. The books that make no mention of parousia are II and III John, Philemon, Galatians, Ephesians. II Peter implies a skepticism.

Christ's descent into hell can be seen as a reflection of the sheol concept of the Old Testament.

The second death is the opposite of the crown of life given to those martyrs. Death and Hades experience this second death (Rev 2:14) with those whose names are not in the book of life (15). This concept is found only in Revelation, as the "lake that burns with fire and brimstone" (Rev 21:8; 20:14).

The *millennium* can be defined as the thousand-year reign of Christ with certain resurrected martyrs. Taken literally, Rev 20:4-6 would mean in the view of some that certain martyrs who refused to worship the

Roman emperor would be resurrected for the millennium (and only these). Revelation's author seems to believe that the millennium was to begin about three and one half years after his prediction. Thus, it would have ended about 1100 AD. There are many other parallels outside Christianity of similar beliefs, but nowhere in the New Testament except in I Cor. 15:23-28 can we find such a concept. There, Paul says that Christ will rule after the resurrection until all the enemies, including death, are abolished. The resurrection of Jesus Christ is not "typical" and is not to be connected in a class with other expectations in the Old or New Testaments. J.A.T. Robinson asserts, "Nowhere in the NT is the resurrection hope deduced from the resurrection of Christ, as if His survival of death were the supreme instance that proved or guaranteed eternal life for others. We are included in His resurrection" (I Cor. 15:22). Mark 12:26-27, "God is not a God of the dead, but of the living," forms the basis of the New Testament hope, just as it pointed the way out of the endless sheol of the Old Testament. In fact, in the resurrection body of Christ the New Testament nowhere sees a type or pledge of our own. Paul does not seem to say that our resurrection body will be like his. Christ is unique Col 1:18.

The noun "anastasis" is never used of other raisings from the dead. Even in the Lazarus story it is used for the general resurrection or by Jesus for himself John 11:24, 25. Those, however, who teach only a realized eschatology are condemned (II Tim 2:18). The Holy Spirit is the link between our resurrection and Christ's, and between our present and future state (II Cor. 5:4-5; I Cor. 15:51ff). Already we are being changed "into His likeness" (II Cor. 3:18). This begins in our baptism (Rom 7:4).

The resurrection body cannot be flesh and blood (I Cor. 15:50). No N.T. writer speaks of the resurrection of the flesh, but only of the resurrection of the body. (I Cor. 15:44). Paul does not discuss the resurrection body of any but those who belong in Christ (I Cor. 15:23). There is a discontinuity of form between our present and our future body (I Cor. 15:36ff). Paul speaks to a situation in which he believes only a minority of Christians will need to be raised from the dead. His focus is the parousia rather than the raising of the dead. It appears that Paul stresses only the resurrection of those who belong to Christ (I Cor. 15:23; I Thess. 4:16). Paul does not seem to connect this resurrection with the general resurrection of the just and unjust (Acts 24:15). Only the writer of Revelation posits two resurrections (Rev 20:4-5), separated by one thousand years. Other writers mention only a single resurrection, for believers and unbelievers, on the last day (John 5:28ff, 6:39ff; 11:24; Lk 14:14).

Finally, as to *universalism*: The New Testament can be seen to give two answers. Some passages appear to posit that all men will eventually be saved (Jn. 12:32; Rom 11:32; I Cor. 15:28 Phil 2:10ff; Lk 15:4). However, these may refer only to a universal *offer* of grace (Matt 12:32; Matt 9:47ff; Matt 25:46ff). There are also those passages which tend to favor annihilationism, the complete destruction of the evil (Luke 20:35; Phil 3:11; I Jn 2:17; Matt 13:40; II Thess. 1:8ff; Jn 15:6). And finally there are passages favoring a twofold division: heaven and hell. We must deny a twofold resurrection—for life and for judgment (John 5:23ff).

Something of a harmony can be inferred in the view that after death the final decision has been made, whether we are with Christ or separated from Him. We (as persons) remain in the grave (sheol of the Old Testament) and divided into Hades and paradise (or the bosom of Abraham in the New Testament), having a foretaste of the real heaven and perhaps the real hell— which only come about after the resurrection and second coming. The dead are with God, for God is everywhere, even in sheol. They are asleep but in Christ.

Bibliography:

Guy, H.A. *The New Testament Doctrine of the Last Things.* London: Oxford Press, 1948.

The Interpreter's Dictionary of the Bible.

Schoeps, H.J. *Paul.* trans by Harold Knight. Phil.: Westminster, 1959.

Strawson, William. *Jesus and the Future Life.* Phil.: Westminster, 1959.

Cullman, O. *Immortality of the Soul or Resurrection of the Dead.* London: 1958.

III

ESCHATOLOGY OF THE EARLY CHURCH

JUDGMENT for Justin seems to be a particular judgment that occurs at death and assigns the soul to any of several places of waiting, more or less comfortable. It does not preempt or preclude the general judgment. The general judgment occurs after the RESURRECTION. Methodius posits that the soul is a corporeal substance and needs to be raised like the body. Jerome stresses the identical character of the resurrection body with the natural body, which we have now in contrast with Origen's idea of similarity only of form. He says our bodies will be spiritual but may not have the same form. In fact people may rise with spherical forms. Ambrose agrees that the body will be spiritualized, but Gregory of Nyssa affirms that our body will be restored to its primitive state (like those of Adam and Eve) —probably to make it feel at home in paradise, which for some is the second garden of Eden. Augustine, in a pastoral note, stresses that the ugliness and deformity will disappear, and the body will be perfect on that day. Those who died in childhood will be raised as adults.

Origen intellectualizes HEAVEN and portrays it in mystical terms. Theodoret and the Latin fathers (Hilary, Ambrose) believe in a gradual progression and a graded blessedness, and Augustine reiterates a theme that will recur again and again in the history of thought about heaven: In heaven, our chief end is the praise of God.

The writer of the *Didache* appears to restrict the resurrection to the good, but most writers in the early church assure us that all will rise. Generally, the early fathers see the resurrection as general—to come just before the parousia. Some, though, believe in an individual judgment immediately after death. Clement says that Peter and Paul and other saints went straight to the holy place. The elders assume that Polycarp has already received the crown of immortality. Generally, the early fathers were on guard against the platonic notion of the immortality of the soul.

HELL was agreed to be eternal, with no end. Gregory of Nyssa, however, wonders whether the idea of eternal punishment might be less than worthy of God. He was, in this as in other things, influenced by Origen.

In the West, Hilary affirmed eternal fire, while Ambrosiaster taught that Christians who have fallen away will eventually be saved (so too say Jerome and Ambrose). Augustine believes in eternal damnation in real fire, but offers the consolation that some may attain pardon. Origen spiritualizes the sufferings and predicts an end to hell. The end of the cosmic evolution will be the same as the beginning. Even the devil will be saved. Hell is distinct from purgatory, but Arnobius, perhaps Justin, Gregory of Nyssa, perhaps Theodore of Mopsuestia, and Diodorus of Tarsus all believed in a termination of punishment. The majority believed it, all the same, that it would be endless.

Cerinthus, Papias, Justin Martyr, Irenaeus, Tertullian, Montanus, Hippolytus, and Lactantius all believed in the MILLENIUM. Some were more "crass" than others. Origen allegorized the millennium: It will be a spiritual kingdom. So did Augustine, who thought the thousand-year reign to be the Christian church. In this connection, it is interesting to note that the Gnostics were against the idea, if not the prospect. Barnabas was one of the first to use see in the six days of creation a clue to the timing of the parousia.

PURGATORY can be seen to begin with Augustine, although the way was prepared for it by prayers for the dead souls (*Civitate Dei* XXI c 13, 24, 26), and by the purifying fire of the intermediate state of Lactantius. It is thought to be certain by Caesarius of Arles (*Homil* VIII) and Gregory the Great (*Dialog Lib* IV c 39f).

The INTERMEDIATE STATE is portrayed with fascinating variety. Ireneaus criticized the Gnostics for their idea that the soul passes to heaven immediately after death. Rather, he says Christians go to an invisible place designated for them. Only the martyrs are excused from the place of waiting. Tertullian agrees and posits a place very much like the sheol of the Old Testament. In any case, each soul receives a foretaste of its final goal. Cyril posits an immediate entry of the soul into heaven or hell. Chrysostom holds to two moments of divine retribution, at death and at the resurrection. Hilary harkens back to the Abraham's bosom concept, in which the righteous rest but the wicked begin to pay for their deeds. Ambrose believes there are storehouses where souls await doom and receive a foretaste of their ultimate states.

In this connection the opinion of Pope John the XXII is of interest. He revived the opinion that saints are not admitted to the vision of God immediately upon death, but only at the resurrection. However, the Franciscans and the Parisian divines made him retract his statement. The Greek church has continued to believe that the fire begins only at the general judgment, not in an intermediate state or after death.

Kelly, J.N.D. *Early Christian Doctrines*, pp. 459=490.
Muenscher, W. *Elements of Dogmatic History* New Haven: 1830.

IV

MEDIEVAL ESCHATOLOGY

(Some of the following is included also in the previous chapter, Chapter Fourteen, to show the sweep of the argument from the earliest Old Testament times to the later theologians of orthodoxy.)

[Since Thomas Aquinas put forward the most developed system, his position will be presented, and as other medieval theologians supplement it, their views will be appended.]

Thomas based his eschatological thought on the dualistic concept of death as the separation of the soul from the body, and recognized two types of death: that of the body is the separation of the soul therefrom; that of the soul is its separation from God. (Interconnected with this dual death is a dual resurrection: the resurrection of the body occurs when the soul rejoins the body, and the resurrection of the soul occurs when the soul is reunited with God (*Comp. Theol.* 239).

Purgatory Aquinas also takes for granted, offering a few practical ramifications of the doctrine. "We should also come to the assistance of our friends who are in purgatory." He stresses the great difference in pains known in this world and in the next. The three measures to bring relief to souls in purgatory are masses, prayers and alms, but fourth, fasting, is added (*Exposition of the Apostle's Creed*).

Judgment occurs after a man has "run his course." Until then no final judgment can be made. Men live on a) in the memories of others and in our reputation for good or ill; b) in our children who are part of us; c) in the results of our actions; d) in the body, which eventually crumbles into dust; e) in the projects in which we had set our hearts, and f) in the soul. All of the above are submitted to the final judgment and are taken into consideration "when everything whatsoever about a man will be manifestly displayed" (*Summa Theologica*, 3a, lix 5). Christ will judge us in His human nature, for to gaze on divinity is a reward. There is also a certain amount of poetic justice in that He who was unjustly punished (condemned) is lifted up to judge the living and the dead (*Compendium Theologiae* 141).

The resurrection of the body is duly stressed and "proven." However, he condemns those who feel that the soul can have no function apart from the body (*Disputations, De Anima*, 14). Our present body will rise and this is supported by "sound reasons." The human soul is immortal, but without the body it is an unnatural condition and what is unnatural can "not go on forever." "The soul's immortality, therefore, seems to demand the eventual resurrection of the body." Another proof for the resurrection inheres in the natural human drive toward happiness, "man's ultimate completion." "Everything made to be perfect desires to be perfect, and a disembodied soul is to that extent incomplete; it is a part out of its whole." We won't have final perfection until our soul quickens our body. In this life perfect happiness is impossible. Therefore, "human completion requires the resurrection of the body."

Finally, he argues the point from the justice of the universe. Wrongdoers must be punished and welldoers must be rewarded. Because the people who performed these acts were flesh and blood, the reward or punishment must also affect their bodily as well as their spiritual lives. Seldom are the scales equalized in this life, and it is sound that the human be "fitly punished and rewarded" (III *Contra Gentes* 79).

The *Compendium Theologiae* (151) adds other "proofs" for the resurrection in a similar vein. "Our wills cannot be quite at peace until our natural appetites are altogether satisfied." The soul has a natural desire to be reunited with the body. Likewise, to achieve ultimate fulfillment the soul must be complete. "Therefore, it must be combined with the body." "What is adventitious and unnatural is not perpetual."

He insists that the humans who rise are identical to those who lived before, "though their vital processes are performed in a different way." However, we are not to understand the resurrection as designed to perpetuate the human species, "for this could be accomplished by "interminable generation." The purpose of the resurrection is rather to perpetuate the individual!

To cover every possibility, Aquinas posits that "even though men were to die again after the resurrection, they would still not remain forever without their bodies." The bodies would rise again, and die, and rise again and so forth, so necessary is the doctrine of the resurrection. Thus Thomas is fairly certain that the more reasonable premise is that "the first resurrection is final."

The bodies we assume are *neither* a heavenly *nor* ghostly kind of body; the material is not altered. Their immortality comes from a divine strength that "enables the soul so to dominate the body (the human body) that corruption cannot enter" (*Compend. Theol.* 155).

Because the soul is the "substantial form of body and its active moving principle," it is the soul that gives the body its "substantial reality" and it is the "principle of the proper characteristics that follow from its union with the body." When the body is entirely possessed by the soul, it will be fine and spirited. It will be noble, beautiful, invulnerable, lissome, agile, radiant, and will be entirely like an instrument 'in the hands of a skilled player.'" He quotes I Cor. 15:42-44 to prove much of the above (*Compend. Theol.* 168).

In Christ's transfiguration we have a type of the resurrected body (Phil 3: 22): the "light-footedness" as when he walked on the waves, the "delicacy" as when He did not break open the Virgin's womb, the "invulnerability as when he escaped unhurt from the Jews who wished to stone Him are also types of the soul and body after the resurrection" (*Summa Theol.* 3 a XLV i, Ad 3).

The resurrected humans will live in a *new heaven and earth* in a city "that lieth four square." "Whatsoever can make us joyful, it is there in heaven, and superabundantly" (honor, knowledge, security, companionship, quoting Job 22:26 in the *Exposition on the Apostle's Creed*).

The angels also can be compared to the resurrected human beings. "With respect to God's love and grace and glory, some angels will be mightier than human beings, and some human beings will be enthroned above the angels." Nonetheless, angelic nature is superior to human nature (*Summa Theol.* I a XX 4, Ad 2).

V

LUTHER ON ESCHATOLOGY

(Parts of this chapter repeat sections of Chapter Fourteen to continue the
"sweep" of how the eschatological doctrines evolved through the centuries.)

At the time of this writing [mid-1960s], there has appeared no adequate
study of Luther's eschatology, putting his thought, rendered in English,
into a context of the Old and New Testament and the history of the church
until his time. It is true that he developed few distinctive eschatological
ideas, and his principle achievement in this area seemed to be a negative,
the denial of purgatory. However, it can be demonstrated that eschatology
is an important theme running through most of his writings. Luther in fact
termed eschatology the chief end of Christian preaching:

> Whatever we teach, appoint, or establish is done to the end that
> the pious may look forward to the coming of their Saviour on
> the last day (Erl Ed. xxii, 12).

Most of his eschatology can be attributed to his own attitude (and
that of many others of the time) that the 16th century was the last times,
and the dominating principle that eschatology must always be seen and
understood in the framework of the "*Evangelische Ansatz.*"

Luther took the conservative approach to the intermediate state. There
are a great many references to the last times in Holy Scripture, but he saw
that there were almost none referring to the time between the death of the
individual and the last day.[1]

Luther views the intermediate state as a kind of sleep in which actual
consciousness has ceased, and the dead will not know they have passed
through death, but they are in a "blissful" sleep, but will think they "have
been asleep only an hour." Although the dead will not have consciousness
of its "life" or "faculties," they will "gain, view, and hear conversations of the
angels and of God, in whose presence they live." In other words, the sleep
will be like a trance (Cf. WA 17:11 w 35 17ff; 36, 252, 10; 37, 149-151; 43
359ff, 480f; and the Erl. Ed. vi: 116-124, 329. also X, 75; xi 141ff; xli 373;
xiv 315). He espouses these views also in his Latin *Commentary on Genesis.*

On the "locality" of this intermediate state, Luther only states that,

> The soul goes to its place, whatever kind of a place that may be, for it cannot be corporeal: it is a sort of sepulcher of the soul, outside of this corporeal world.

In the same vein he writes,

> What paradise is, I do not know. It is enough for us to believe that God has a place where He perhaps preserves also the angels. Things are not as they are here. (Erl Ed. XXI 193ff; xxxiii, 156).

Both statements (and for that matter most of his eschatological remarks) have rich overtones of Old Testament theology. Usually, the Christian church has neglected (or ignored) the Old Testament statements on eschatology, but Luther took them seriously. He thus is able to describe sheol in his *Ennarratio* of Psalm xvi of 1530 as, "Everything that there is in the existence upon which we enter after life" which includes the "fire" of the rich man, and the "bosom of Abraham" (Erl. Ed xvii, 125ff; xli, 378; x 206ff.) Strongly reminiscent of the Old Testament are such statements as the "grave of souls" and the "promises in which we fall asleep" (Erl Ed x 208, xi 302, vi 121). There is no dogmatism in his views, however, except where they explicitly deny a fundamental article of the Roman Catholic church (such as purgatory).

Purgatory fails because it conflicts with the doctrine of justification by faith. His "doctrine" of the intermediate state can be seen to have originated in the discarded doctrine of purgatory. "The final decision on salvation has already been made." Early in his career, he could say,

> I have never yet denied that there is a purgatory, and I still hold that there is, as I have many times written and confessed, though I have no way of proving it incontrovertibly, either by Scripture or reason. I find in the Scriptures, indeed, that Christ, Abraham, Jacob, Moses, Job, David, Hezekiah, and many others tasted hell in this life. This I think to be purgatory, and it is not incredible that some of the dead suffer in like manner. Tauler has much to say about it, and in a word, I have decided for myself that there

> is a purgatory, but cannot force any others to the same decision (*Brief,* Jan 13 1529 to Amsdorf).

He could not countenance a view that understood purgatory to be a place of development as though salvation was not sufficient, but as a place of purgation for those saved by grace, perhaps!

Luther was driven to this mediating position by the many problems involved, such as those who died without faith. God could save them after death, but does He? (WA 10, II 325, 3). At any rate, he hoped God would be gracious to Cicero (Tisch. 3925). Naturally, masses, good works, or prayers meant to influence the fate of the dead are likewise rejected. He does allow a short prayer of intercession for them recommending them to the mercy of God (Confession of 1528).

He posits that the majority of the dead are in the intermediate state, but does not venture to regard this sleep as universal.[2] Because scripture presents varying, attitudes toward life after death, Luther is constrained to do likewise.

Connected with his feeling that the last times are "now," Luther's interpretation of the political and ecclesiastical situation of the times led him to connect scripture's picture of the last times with current phenomena (Tischr 4979, 5130, 5239, 5488, 6984). When an astronomer predicted a great flood for 1524, Luther hoped that this was a sign of the second coming.[3] In the beginning of his *Church Postils* Luther looked for the conjunction of the planets scheduled to occur in 1524 as another sign of that day, but warns against a too-precise reckoning. A fascinating bit of Luther lore occurs in the *Supputatio Annorm Mundi*. Luther there calculated the end of the world by asserting that the year 1540 AD corresponded to the year 5550 after Creation. Using Patristic logic, Luther then posited that as there were six days of creation and the seventh of rest, and a day was as a thousand years, therefore in the year 6000 after creation (or about 2000 AD), God would bring creation to an end. This work was printed in 1541 and reissued in 1545. Any discerning reader might ask, did not Luther realize he was five hundred years off? Luther replied that the Lord promised to shorten the days for the sake of the elect, and, therefore, the day could come at any time.

Luther looked to Daniel and the book of the Revelation of St John for material on signs of His coming. For example, in Daniel the end of the fourth world kingdom is interpreted by Luther to mean the end of the Roman Empire, and the Antichrist (the Turk) is to overthrow the third of ten horns (rulers) of the Roman empire (Erl Ed, xli 233, 243sqq; xxxi 83 ff).

Luther did the same with Revelation. The thousand years mentioned therein he counts either from the date of the book itself or from the birth of Christ. It is not necessary to be minute, but he sees God and Magog as possibly the Turk. The luxury and signs in the heavens are signs of that day (Jena iv 741). In conjunction with his thoughts on the last day and occurrences connected with it, he hoped for a general conversion of the Jews (Erl Ed. x 231ff), but later in his writings we find no such references but rather disillusionment with and antipathy toward the chosen people.

As to the *millennium*, Luther expressed varying views on it, but none approximated Chiliasm and Jewish hopes. For example, Luther said that the one thousand years mentioned in Revelation represent the thousand years Satan is bound, which corresponds to the first thousand years of church history, during which time the church was comparatively free of heresies. Satan is released in the form of the Antichrist (the Pope) and the nations Gog and Magog (the Turks) (*Brief.* March 7, 1529 to W. Link; Oct 26, 1529 to N. Hausmann; Nov 10, 1529 to J. Probst). The new world is to be brought about by the action of Christ and not by human development or force. We will always have strife on that day (Erl Ed XI 85; xlv 110 sq).

In his sermons and writings, Luther described that day and the last judgment with biblical expressions (the last trumpet, Christ coming in the clouds), but he adds, "These are only allegorical words . . . as we have to picture it for children and simple folk" (WA 10 I (2) 93-120 and Erl Ed. xix, 153ff; xviii 342ff.). The believers will meet the Lord in the air "and unite with Him in passing judgment on the wicked" (Erl Ed xxx 372; xix 345). We will look on the naked Godhead, no longer enshrouded with words (Erl Ed xxxii 307).

After the resurrection, the "places" heaven and hell become a reality. Paradise is a condition, not a place (Erl Ed. i, 110ff). Abraham's bosom means that the dead were asleep in faith and are embraced and preserved in the word of God (Erl Ed xiii, 10; xviii, 266 and vi 116;). The hell of Dives was an evil conscience (Erl Ed xiii, 11; xviii 267). After the resurrection, we will be exempted from places and times (Erl Ed xxi 199). The body is still the body, however, even though it is above limitations. The distinction of sexes is perpetuated, but the form of the body will be transformed and made beautiful, healthy, not weary, perfect (Erl Ed xix 133f; iv 2, 411; xviii 346). Our bodies will be able to pass quickly from place to place. Our eyes will be able to look through mountains. Our ears will be able to hear from one end of the world to the other. We will then travel like a flash (Erl Ed iv 2ff; xix 135; li 183). Christ attests our resurrection by His own. We will "no longer be subject to disease and pain, to the limitations of time and place, no longer perishable and changeable. But everyone will have his own body, a spiritual body as described in I Cor 15" (Large Catechism).[4]

The whole world will be transformed by fire, and the sun will then shine seven times more brightly than it does now. Everything will be more beautiful. The moon will then be as bright as the sun is now. "Now heaven and earth wear their working clothes, but then they will be in their Sunday clothes" (to his son Hans, Brief June 19, 1530). There will even be "new animals" with golden hair (Erl Ed. x 74; xxxix 35; li 243; lx 106; *Tischr* lv 289ff). We will live on the earth (lII 270; xxxix 37ff).

However, these comforting words on "heaven" should not mislead anyone as to Luther's eschatology. As early as 1523 he disagreed with those who thought that hell was too harsh a doctrine. He does say that God is even in hell and that the ungodly are punished only by their own consciences, but he warns against further prying (Brief ii 453ff; Erl Ed xxx 372; Jena iv 482; xxxiv 207; Erl Ed v 179; xxxiv 207). For the ungodly, the greatest "pain consists in the feeling of God's wrath and the knowledge of being separated from Him"(*Tischr*. 6982). In his Latin commentary on Genesis, Luther won't take a position or express a positive opinion as to whether the torments of hell begin at once after death or after the judgment. He says this should be left to God (Er. Ed xiii 22; vi 122, 124; x 208 213).

There is no doubt that the Anabaptist excesses led Luther to tread lightly on so controversial a subject. After 1530, his interest in eschatology is more notable and taken in conjunction with his statement that the world could not last much beyond 1550, one could say that it did not, for Luther died in 1543. The world ended for him, and perhaps as he grew older, this nearness to death influenced his interest.

Perhaps more than any other man of the Middle Ages, he had the eschatological gift. He knew where to speak and when to keep silent. In view of the "after death" excesses which preceded him and surrounded him, Luther stands out refreshingly not only in the New Testament tradition, but more important as a synthesizer of the Old and New Testament views.

Endnotes:

[1] Kramm, H.H. *The Theology of Martin Luther.* London: James Clarke, 1947, pp103, 104.
[2] Köstlin, Julius, *The Theology of Luther.* Vol II, Philadelphia: Lutheran Publishing Society, 1897, p. 471
[3] Kramm, p.103.
[4] Kramm, pp. 659, 1007.

Other sources:

Watson, Philip.   *Let God be God*

Althaus, Paul.   *Die Letzten Dinge.* Gutersloh: Bertelsmann, 1949.

Rupp, Gordon.   *The Righteousness of God.* London: Hodder and Stoughton, 1953.

Hall, George.   "Luther's Eschatology," in *Augustana Quart.*, Vol 23, 1943 Rock Island: Aug. Book Concern. Pp. 13-21.

VI

PRE-CONFESSIONAL STATEMENTS ON ESCHATOLOGY AND ECK'S *404 THESES*

(Again sections of these last parts of this chapter are also included in Chapter Fourteen of this volume to give a fuller picture of the development of this doctrine.)

The *Schwabach Articles* of 1529 and *The Marburg Confession* along with Luther's Confession of 1528 form the basis for this pre-confessional study.

Perhaps, the majority of eschatological references of these pre-confessional documents reiterate the Catholic position of the evangelicals. For example Luther asserts that "outside this Christendom there is no salvation nor forgiveness of sins, but everlasting death and damnation" (p. 29), thus stressing the crucial character of Christianity in eschatology. All his doctrine he realizes will be judged in the light of the last judgment and so even "teachings" take an eschatological character. He realizes "full well what it will mean (for (him) upon the return of the lord Jesus Christ at the last judgment" (p. 24).

The *Schwabach Articles* in Article XIII repeat the Catholic creedal stand,

> That the Lord Jesus Christ will come at the last day to judge the quick and the dead, and to deliver those who believe in Him from all evil, and bring them to everlasting life; and to punish the unbelieving and godless, and to condemn them eternally, with the devil in hell. (p 43)

He thus affirms the traditional belief in heaven, hell, and judgment. This article is intimately connected with civil power in XIV, which begins: " . . . until the Lord come to judgment and will do away with all power and rule, we should honor worldly magistrates and rulers, and be obedient to them."

Marburg includes similar statements, which are also reminiscent of the creeds. "Thirdly . . . will come to judge the quick and the dead.

Fourthly . . . (on account of original sin) we must on that account have died eternally and could not have entered God's kingdom and salvation. Fifthly, we believe that we are delivered from this sin and all other sins, as well as from eternal death, if we believe in this Son of God, Jesus Christ, who died for us . . ." (p 45)

The controversial issues later taken up in the confessions are considered mainly in Luther's Confession of 1528.

> As Scripture mentions nothing about the matter, I do not regard it a sin to pray for the dead, as our devotion may direct, either as follows or in some similar fashion: Dear God, if the soul be in such a state that it may be helped, be gracious to it. etc. And when this has been done once or twice let that suffice. For the vigils and masses for souls and annual requiems are useless and the very devil's auction. Neither is there anything in Scripture concerning *purgatory*, and it has been originated by the hobgoblins, so I hold that it is not necessary to believe anything concerning it, even though all things are possible to God and, if He wished, He could rack *the souls after they have left the body*, but as He has caused nothing to be told or written concerning it, He does not wish to have it believed. I know indeed of another sort of purgatory but this is not a subject for teaching in the congregation nor will pious endowments and vigils avail against it (p 30).

(Luther here is referring probably to the sufferings in this life.) He strongly emphasizes the finality of death, the nonexistence of purgatory, and suggests the body/soul dualism. However, also important is the relative paucity of eschatological comment and speculation in these quasi-confessional statements.

Eck's *404 Theses* had a conjunctive influence on the Lutheran confessions, if only a negative one. A random sampling of Eck's citations of eschatological "tidbits" which he said he found in the writings of Luther and the Lutheran reformers reveals the usual mixture of truth and error in Eck.

Thesis: 37:   Purgatory cannot be proved from the canonical scriptures (Luther)

39:     Souls in purgatory sin without intermission, as long as they seek rest and dread punishments.

40:     Souls delivered from purgatory by the intercession of the living have less happiness than if they had made satisfaction of themselves.

(Eck, however, counters with his own thoughts on the subject at Baden.)

56:     They (the true body and blood of Christ) are truly offered in the office of the Mass for the living and the dead.

57:     We ought to invoke Mary and the saints as intercessors.

59:     After this life there is a purgatorial fire.

(He continues with the "errors" of the Lutherans.)

113.   Prayers to the saints for avoiding any temporal evil are to be shunned since they cannot aid us (Melanchthon).

114:    Only through Christ do we have access to God; accordingly, confidence in the saints falls.

123:    Since the ascension of Christ, no one has gone to heaven or will go until the end of the world (Luther).

149:    Christ descended ad infernos not to a *limbus patrum*, a term unknown in the Holy Scriptures, but truly to hell, in order to see all places full of despair (Bugenhagen)

150:    That the fathers in the Old Testament descended to hell is fictitious. (Haller)

151:    Abraham's bosom is nothing but the word of God (Luther)

326:    We have no command to pray for the dead. You may, therefore, pray once or twice for a dead person, but afterwards, cease lest you tempt God or distrust him (Luther).

The quotations from pre-confessional sources are from the *Collection of Sources, Augsburg Confession.* St. Louis: Concordia Seminary Print Shop.

"An English Translation of the 404 Theses", by H.E. Jacobs, pp. 37-85. *Papers of the Amer. Soc. of Church History.* Second Series, Vol I Ed. by S. Jackson, 1910, New York: Putnam and Sons, N.Y.

VII

THE ESCHATOLOGY OF THE LUTHERAN CONFESSIONS

The Confessions speak of three kinds of death: the *spiritual*, the *physical*, and the *eternal death*. Physical death is not dealt with at any length (cf. Ap. IV 302 and XII 153). Luther, like the writers of the Old Testament, saw that evil people rarely died a proper or a timely death, but this thought, too, is little treated (LC I, iv 137).

The last times, "they are now" (Ap. XII: 126; AC XXIII, 14; Ap XXIII 53). This is said not only in view of the eschatology which continually breaks into the life of a Christian due to the forgiveness of sins, excommunication, the Sacraments, the preaching of the law and Gospel, and death, but the confessors noted signs of the times which denoted these as "the last times." "Sins and vices are not decreasing but increasing daily." (Ap. xxiii, 53). "We see that these are the last times, and just as an old man is weaker than a young man, so the whole world and nature is in its last stage and is fading" (Ap. XXIII, 53). The church is also in a poor state. The Smalcald Articles end with the prayer, "O dear Lord Jesus Christ, invoke a council yourself and deliver your servants through your glorious advent." (Note in this connection SA II, iv 15 for the urgency of these last times and their effect on sound doctrine.) The second coming was often invoked as it was in Luther's Confession, "This is our faith, doctrine and confession, in which we are also willing, by God's grace, to appear with intrepid hearts, before the judgment seat of Christ and give an account of it" (S.D. VII 31, 29, 40, also Melanchthon's *Erster Entwurf fuer den Beschluss*, and Ap. XXVIII 5, AP XI 124).

Also significant for an introduction to the eschatology of the Lutheran confessions is their "realized eschatology," as it were.

> The Gospel (which is preached in the church) brings not merely the shadow of eternal things, but the eternal things themselves.... But every true Christian is even here upon earth a partaker of eternal blessings, even of eternal comfort, of eternal life, and of the Holy Spirit and righteousness which is from God, until he will be completely saved in the world to come (Ap. VII 15).

The urgency of the last times and the realization even here and now provide the framework and the working principle of any approach to the confession's eschatology.

Because the church of the Augsburg Confession considered itself a Catholic Church, the creeds are reaffirmed and provide the "*Grundbekenntnis.*"

To be complete, these creedal statements should be summarized. The Apostle's Creed affirms the eschatological doctrines, "He descended into hell, He ascended into heaven, thence He shall come to judge the living and the dead, and the resurrection of the body and the life everlasting." A historical study of the "descent" should prove that Christ did not *necessarily* descend to a "place." The heaven to which He ascended was not a spatial heaven but in the skies, at the right hand of God. Hell, likewise, was not a place but a banishment from God and His sight. However, there can be no doubt on the resurrection of the body and everlasting life.

The Nicene Creed affirms in a similar manner,

> He ascended into heaven, He shall come again with glory to judge both the living and the dead, and His kingdom shall have no end . . . and I look for the resurrection of the dead and the life of the world to come.

Here again the judgment, the everlasting kingdom, the resurrection are affirmed.

The Athanasian Creed adds a few concepts:

> He descended into hell, ascended into heaven, whence He shall come to judge the living and the dead. At His coming all men shall rise with their bodies and give an account of their own deeds. Those who have done good will enter eternal life, and those who have done evil will go into everlasting fire.

The concept fire, criteria of judgment and the giving account "of their own deeds" are added to the affirmations of the other creeds.

To be complete the other articles in which these creeds and similar statements are reaffirmed are listed: SC, second article and the LC. SA lists the three creeds and states that Christ will come I, iv; "These articles are not in dispute" (*cf* AC III: 4,5,6).

The only article which deals exclusively with eschatology in the confessions is AC XVII.

> It is also taught among us that our Lord Jesus Christ will return on the last day for judgment and will raise up all the dead, to give eternal life and everlasting joy to believers and the elect but to condemn ungodly men and the devil to hell and eternal punishment.
>
> Rejected, therefore, are the Anabaptists who teach that the devil and condemned men will not suffer eternal pain and torment.
>
> Rejected, too, are certain Jewish opinions which are even now making an appearance and which teach that, before the resurrection of the dead, saints and godly men will possess a worldly kingdom and annihilate all the godless. (The Latin is similar in meaning differing only in wording.)

The *Roman Confutation* accepted article XVII with no exceptions, and, therefore, the Apology merely reaffirms part of the article,

> There we confess that at the consummation of the world Christ will appear and raise all the dead, granting eternal life and eternal joys to the godly but condemning the ungodly to endless torment with the devil.

As mentioned above, the Christian's life is filled with eschatological events beginning with his baptism (SC IV 2). The Lord's Supper, likewise, is inescapably connected to the last things and to JUDGMENT (SD VII 77; LC VI 22). It can be seen as a medicine (of immortality?) (LC VI 68; and esp. Ep. XI 13 and SD XI 13). Judgment is made whether for life or death (Ep VII 2, 17). However, all history points to the second coming, the judgment. The purpose for which Christ will come will be to judge the living and the dead (AC III and XVII; SA I 4 and the Creeds). There will then be a division made, those who have done good, and those who have done evil. It would seem that this contradicts the Ap. IV, but see part 278. Only faith justifies (Ap. IV 189). Heaven is not gained by works (Ap. IV 195; Ap. XXVII 32) nor through monasticism (Ap. XXVII 21). It would seem that the easiest way to reconcile this seeming contradiction is to invoke the traditional definition of a living faith, showing forth fruits! Every faith will have works to show, and these will be evaluated in the judgment. Both the Solid Declaration (XI 13) and the Ap. (XII 157) mention Christ as the book of life in which Christians are written. He guarantees our salvation. We are not to be misled, however, by the mention of the salvation and destruction of "souls" (Tract 52:3 and SA *Vorrede* 409). *Soul* as defined by Luther (in his explanation of Psalm 16:10 in the *Torgau* which is referred to in Article IX of the Solid Declaration),

> according to the scriptural use of the term, does not mean, as we usually think, a separated essence in distinction to the body, but the entire man, as it is called by the saints of God.

> This judgment will occur after the resurrection as the Small Catechism states, and at the last day He (the Holy Spirit) will raise up me and all the dead, and will give to me and all believers in Christ eternal life, that I might be his own and live under Him in His kingdom and serve Him in everlasting righteousness and blessedness even as he is risen from the dead and lives and reigns to all eternity.

It is Christ's resurrection which guarantees ours. It is the Holy Spirit who raises us according to the Large Catechism, but other statements (*i.e.*, AC Athanasian Creed) seem to predicate the resurrection to Jesus Christ. This is not a contradiction, if we see Christ working through the spirit and the same God doing all works.

In the resurrection the sinful aspects of the flesh will be destroyed and the flesh will come forth in perfect holiness in a new and eternal life (LC iii 57). In the Large Catechism (II 57, 60), Luther criticizes the term "resurrection of the flesh," yet the bodily resurrection is vehemently asserted. As Schlink so aptly notes, all the dead will rise, but only the believers have bodies predicated of them. It is hard to say exactly why this was stated, or whether it was purposeful.

Death destroys the original sin in our nature (Epitome I:10). We will be completely renewed (Ap XII 153). Thus the "substance of our flesh, but without sin shall arise, and . . . in eternal life we shall have and keep precisely this soul, although without sin" (FC:SD I 46ff). We will have a new will (Ep II I). Thus, in the resurrection, the eternal life already begun in us will be brought to completion in our glorified body (LC II ii 57; Ap. VI 56).

In the *life* the believers will be given on the resurrection, the law and the Gospel will no longer be necessary (LC II 57). This is why the Pelagians, Schwenkfelders, and Papists are condemned —for they think that man does not have to wait for Christ's return but can already be perfect (Ep. I 5). The means of grace will also not be needed in life eternal (SDVII 44). We will be made perfect and preserved (LC II iii, 162). We will be peaceful (AP XXIV 60) and eternally rich (LC I iv 164). All our doctrinal and theological problems will be solved (Ep. IX 4). There will be distinctions of glory among the saints in light. (Ap. IV 355)

Hell, unlike the salvation to life, is not further described. Damnation cannot be compelling in its own right, nor divorced from the Gospel. AC 17 affirms that punishment is everlasting. God desires that no one should perish but that all should be saved (SD II 49). God is not the cause for damnation, but sin is. Inherited sin brings about this condemnation (SD XI 81; SD V 23; AC II).

The punishment given in hell is variously described. It is perishing (SD II 58). It is eternal wrath and death (AP IV 161). In addition it is misfortune and heartache (LC I 140). It is eternal anger and condemnation (LC II iii 66). It is like paying God the penalty for a crime (Tract 82). It is an eternal burden on their shoulder (SC *Vorrede* 4). It is a destruction of souls (Tract 48). It is being held in the jaws of hell (Ep. IX 4). It is hellfire (SD V 20). It is an eternal fire (*Quincunque vult*). It is hell's vengeance (LC II ii 30). However, hell is nowhere explicitly defined. Rather, it is viewed as a state of eternal sufferings from which there is no hope of relief. Even the devil can't escape (SC XVII; LC II ii 30). They cannot repent (SD II 22; AC XX). In spite of the Exposition to the Lord's Prayer,

> We pray in the Lord's Prayer that the devil's kingdom may be overthrown, and he may have no right or power over us, until finally the devil's kingdom shall be utterly *destroyed* and sin, death, and hell *exterminated*, that we may live forever . . . .

The confessors made it clear that hell is eternal! It would take considerable eisegesis to prove otherwise. The critique of the Prussian theologians requested that eternal damnation be especially mentioned that "people would know that original sin merits not temporal but also eternal death and condemnation." (S.D.). Schlink says the symbols nowhere consider those who have not heard the Gospel (in relation to hell). However, the heathen, the Turks, the Jews, the false Christians, and the hypocrites stay in eternal anger and condemnation (LC II iii 66).

The "damnamus" clauses would appear not immediately relevant to the question of eternal damnation but only ultimately.

The first of the antitheses of Article XVII can be seen to deal with *annihilationism* and/or UNIVERSALISM. Both these doctrines are disavowed in other articles of the confessions. The confessions are explicit that only those who are elected, called and justified will be saved (SD XI 22,. see also SD XI 5, Ep. XI 9). Also, the confessions, as mentioned under the section dealing with hell, confess eternal damnation (see especially SD I 13 and 19 and notes, also Ap. IV 128). Statements which sound like the evil ones will be annihilated must be seen in the light of the above passages.

The second antithesis deals with the *chiliasts*. Due to the tension of the times, the reformers did not think out chronologies or details of the end. Because of the Anabaptist excesses, they were led to disavow "crassMILLENNIALISM." However, it is to be noted that only *crass* millennialism is to be disavowed and perversions forsaken. The confessions are conservative in their outlook, and thus do not speculate. Notice in this connection that the idea, once espoused by Luther, that all the Jews would be saved or all the world would have heard the Gospel before Christ came, are both omitted from the confessions. It would be an intriguing study to inquire as to whether any concept employed by the writer of Revelation was used by the confessors without verification via another book of Holy Scripture.

The objection to purgatory was not at all that it was an intermediate state, but that it was in contradiction to justification in Christ Jesus. Just as the 39 Articles (Episcopal) reject the "Romish doctrine of purgatory," so also the confessions reject the Roman doctrine of purgatory. As the SA put it, "Purgatory, too, is contrary to the fundamental article that Christ alone, and not the work of man, can help souls. Besides, nothing has been commanded or enjoined upon us concerning the dead" (SA II, 12). It "may" consequently be discarded, "apart entirely from the fact that it is error and idolatry" (SA II, II, 13 and see also Ap. XII, 13ff, 134ff; XXIV, 90ff; SA II, ii 12ff)

It is interesting that the confessions say nothing directly about the INTERMEDIATE STATE, although Luther seems at times to affirm such a doctrine. Likewise nothing is said about further purgation or sanctification of the Christian dead, although Luther suggested their possibility. The dead are spoken of as in the grave, *and* in heaven (SA II ii 25) The Formula says that Christ "ascended into heaven, not just like some other saint" which appears to favor the notion that when a person dies his soul goes to heaven (SDVIII 27). It is also mentioned that Peter, Paul, and all the saints are in heaven (SDVIII 77), and Mary prays for the church so they have an active existence there (AP XXI 27). Likewise, the other saints pray for the church in general, although only Macc. 15:14 refers to this in Scripture (AP XXI 8). They may not understand our prayer (Ap. XXI 12) but they even may pray for individuals (SA II ii 25). We are not, however, to pray to them, have celebrations for them, or masses to their honor (SAII ii25) since there is no example of this in Scripture, and a prayer to Christ is a thousand times better (See SA II ii 24; Ep. VII 23; and SA II ii 21). It would appear that Cullman's theory of a difference in time conception between that of God and ours breaks down when we discuss prayers for the dead. It helps in some instances to explain some of the confessional examples, if one wishes to maintain an intermediate state, but the theory does not cover all instances in the Confessions (and I feel in Scripture, as well). Metaphorical speech may also provide a "way out" of the body/soul dualism which some of the passages seem to favor.

The text would seem to require limited critical study. It lists various antecedents such as Luther's *Confession of 1528*, which has been cited above. He added thoughts on prayer for the dead, vigils, masses, purgatory, and he stresses his disbelief in the ultimate salvation of the devil. Since I did not include this paragraph of the 1528 Confession in my pre-Confessional study, it is here reproduced.

> I believe in the resurrection of the dead, both the good and the evil, at the last day, when each shall receive in his body what he deserves; the righteous eternal life with Christ, and the wicked eternal death with the devil and his angels, for I do not agree with those who teach that finally even the devils will be saved.

The resurrection is not specifically mentioned in the Schwabach articles and there is no mention of the "deliverance from all evil" in AC. The followers of Origin are condemned by name in Na.

In the years of the Reformation, Hans Denck was the most important champion of universalism for the Anabaptist movement. He makes reference to it in chapters 16, 17, and 28 of *Wer die Wahrheit wahrlich lieb hat, Vom Gezetz Gottes, and Ordnung Gottes und der Kreaturen Werk*

(1527) 8f. Because God is love and mercy, He cannot be angry forever. The Mennonite Encyclopedia says that the Augsburg Confession wrongly attributes universalism to all Anabaptists. It was never really accepted in those circles. "It is found nowhere else except perhaps in Jakob Kautz and Hans Hut." (p 783 Vol IV). In fact, he won Hans Hut to the "cause." Urban Rhegius (1500-1527) was his chief opponent.

Melchior Rink (1494-1546) appears not to have been involved in universalism, although J. Menius in his book *Der Widderetufer und Geheimnis* (1530) attributes this doctrine to him.

Chiliasm is rejected in the second antithesis. This was rampant among the Anabaptists. (Incited by Hans Hut and some Jews in Worms, Melchior Rinck predicted that the millennium would be ushered in during Easter 1630.) Hans Hut is quite an individual, one of the most colorful of the period. He preached the imminent coming of Christ. In addition, he saw in the Turks a sign of Christ's return and said that the Lord had given three and a half years more for repentance, as shown in Rev 13 and Dan 12. Those that repented would rule the earth.

Charles V was interested in the article merely as a matter of government. The Anabaptists were often anti-government.

Sources in addition to Tappert's The *Book of Concord*:

Elert, Werner *The Structure of Lutheranism.* St. Louis: CPH

Muenscheer, W. *Elements of Dogmatic History.* New Haven: 1830.

Pieper, Charles Walter, *The Eschatology of the Lutheran Confessions*, an STM thesis.

Schlink, Edmund *The Theology of the Lutheran Confessions.* Philadelphia: Muhlenberg, 1961.

VIII

THE ESCHATOLOGY OF THE COUNCILS OF TRENT

(For the sake of completeness parts of this section are repeated from Chapter Fourteen in this volume.)

The Council of Trent (1545-63) was called to redefine Roman Catholic teaching, in part to counteract Protestant teaching. It pronounced on eschatological matters succinctly:

Canon 30: If anyone says that after the reception of the grace of justification the guilt is so remitted and the debt of eternal punishment so blotted out to every repentant sinner, that no debt of temporal punishment remains to be discharged either in this world or in purgatory before the gates of heaven can be opened, let him be anathema (p. 46).

22nd Session: (This session stresses that Masses are effective for the dead, and the sacrifice of the Mass is not offered to the saints, but to God.) The Mass gives "thanks for their victories and implores their favor that they may vouchsafe to intercede for us in heaven whose memory we celebrate on earth" (p. 146).

Chap. 9 "Those who say the mass ought not to be offered for the living and the dead . . . let him be anathema" (p. 149).

25th Session: "There is a purgation and that the soul there detained are aided by the suffrages of the faithful and chiefly by the acceptable sacrifice of the altar . . ."

"The more difficult and subtle questions, however, and those that do not make for edification and from which there is for the most part no increase in piety, are to be excluded from popular instructions to uneducated people."

"Likewise, things that are uncertain or that have the appearance of falsehood, they [the bishops] shall not permit to be made known publicly and discussed" (p. 214).

"That they think impiously who deny that the Saints who enjoy eternal happiness *in heaven* are to be invoked or who assert that they do not pray for men, or that our invocation of them to pray for each of us individually is idolatry or that it is opposed to the Word of God, let them be anathema" (p. 215).

" . . . the holy bodies of the holy martyrs . . . to be awakened by Him to eternal life and to be glorified, are to be venerated by the faithful" (p. 215).

IX

ESCHATOLOGY IN LATER ORTHODOXY

(Again for the sake of completeness parts of this section are repeated from Chapter
Fourteen in this volume.)

With the dogmaticians of later Orthodoxy the development of
the doctrine of eschatology circles around once again, approximating
pre-Lutheran attitudes (and also foreshadowing later returns). By this point
of the present study, it must be clear that concerns beyond tracing the course
of eschatology in the church have entered the inquiry. The development of
doctrine, the cyclic character of systematics, progressive revelation, and the
allowance of diversity of opinion are all side assumptions which may indicate
the (too-wide) swath this paper has cut through history, sources, and ideas.

An attempt will be made to approximate the outline the *Grundbekenntnis*
(AC) set forth in article XVII (mainly for ease of comparison).

Death is defined as the separation of the "soul from the body" by Baier
(354), Gerhard (XVII, 149), and, Quenstedt (I v 535). Baier adds that it
was a consequence of the fall (354). Hollazius seems to approximate the
Hebrew conception of death when he says, "The death of the body formally
consists in the deprivation of natural life" (1225). Gerhard underscores his
basic stance with such statements as, "Death is the release of the soul from
the body" (XVII 51) and "Death is nothing else than the taking off of this
garment" (the body) quoting Aristotle for proof (628).

As preparation for the discussion of heaven, hell, and the intermediate
state, it would be well here to briefly outline the understanding of the "soul"
in the dogmaticians. Baier believes that the "soul . . . survives and performs
its operations separately outside of the body; for example those things
which pertain formally to the intellect and will" (368). Quenstedt proves
the immortality of the soul from such arguments as "From the opposition
of the soul and body." "From the original creation of the soul." "The souls
of the brutes were produced from the same material as their bodies, whence
when their bodies perish the souls themselves likewise perish" (Gen 1:20).
"Into man He breathed a soul" (Gen 2:7). Gerhard adds the concept that
the difference between our immortality and God's is "He is essentially and
independently immortal." Ours is given *to* us. (631). He adds numerous

natural, metaphysical, teleological, cosmically, analogical, and moral arguments to the ethical, argument to the juridical, empirical, traditional (which include the *consensus gentium* which includes Homer, Virgil, and others), and the arguments from the New Testament and history.

At the *final judgment* the men that are alive will not experience death, for they are unified in body and soul. Instead they will be transformed. The precise time of His coming is not known, but it is known that Christ will judge, and that all will see Him. All will be judged according to the norm of revelation which is given them on earth (Schmid, p 643).

Gerhard lists five reasons for a universal judgment; these reasons are necessary because the particular judgment has already taken place: (1) "the manifestation of divine glory," (2) "the glorification of Christ," (3) "the exaltation of the godly," (4) "the completion of rewards and punishments," and (5) "the continued consideration of good and evil works." Finally, as a practical concern, Hafenreffer adds that the dead will rise before we are transformed (682).

The signs of the times can be divided into five happenings according to Gerhard: (1) The multiplication of heresies, (2) seditions, (3) the persecution of the godly, (4) careless security, and (5) the universal preaching of the Gospel (XIX 246). Gerhard notes that the dogmaticians see this last aspect as a sign of the last day, but not the general conversion of the Jews—which Hollazius [1263], along with others, explicitly rejects. (The confessions are silent on both issues). Gerhard also deals with such questions as whether the return will be local, why He is coming in the clouds, and in what form He will be seen.

Quenstedt has a representative concept of the resurrection.

> The subject of the resurrection is the entire man as had previously died and been reduced to ashes. The subject from which, is the body, the same in number and essence as we have borne in this life, and as had perished through death, yet clothed with new and spiritual qualities. (IV 582)

Thus the body that will rise will be spiritual in quality and endowments, but not in substance. Hollazius notes the difference lies in duration, outward form, vigor, activity, and endurance. (1243).

In the resurrection the wicked and the godly will have incorruptibility and immortality in common, but the godly alone will have glorified bodies which are powerful, spiritual, heavenly like the angels. The wicked will not be impassible, but will be foul and ignominious (Gerhard XIX 38)

Many of the dogmaticians posit the immediate entry into either heaven or hell. It must, therefore, be remembered in discussing heaven and hell that these "exist" both before and after the resurrection, even though in *outline* form the *Augustana* places these after the resurrection. Therefore, objectivity does not enter into the relative placing of these topics.

Melancthon had viewed heaven as an academy wherein he hoped to converse with the apostles, prophets, and church fathers about pure doctrine. (CR 7, 319). Hollazius, however, stresses the chief aim of heaven. "Our eternal and highest blessedness consists in the perfect sight and enjoyment of God" (456). Quenstedt divides the blessings of heaven into privative and positive blessings. Privative blessings are absence of sin and its causes (death), and the positive blessings consist of internal and external blessings. The internal blessings are further divided into those benefiting the soul and the body. For the soul it will have 1) the perfect enlightenment of the intellect, 2) the complete righteousness of will and appetite, 3) the highest security. For the body, there will be 1) spirituality, 2) invisibility, 3) impalpability 4) illocality, 5) subtlety, 6) agility, 7) impassibility, 8) immortality and incorruptibility, 9) strength and soundness (I 553).

Further questions are answered with some degree of assurance.

> Infants departing without baptism, either believe or do not believe. If the former, they are in the grace of God, and obtain the remission of their sins; if the latter they remain children of wrath under condemnation, exile from the heavenly Jerusalem and are cast into the lake of fire (Gerhard XVII 189ff).

Our joy shall not be marred by seeing our friends and relatives tortured in hell. We will have perfect wisdom and know that God is just even in this. We will likewise recognize one another in heaven(HFr 699). The practical significance of heaven is that in

> considering the joys of eternal life every day, we may keep closely to the way leading thither, and carefully avoid all that can cause delay or recall us from entrance into life eternal (Ger. XX 528).

In heaven, the godly "will enjoy according to the degree of their godliness the highest and completely undisturbed happiness in beholding the face of God" (Holl 978). Thus there will be degrees in heaven.

Likewise the ungodly suffer in hell "according to the degree of their ungodliness, in bodily and spiritual pains for their sins eternally" (Holl 990 978). Quenstedt divides the sufferings of hell into privative and positive punishments which will be experienced with the devils (Quen. I 565, Hfr 691). Gerhard delineates two kinds of hell: the internal and formal hell (which is the conscience) and the external, objective, and local hell (which is the real hell XX175). He goes into detail on the tortures of hell: 1) There will be every kind of torture because in hell there is the presence of all evil and the absence of all good. 2) The torture will be most "exquisite" like those pains criminals experience. 3) They will feel the anguish of belonging to those who feel the "pains of childbirth." 4) They are burned not lightly and superficially, but in the midst of flames penetrating *ad medullas*a." 5) They are not even given a drop of water to cool their body, "much less the least consolation for their soul." 6) They are able to see the elect in glory, "and hence, from envy, are seized with horror and indignation." 7) Their sorrow is increased by remembering former good things. 8) They will know that their punishment is eternal. 9) They will be tortured by seeing the pains of their relatives. 10) They will resist and contend against God, and this is the gnashing of teeth mentioned in Matthew 13. Although they will not receive the full measure of their pain immediately after death, the experience is begun right after death (Gerhard XVIII 21).

Metempsychosis is entirely rejected (Grh. XVII, 171), as are the Papists' five receptacles for the soul: hell, purgatory, *limbus puerorum*, *limbus partum*, and heaven, as they understand them. There are only two such repositories. From the above, it is no doubt obvious that the dogmaticians reject both *annihilation* and *universalism*.

As to any *millennium*, Quenstedt and the others deny it. The general resurrection, the final judgment follow one another with no time interval (Iv 649). They (dogmaticians) make a distinction between "gross and subtle chiliasm".

> The former estimates the millennium as happy because of the illicit pleasure of the flesh; the latter, because of the lawful and honorable delights of the body and soul. Both are rejected. (Holl. 1256, Grh. XX, 109)

The different views are elaborated upon, and rejected. Gerhard's explanation of the one thousand years of Revelation is that they begin in the empire of Constantine. The Antichrist is thus the Turk. Holl argues that the millennium can be explained away by the allegorical and quasi enigmatical character of the book of Revelation (1259).

Nothing would be gained by a listing of the theologians of orthodoxy's views on purgatory since they approximate both Luther's and the confessions'.

The intermediate state is categorically denied by most of the theologians of orthodoxy.

> Neither, after death, do the souls of the godly live in a cool and tranquil place, and possess only a foretaste of heavenly happiness, but they enjoy full and essential happiness. Neither, after death, do the souls of the wicked feel only the beginnings of tortures, but perfect and complete damnation (Quen. IV, 538).

(What, therefore, is left for the resurrection of the body? Does the resurrection mean nothing, or only a difference in degree?) Baier is just as explicit:

> Yea, we believe that the souls of the godly attain essential blessedness immediately after they have been separated from the body, but that the wicked undergo their damnation (364).

Gerhard, likewise, agrees in substance. After death, the soul

> returns to God, to whose judgment it is committed from which it is either borne by holy angels into heaven, or is delivered to evil spirits to be cast into hell (Gerhard XVII, 149).

His additional comment that the soul

> is preserved somewhere (*pou*) until, on the appointed day of the general resurrection, the body raised up by divine power will be joined again to the body, Gerhard XVII, 149).

The "somewhere" is thus heaven or hell. Likewise, Quenstedt's statement allows no alternative interpretation:

> Following death is the judgment, whose forerunner is the general resurrection of all men, and whose following attendant is the end of the world (IV 534).

Even Gerhard makes a statement that could be interpreted in Luther's sense of the intermediate state, that after death comes the "resurrection, the judgment, and finally the eternal state in heaven or hell" (XVII 8). However, in the light of his other writings, this statement does not explain his full attitude toward "life after death." Hutter, however (and perhaps only because his other writings have not been fully examined), makes a statement more in harmony with the Old Testament and Luther,

> The souls of the godly are in the hand of God, awaiting there
> the glorious resurrection of the body, and the full enjoyment of
> eternal blessedness. (Loc Th. 297).

Contrast this statement of Hutter's with this of Gerhard, which comes much closer to describing the "furniture of heaven and the temperature of hell":

> Of receptacles and habitations, Scripture, by a general appellation,
> speaks of a place. Not that it is a corporeal and physical place
> properly so called but because it is a "where" (*pou*) into which
> souls separated from the body are brought together . . . . Scripture
> enumerates only two such receptacles, one of which, prepared
> for the godly, is called by the most ordinary appellation heaven,
> and the other, intended for the souls of the wicked, is called hell
> (Ger XVII 17 and see the IDB for uses of heaven in the Old and
> New Testaments).

Luther, as so often has happened in the intervening centuries, came close to being called "heretic" by the theologians of the church in which he did his confessing. Gerhard, in his critique of psychopannichists who hold a doctrine similar to that of Luther (and many others in the church), comes in for damning criticism by Quistorp, the Calvinist theologian (damning from the Lutheran point of view).

> It is especially typical for the development of Protestant
> eschatology that the great architect of Lutheran orthodoxy, John
> Gerhard, in his doctrine of the state after death, represents not
> the standpoint of Luther but that of Calvin. Heinrich Quistorp,
> *Calvin's Doctrine of the Last Things.*

His arguments follow a definition of the psychopannischists' position.

1) The dead are said to sleep. Answer: As sleep holds only the members and outward senses while the soul exercises its inner operations, as is inferred from dreams; so in death the body alone perishes, while the souls of the godly are transferred to Abraham's bosom, and enjoy consolation.

2) The dead shall not praise thee. Answer: These passages refer to the proclamation and propagation of true doctrine, and the celebration of divine blessings through which, in this life, others may be invited to true conversion and the glorification of the divine name.

3) (Posits a general and a particular judgment.)

4) The rest of souls must be understood with respect to the *terminus a quo*, *i.e.*, they rest from labors and troubles . . . but not with respect to the *terminus ad quem*, as though the souls of the godly rest after death in the stupor of sleep. (Gerhard XVIII 26ff).

As to the knowledge of the dead, in the place cited, Gerhard makes some general comments:

> It is a pious and good thought to hold that they have a general knowledge of what is occurring to the church militant here on earth, and therefore they beseech Christ with whom they are present in heavenly glory, for some good for the church . . . . Meanwhile, it must not be inferred from this, that they have in full view the individual circumstances or calamities to the godly.

Schmid, Heinrich	*The Doctrinal Theology of the Evangelical Lutheran Church.* MLPS: Augsburg, 1875.
Burtness, James H	"Immortality and/ or Resurrection," *Dialogue*, Easter 1962, pp. 46-52.
Smits, Edmund	"Blessed Immortality, a Study in Gerhard," *Dialogue*, Easter 1962, pp. 40-45.

NOTES TOWARD A CONCLUSION

These individual study chapters on eschatology in the Old and New Testaments, the apocrypha, the early fathers, the medieval church (Aquinas), Luther, the pre-Confessional documents, the Lutheran confessions, the Articles of Trent, and later Orthodoxy, while tentative and sketchy at best, show the wealth of ideas and often contradictory understandings, handed down throughout the history of the church, about the last things.

And this surveys shows, as a work-in-progress, how a young seminarian works through the sources in examining just one of the doctrines of the church.

Marvell's hope of "having world enough and time," may indeed be extended, even into all eternity.

GENERAL BIBLIOGRAPHY

Althaus, Paul   *Die Letzen Dinge.* Gutersloh: Bertelsmann, 1949.

Aquinas, Thomas   *Complete Works*

Burtness, James   "Immortality and/or Resurrection," *Dialogue,* Easter 1962, pp. 46-52.

                         Collection of Sources: Augsburg Confession. St. Louis: Concordia Seminary Print Shop.

Cullmann, Oscar   *Immortality of the Soul or Resurrection of the Dead.,* London, 1958.

Elert, Werner   *The Structure of Lutheranism.* CPH, St. Louis.

Guy, H.A.   *The New Testament Doctrine of the Last Things.* London: Oxford Press, 1948.

Hall, George   "Luther's Eschatology," in *Aug. Quart.* Vol. 23, 1943, Rock Island: Aug, Book Concern, pp.13-21.

Interpreter's Dictionary of the Bible Various articles.

Jacob, H.E.   *Theology of the Old Testament*

Jacob, H.E.   "Eck's 404 Theses." Papers of A.S.C.H., Putnam, N.Y

Kelly, J.N.D.   *Early Christian Doctrines.* pp. 459-4901

Knight, George   *A Christian Theology of the Old Testament*

Köstlin, Julius   *The Theology of Luther.* Lutheran Publishing Society, Phil, 1897.

Kramm, H. H.   *The Theology of Martin Luther*. London: Clarke, 1947,

Quistorp, Heinrich   *Calvin's Doctrine of the Last Things*. trans by Knight, Richmond: John Knox, 1955.

Rupp, Gordon   *The Righteousness of God*. London, Hodder and Stoughton, 1953.

Shlink, Edmund   *The Theology of the Lutheran Confessions*.

Schmid, Heinrich   *The Doctrinal Theology of the Evangelical Lutheran Church*. MLPS: Augsburg, 1875.

Schroeder, H.J.   *The Canons and Decrees of the Council of Trent*.

Smith, Ryder   *The Bible's Doctrine of the Last Things*

Smits, Edmund   "Blessed Immortality, a Study in Gerhard," *Dialogue*, Easter 1962, pp 40-45.

Strawson, William   *Jesus and the Last Things*

Tappert, T.   *The Book of Concord*

ACKNOWLEDGMENTS

In view of the theme of this volume, "time's winged chariot," the acknowledgments are just a brief, eclectic selection, in no particular order or ranking, of those who have influenced me through the years, and limited to those who have (to use Marvell's word) entered "vast eternity."

The earliest, strongest, and most continuing influence is my mother, ANNA LOUISE GALL (Sluberski, Wood) CZNADEL, who inspired me to be my best, be adventuresome, be my own person, love travel and experience as much as possible. She modeled in her own life and person someone who survived and surmounted society's and her own family's mores against great odds, rearing a talented family, living a fascinating life, and dying in surprisingly good health at age ninety-four on January 24, 2011.

My younger sister, NANCY LEE WOOD (Plouse) Hixson, challenged me on almost every level, continually raising the bar and changing the playing field. Probably the most astonishing person I have known. Her obituary (2009) went viral on the Internet.

TED CZNADEL was a stepfather sent from heaven. My mother remarried for the third time when I was in my early teens, and Ted became a supporter in all my choices. This marriage lasted for over 45 years, "till death do us part."

DAVID BLEIFUS, Nancy's partner for thirty years, became by sheer dint of character and integrity a part of our family.

BEA RICHARDS was my most memorable and influential Sunday school teacher at Redeemer Lutheran Church in downtown Cleveland. She later went into missions in Hong Kong.

ELLEN FLORENCE HALTER, a close friend along with her husband Howard and a longtime housemate and frequent travel companion: encouraging, adventuresome, adaptable, energetic, enthusiastic even in the most difficult situations. She died at age ninety-three, in 2003, at home with her beloved dogs.

KATHERINE BOERWINKLE, an all-important next-door neighbor, my Latin and English teacher in high school, offered a model of the educated Christian (as a graduate of Wheaton College) at an important time in my life. Her husband, children, aunt, and circle of friends provided essential support and constant encouragement.

LANNY KEPES had an amazing knack for knowing interesting people and discovering important events. I still marvel at how much he taught and showed me in our brief friendship in Brazil.

ARTHUR CARL PIEPKORN, a demanding and admirable professor, expected the best: rigorous scholarship and ways of living and believing, never quite the norm.

MARGARET (my mother's sister) and CHET ELLIS led dramatic lives overseas. Their frequent letters and stays in our home on furlough were the stuff of dreams and the inspiration to "do likewise."

PROF. PAUL MANZ first made real to me how and why to love, appreciate, and understand great music, art, and literature. His is the model I strove to follow in all the courses in humanities I subsequently taught.

LUIZ HENRIQUE CRUZ and ALEXANDRE PAGNANI paved the way for my experiences in Brazilian sports and society, getting me visas and introducing me to the complexities of judging and navigating in a world so often foreign to me.

IVAR ASHEIM, chairman of the department at the Lutheran World Federation in Geneva, Switzerland, hired me at a turning point in my life. My own church was not a member of the LWF, but he and Jack Preus made possible my appointment as researcher and literary survey editor.

JACK PREUS, a president of the Lutheran Church—Missouri Synod and an unexpected and constant supporter, enabled me to get ordained and accept posts at the Lutheran World Federation, at Valparaiso University and at St. Matthew's (Hastings-on-Hudson), in difficult years for the church.

RICHARD JOHN NEUHAUS, an early role model, "turned me on" to the inner city, though our political and social viewpoints diverged in later years. He provided real support in my post as executive director of the American Lutheran Publicity Bureau.

MARTIN SCHMIDT, my *Doktor Vater*, enabled my transition from the University of Erlangen-Nuremberg to Heidelberg University. A foremost scholar on English church history, he suggested the topic of my dissertation and guided me through to the doctorate with honors—an unusual accomplishment in those days for a foreigner.

MARTIN NEEB served as first president of Concordia Senior College, and guiding hand in its founding. The institution he fostered provided simply the finest education I have experienced anywhere.

THANKS FOR PREPUBLICATION ASSISTANCE

FLAVIA AZEVEDO— Niteroi, Brazil—publishing consultant
TIM AND SUSAN GALL— Cleveland, Ohio—publishing and editing
CHRISTOPHER HIXSON— Akron, Ohio —cover design
Cj CRAWFORD— Warsaw, Ohio—typing and transmission
SIGART REIN— Cleveland, Ohio—translating
WARREN DAY—Fort Lauderdale, Florida—editing
THOMAS PENN JOHNSON—Fort Myers, Florida—editing

And especially Jess Nelson Taylor—São Paulo, Brazil—who tried to bring order to this collection and encouraged me to continue the task.

TOM'S TIMELINE

(annotated to illuminate the essays)

1939. Born December 7 at Margaret Hague Hospital, Jersey City, New Jersey.1940. Baptized at St. Paul's Lutheran Church, Valley City, Ohio, (surreptitiously) on a quick trip back from New Jersey. (This took place during the day, which explains my having two godmothers—all the men were at work. Evidently, I had also been baptized prior to that as a Roman Catholic in New Jersey.)

1943. Parents divorced; Mother remarried, in Cleveland.

1944. Second divorce. Family in hiding with relatives in Brunswick, Ohio, because of a court restraining order against a stepfather. Sister, Nancy Lee, born.

1945. Moved to the projects on Cleveland's South Side and lived on public assistance. Attended Tremont Elementary and Lincoln High School.

1950. Mother married for the third time. (This time it was till death do us part—over forty-five years). Sister, Linda Rose, born.

1951. Confirmed Congregational at Pilgrim Congregational Church in Cleveland, Ludwig C. Emigholz, pastor, who kept in touch for many years.

1952. Began confirmation classes at Redeemer Lutheran Church in Cleveland. Joined an inspiring Lutheran scout troop and a Sunday school class led by Miss Bea Richards.

1953. Brother, Gregory Theodore, born. Moved to Independence, Ohio. Confirmed Lutheran at St. John's Lutheran Church, Independence. Attended Boy Scout and church camps every summer; worked at Camp Cherith. Active in Youth for Christ; attended various Lutheran youth gatherings; saw Concordia Seminary and sites in St. Louis for the first time. Attending Independence High, played junior varsity basketball, worked on the school paper, and wrote a gossip column, "Tom About Town."

1957-'58. Scholarships for two summers at the Cleveland Institute of Art, in life drawing and watercolor. Finalist in the Higbee Art Competition.

1958. Graduated Independence High as a National Merit Scholar finalist, offered seventeen scholarships, turning down all but one to attend Concordia College, St. Paul, Minnesota. (Concordia made German a prerequisite, so I went a summer to Western Reserve University to study that language.)

1959. While at Concordia College, active in drama, on the school paper, and in the traveling Minnesota Centennial of Lutheranism Pageant; awarded a "Promising Student Award." Worked summers at Tricker's Aquarium, Independence, as an assistant ichthyologist.

1960. Transferred to one of America's most beautiful campuses, Concordia Senior College—designed by Eero Saarinen—in Ft. Wayne, Indiana. Worked on the college newspaper and spent a summer building army trucks for International Harvester in Ft. Wayne.

1962. Bachelor of Arts in English Literature and Classics, *cum laude*. Transferred to Concordia Seminary, St. Louis; helped edit student journal; involved in interfaith dialogue; inner city work. Aide to Dr. Norman Habel, Professor of Old Testament.

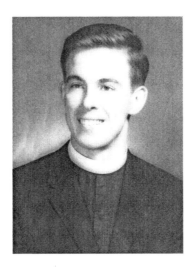

1963. Summer intern for the soon-to-be-named Faith Lutheran Church, Mansfield, Ohio; effectively started a congregation.

1964. After classes ended in June, hitchhiked to California, following a trail blazed by my sister, Nancy, the year before.

1964-'65. Vicarage (pastoral internship) at Zion Lutheran Church in Wausau, Wisconsin. Three thousand-member parish with a parochial school, Pastor Dale D. Hansen, supervisor.

1965. First nephew, Christopher Daniel, born to Nancy.

1966ff. Graduated with a masters in divinity from Concordia Seminary, St. Louis, *magna cum laude*. Granted a bonanza of scholarships and fellowships. Studied at the University of Vienna, then with the Experiment in International Living in Bonn, and finally at the University of Erlangen-Nuremberg, living at the famed Martin Luther Bund Heim (originally intended for students from Poland and Eastern Europe—my last name helped.) Three study tours to Berlin; others to Bavaria and

Auslands- und Diasporatheologenheim
des Martin Luther-Bundes in Erlangen

Rhineland Pfalz. Travel on my own to Turkey, Greece, Italy, France, Spain, Morocco, East Germany and Czechoslovakia. (The day the Soviets marched in with tanks and troops, I escaped by hitchhiking with a German national, via the last border crossing open to West Germany.)

1967-'68. Two extended study periods at Cambridge University, where Dr. Norman Nagel was provost of Westfield House. (He later arranged my call to Valparaiso University and ordination.) Tours of Holland, Belgium, England, Wales, Scotland, Ireland, and France.

1968. Hired by the Lutheran World Federation in Geneva, Switzerland, as researcher in the Department of Theology and literary survey editor for the *Lutherische Rundschau/Lutheran World.* The department was directed

by Paul Hoffman, Ivar Asheim and Sig Aske. As a member of "The Group," an international young people's association, visited Francis Shaefer's center at L'Abri, Switzerland, and the Taizé Community in France.

1969. Was to attend the Lutheran World Federation Assembly in Porto Alegre, Brazil. Due to increasing difficulties with the reigning military regime, LWF moved the Assembly to Geneva (inadvertently postponing my first visit to Brazil by forty years). Christmas, mother visits Europe; tour of Switzerland, France, and Spain. (She wanted to know why I had not returned to the U.S. By way of reply, and as a Christmas present, I show her my signed contract for a post as instructor at Valparaiso University, Indiana.)

1969. Assistant to the dean of the chapel and instructor in the Department of Theology, Valparaiso University. A year of upheaval in the USA—underground happenings; universities closed; Kent State. Valpostock, Valparaiso's answer to Woodstock.

1969 November 9. Ordination, the first permitted by Lutheran Church—Missouri Synod to be performed at a university. Chaplain Nagel and Indiana District President Zimmerman officiate.

1970. Returned to Heidelberg University with a *Deutscher Akademisher Austaushdienst Fellowship*; lived at *Rheino Arminia*, a swordfighting fraternity. Toured Denmark, Norway, and Sweden, declining a position as campus pastor offered by the Swedish Lutheran Church.

1971-'73. Elected Board of Directors, Society for Worship, Music, and the Arts.

1972. Accepted assistant professorship, Concordia College, Bronxville, New York (Robert Schnabel, president).

1972. Awarded Master of Arts in English Literature, Washington Univ., St. Louis, Mo.

1973. Doctorate *cum laude* (unusual for a foreigner), Heidelberg University, Theology, Literature, and the Arts. Moved to Greenwich Village, New York. First of two summers as a scholar in residence at the Edward Albee Center for Creative People in Montauk, New York.

1974. Certificate in Fund-Raising, New York University.

1974-'75. Led Concordia tour groups to England, Germany, France, Spain, and Italy. Second summer at Albee Foundation.

1976. Led "In the Footsteps of Columbus," a memorable student tour of the Caribbean. (Off Tortola, British Virgin Islands, the crew of our schooner, the *Tiki*, mutinied, threw the ship's motor overboard, and took the lifeboats—leaving us on what we believed to be a sinking ship. Rescued

SCHOONER "TIKI"

by the British Coast Guard. The college was unable to sue because under British maritime law, the Tiki was considered a "pirate" ship.)

1976-87. Member of the American Film Institute and juror for the American Film Festival.

1976. Fellow, Christian Writer's Institute, Bronxville, New York.

1977. Called as part-time pastor of St. Matthew's Lutheran Church, Hastings-on-Hudson, New York. The congregation's church building was

ST. MATTHEW'S
LUTHERAN CHURCH
HASTINGS-ON-HUDSON, NEW YORK

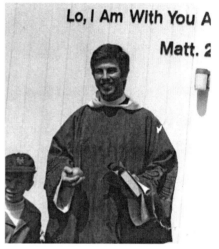

Lo, I Am With You A
Matt. 2

the only Lutheran church in New York featured in *Architecture in America*, and its historic twelve-room parsonage was reputed to be haunted. Began a ten-year tent-making ministry enabling the congregation to pay off its $100,000 mortgage, remodel its buildings, and secure a $100,000 grant for the Village of Hastings-on-Hudson. Started Crossroads College and a joint Sunday school with the Reformed Church and Episcopalians. Initiated a lay ministry program with the first woman lay minister in the LCMS; employed pre-seminary students as youth workers. (My photo appeared in *People* magazine in connection with the famed Hastings Center.)

1982. Chair of the Northeast Conference on Christianity and Literature held at Concordia.

1983-'87. Qualified as a National Physique Committee judge and judged more than fifteen bodybuilding and fitness contests in U.S. Extended trips to Japan, Korea, Hong Kong, Macau, Thailand, Korea, India, Nepal, Spain, Russia, Kazakhstan and Uzbekistan.

1983. Second nephew, Matthew, born to Linda.

1985-'88. Founder of Concordia's chapter of the Alpha Chi National Honor Society.

1987. Resigned as pastor of St. Matthew's after its gala 125th anniversary to become executive director of the American Lutheran Publicity Bureau and managing editor of *Lutheran Forum/Forum Letter*, edited by Richard John Neuhaus and Glenn Stone. Held two forum banquets, including one hosting the first president of the new Evangelical Lutheran Church in America (Herbert Chilstrom); moved the ALPB offices to Mt. Vernon, New York. Resigned ALPB when Neuhaus became a Roman Catholic. When Concordia colleague and friend Florence Halter suffered heart attack and stroke, I moved to Bronxville to live with and care for her.

1988. Performed nephew Chris's wedding at Lyndhurst Castle, New York.

1991. Called by LCMS to be its first Russian Ministries consultant, and the first American Lutheran missionary to Russia since the Revolution of 1917.

1992. January. A fact-finding tour of Russia led me to numerous possibilities for work there and to the locations of many of St. Petersburg's remaining

Lutheran churches (more than nineteen) taken over by the Communist government, recently toppled.

1992. February. A wake-up call just prior to my installation as a missionary to Russia prompted me to defer for six months. I returned to Russia in August. Five student volunteers worked with me over the ensuring year. Served as visiting professor at the University of St. Petersburg and Alexander von Herzen University; advisor for the Russian/American Press Center; on the board of the Peterschule and the Ben Weider College of Bodybuilding; warden for the US Consulate. First foreign judge of Mr. Russia contests (in Moscow, St. Petersburg and Omsk) for the Russian Federation of Bodybuilders; interviewed frequently for TV, radio, and print. Worked

with a major Russian film company (Ruskoi Film Video). Was provided an apartment at the Academic Hotel, a remodeled palace on Millionaire's Row, near the Hermitage; gave a series of parties for hundreds of Russians in the huge apartment (40 overstuffed chairs in the living room, 15-foot ceilings, ceramic fireplaces). One such party was broadcast live on Radio St. Petersburg.

1993. Investigative tour of Russia's eleven time zones, in search of other remnants of Lutheranism; lectured (many times as the first American to do so) at five universities (in addition to those in St. Petersburg, the universities of Omsk, Khabarovsk and Vladivostok), at the Merchant Marine Academy

in Vladivostok, the reopened Lutheran Seminary in S.P. and the new Deacon's Training School. Visited Latvia, Estonia and Lithuania as a guest of the Lutheran World Federation.

1994. Co-produced televised Easter service, live from four continents (linking Lutheran churches in Ghana, Korea, Russia, and US); according to ABC, the first broadcast of its kind. Trained volunteers for the 1994 Goodwill Games. Gave a popular series of lectures, "Sports Reporting for

the Western Media." Among those attending was Thomas Rosandich, president of the United States Sports Academy. During a tour of athletic institutions, he offered me a position with USSA, but I could not see myself teaching sports journalism full-time.

1994. August returned to Concordia, Bronxville. Named to the national faculty of the US Sports Academy and did not have to be on their campus. Elected to the National Academy of Television Arts and Sciences and began judging the Emmy Awards.

1995. Under the aegis of the US Sports Academy, taught "Sports Marketing" (for me, a new academic discipline) for the sports and Olympic committees of Singapore, Hong Kong, and Malaysia.

1996. Served on the executive board for the 15th Annual Workshop on Jewish/Christian Relations, held in Stamford, Conn. Continued to lead numerous workshops and lectures around the country on Russia, theology and literature, film, and television.

1995. Elected to the Polish Academy of Arts and Sciences.

1996. Elected to the historic Salmagundi Club, NYC.

1999 Led a series of presentations for a Bronxville group called "Books and Coffee": "Books and Coffee goes to the Movies"; "Great Movies Based on Great Books"; "Sleuthing and Cinema"; "Sex and Cinema"; "Science Fiction and Cinema"; "Spirituality in Cinema."

2003. After leading a series of overseas study trips through the years (France, England, Germany, Spain, Italy, American and British Virgin Islands, Puerto Rico) I was given an award trip to Brazil. Taking it altered the direction of my life.

2004. Returned to Brazil on a sabbatical, to teach at ULBRA, the Lutheran University of Brazil, in Canoas, Rio Grande do Sul. ULBRA has more than twenty campuses, with 150,000 students. Under its auspices participated in

a month-long medical, governmental/academic trip by ship up the Amazon, as the only foreigner in working group of 95.

2004. Retired from Concordia University, New York (after thirty-one years on the faculty). Deployed to Brazil.

2004-2007. Judged the 35th, 36th, and 37th National Contests of the Brazilian Federation of Bodybuilding and Fitness: Goiânia, João Pessoa, Rio de Janeiro, São Paulo.

Presenter for the 6th International Congress on Literature and Language in Mercosul/Mercosur countries (2004) and the first International Congress for Executive Secretaries (2004) in Canoas.

2005. Visited Paraguay and learned of former U.S. president Rutherford B. Hayes's connections with that country. (My sister had been librarian at the Hayes Presidential Library in Fremont, Ohio.) Memorable meetings and visits because of that connection.

2006. Elected to the board of governors of the American Society of Rio de Janeiro and participated in the annual conference of ABRALIC (the Brazilian Comparative Literature Association), giving a presentation titled "Brazil and *Brokeback Mountain.*" Issued a *visto permanente* and a *visto empresarial* by the Brazilian government (permanent residency with a business visa). Company's official name: "*Sluberski Serviços de Consultaria e Empresarial Ltda.*"

2006-'07. Research and reported for Brazilian authorities on drugging and doping in athletics, especially in connection with the Pan American Games held in Rio de Janeiro in July of 2007.

2008. Published *A Mind in Frame: The Theological Thought of Thomas Traherne, with* Lincoln Library Press (a Division of Eastward Press), Cleveland, Ohio.

2009. My younger sister, Nancy, died at age 65 on June 30th, in Danville, Ohio.

2010. Changed official US residence to Florida (necessary for voting and paying taxes) and took up part-time residence in an oceanside condo in Fort Lauderdale, but retained my Brazilian residence visas.

2011. My mother, Anne Cznadel, died at age 94 on January 24th, in Brookpark,Ohio. David Bleifus, sister Nancy's partner of thirty years, died June 15 in Wooster, Ohio.

2012. Dedication of a 28 Bell Carillon in my honor at Village Lutheran Church and Concordia College, Bronxville, New York.

2013. Moved to Oviedo, Florida.

To be continued, God willing.

+ + +

NOTES:

Baptized twice, confirmed twice, certified, ordained, commissioned, inducted, installed (the "sacred seven," or nine, depending on how you count)

Almost all my education, undergraduate and graduate, was underwritten by generous scholarships from the Deutscher Akademescher Austaushdienst, the Bavarian State, the Austrian State, the William and Tona Shepherd Travel Grant, the University of Vienna, the Martin Luther Bund Heim, the Lutheran World Federation, the World Council of Churches, the Aid Association for Lutherans, the Kiwanis Club, and the Institute of International Education, among others.

Where I've lived underscores what I've done and what I've thought. I have seldom lived in the same place for long. While some consider "a rolling stone gathers no moss" a negative judgment, I have found that there are always interesting and exciting possibilities elsewhere, and wanted to experience them first hand. As e. e. cummings put it, "there's a hell of a world next door . . . let's go." Or "When you come to a fork in the road, take it." Or 'Two roads diverged in a yellow wood, take both."

The stone began rolling in early childhood. After my mother divorced my father, when I was a baby, we moved from New Jersey to Ohio, and lived in a series of relatives' homes, just briefly settling down, on her second marriage, when I was four. After my sister Nancy's birth and my mother's subsequent divorce from her father, we went on welfare and moved to the projects on the Southside of Cleveland. After my mother's third marriage, when I was in my early teens, we moved to a Polish immigrant neighborhood, and from there to Independence, Ohio, a Cleveland suburb. Since then, I've lived: at a veteran's club; in the oldest dormitory on Concordia, St. Paul's campus (five to a room); on an ultra-contemporary campus designed by Eero Saarinen in Ft. Wayne, Indiana; at the YMCA in Mansfield, Ohio for a summer vicarage; at the summer school of the Univ. of Vienna in Strobl am Wolfgansee, Austria; in a *Bund Heim* meant for students from Eastern Europe in Erlangen, Germany; at a swordfighting fraternity (*Reino Arminia*) in Heidelberg, Germany; at a multitude of youth hostels all over Europe; in a maid's apartment in Geneva, Switzerland; at a former waystation of the Underground Railroad in Valparaiso, Indiana; at 17 Downing Street, Greenwich, Village; at the Rupert Brewery Towers in NYC; in a certified haunted twelve-room house in Hastings-on-Hudson, NY; in a spectacular apartment at the Academic Hotel in St. Petersburg, Russia; in an oil workers' dormitory in Omsk, Siberia; in officers' quarters

in Vladivostok; faculty housing in Bronxville, at an athletic dorm at ULBRA in Brazil; in a penthouse in Glória, Rio de Janeiro, and another in Copacabana; in an beachfront highrise in South Florida.

On five continents, where I had to manage in five or six languages, I've never acquired any property. The only real estate I've ever owned is my intended garden gravesite, in the *Cemitério dos Ingleses do Rio de Janeiro*, the English Cemetery of Rio, at the intersection of three paths behind the chancel wall of the cemetery chapel across the street from the Museum of Samba.

CPSIA information can be obtained at www.ICGtesting.com
Printed in the USA
LVOW08*2323071013

355885LV00002B/2/P